D1293451

Early Modern Tragedy and the Cinema of Violence

Also by Stevie Simkin

REVENGE TRAGEDY: A New Casebook

MARLOWE: The Plays

A PREFACE TO MARLOWE

Early Modern Tragedy and the Cinema of Violence

Stevie Simkin

Senior Lecturer in Drama, University of Winchester

© Stevie Simkin 2006

All rights reserved. No reproduction, copy or transmission of this
publication may be made without written permission.

No paragraph of this publication may be reproduced, copied or transmitted
save with written permission or in accordance with the provisions of the
Copyright, Designs and Patents Act 1988, or under the terms of any licence
permitting limited copying issued by the Copyright Licensing Agency,
90 Tottenham Court Road, London W1T 4LP.

Any person who does any unauthorised act in relation to this publication
may be liable to criminal prosecution and civil claims for damages.

The author has asserted his right to be identified
as the author of this work in accordance with the Copyright,
Designs and Patents Act 1988.

First published 2006 by
PALGRAVE MACMILLAN
Houndmills, Basingstoke, Hampshire RG21 6XS and
175 Fifth Avenue, New York, N.Y. 10010
Companies and representatives throughout the world

PALGRAVE MACMILLAN is the global academic imprint of the Palgrave
Macmillan division of St. Martin's Press, LLC and of Palgrave Macmillan Ltd.
Macmillan® is a registered trademark in the United States, United Kingdom
and other countries. Palgrave is a registered trademark in the European
Union and other countries.

ISBN-13: 978–1–4039–4411–5
ISBN-10: 1–4039–4411–3

This book is printed on paper suitable for recycling and made from fully
managed and sustained forest sources.

A catalogue record for this book is available from the British Library.

Library of Congress Cataloging-in-Publication Data
Simkin, Stevie.
    Early modern tragedy and the cinema of violence / Stevie Simkin.
        p.   cm.
    Includes bibliographical references and index.
    ISBN 1–4039–4411–3 (cloth)
    1. Violence in motion pictures.   I. Title.
    PN1995.9.V5S55 2005
    791.43′6552—dc22   2005051214

10   9   8   7   6   5   4   3   2   1
15   14   13   12   11   10   09   08   07   06

Printed and bound in Great Britain by
Antony Rowe Ltd, Chippenham and Eastbourne

Contents

Conclusion: Gendered Revenge

List of Illustrations

Acknowledgements

First of all, I wish to thank my editors at Palgrave: Emily Rosser, who commissioned the project in the first place, and Paula Kennedy and her assistant, Helen Craine, who saw it through to completion. Thanks also to Keith Povey and Elaine Towns for their excellent copy-editing.

My thanks go to the University of Winchester (formerly King Alfred's College) for research support, my colleagues in the School of Community and Performing Arts, and in particular Ronan Paterson, Drama Programme Leader, who helped to facilitate a valuable period of research leave.

I owe a special debt of thanks to friends and colleagues who kindly offered (or agreed under duress) to read draft chapters and provided constructive feedback and new leads to pursue. I am particularly indebted to Marianne Sharp for her sensitive readings of Part II, and to Roger Richardson, who brought a keen historical eye to bear on Part I. Rob Conkie provided some close reading of several chapters just when 'we' really needed it, but his influence runs much deeper after the five years we have spent teaching together. Special thanks to Brian Woolland for his careful reading of most of the project in draft form, and for the invaluable, sometimes usefully spiky, debates over pub dinners. Thanks are also due to Brian for offering the opportunity to present some of this material at Reading University, where Jonathan Bignell and Doug Pye provided provocative feedback about the conception of the project, and the analysis of *Straw Dogs* in particular.

Thanks to my students who have taken the module 'Body Parts: Early Modern Tragedy and Millennium Cinema' at Winchester since 1999: your responses to the texts in sometimes heated discussions have provided the ongoing inspiration for the book. I would like to thank in particular those whose eye-opening independent research fuelled my own thinking and rethinking, among them Maz Baxter, Bethyn Casey, Rik Hartley, Theresa Heath and Hayley Yates.

Finally, thanks to Aileen, Jamie and Matty for helping me keep things in perspective and kicking me off the computer at regular intervals. This one is for the three of you.

STEVIE SIMKIN

Introduction: Worlds Apart

'A Klee painting named "Angelus Novus" shows an angel looking as though he is about to move away from something he is fixedly contemplating. His eyes are staring, his mouth is open, his wings are spread. This is how one perceives the angel of history. His face is towards the past. Where we perceive a chain of events, he sees one catastrophe, which keeps piling wreckage upon wreckage and hurls it in front of his feet. The angel would like to stay, awaken the dead, and make whole what has been smashed. But a storm is blowing from Paradise; it has got caught in his wings with such violence that the angel can no longer close them. This storm irresistibly propels him into the future to which his back is turned, while the pile of debris before him grows skyward. This storm is what we call progress.'

Walter Benjamin, Theses on the Philosophy of History[1]

The angel of history

In a report on so-called 'honour killings' in Pakistan, published in 1999, Amnesty International noted that, 'For a woman to be targeted for killing in the name of honour, her consent – or the lack of consent – in an action considered shameful is irrelevant to the guardians of honour. Consequently, a woman brings shame on her family if she is raped.' The report gives a number of examples, including the case of Lal Jamilla Mandokhel, a 16-year-old mentally retarded girl who was reportedly raped by a local government employee in a hotel in Parachinar in the North West Frontier Province. The official accused of the crime was

1

arrested and the girl returned to her tribe. The report continues: 'A *jirga* of Pathan tribesmen decided that she had brought shame to her tribe and that the honour could only be restored by her death. She was shot dead in front of a tribal gathering.'[2] In July 2004, Amnesty also reported that, in the same country, the victims of rape often become victims of the law: in the case of so-called *Zina* crimes (unlawful sexual intercourse), rape can only be proven on the confession of the rapist, or on the testimony of four men; the victim's testimony is immaterial. As a result, some women who report that they have been raped are imprisoned, or worse: sentencing for *Zina* crimes includes death by stoning.[3] In the climactic scene of Shakespeare's *Titus Andronicus* (1592), Titus, hosting a banquet for representatives of the Roman Empire and their enemies the Goths, asks the Roman emperor Saturninus whether the Roman centurion of legend, Virginius, was right to slay his own daughter because 'she was enforced, stained, and deflowered' by the corrupt official Appius Claudius (5.3.38).[4] Saturninus, unaware that Titus's daughter Lavinia was the victim of brutal rape and mutilation at the hands of his stepsons, blithely replies that it was, explaining that 'the girl should not survive her shame, / And by her presence still renew [her father's] sorrows' (40–1). To the horror of the assembled company, Titus promptly slays his daughter.

To a reader who has grown up in a liberal democracy, where the rhetoric (though rarely the reality) of equality between men and women prevails, hearing or reading about different practices in other parts of the world, or in earlier incarnations of our own society, may still shock us (and may also tempt us to dismiss the cultures where such things are still common as primitive, barbaric, or the result of religious fundamentalism). However, it is also important to recognise that among the emotions that victims of rape in Western society still record when attempting to come to terms with what has happened to them, guilt, shame and self-blame remain significant, and particularly cruel, symptoms. It is estimated that in the USA in 2001, for example, only 39 per cent of rapes were reported, and the most commonly recorded reasons for failure to do so were fears of reprisal and the feeling that it was a private matter.[5] While it is impossible to rationalise the emotional trauma rapists inflict on their victims, it is not difficult to trace a connection between feelings of guilt and shame and the cultural legacy of hundreds of years of patriarchy that has consistently cast women as being inferior to men, and laid claim to female sexuality as the property of the male to use and abuse as he pleases. Even after forty years of high-profile feminism, since the 1960s, in Western culture, the lies men have told about women through the ages, and which have, historically, been taken at face value by men and women alike, die hard.

This book is an attempt to interrogate a tension between historical specificity and what some might call universalism, but which I choose to refer to as transhistoricism. The simultaneous familiarity and strangeness of the past has become something of a preoccupation for critical thinkers in various fields, notably history and historiography, social studies, literary and drama studies. The large-scale rejection of any hope of objectivity in our approach to the past has provoked varied responses, from the tendency to rely on micro-stories and their extrapolations, which characterises the work of new historicists, to the political commitment and upfront agenda of cultural materialists, and to the profound scepticism of various forms of postmodernism. Jean Howard has proposed that, 'since objectivity is not in any pure form a possibility, let us acknowledge that fact and acknowledge as well that any move into history is an *intervention*, an attempt to reach from the present moment into the past to rescue both from meaningless banality'.[6]

This two-way process that Howard hints at – the way in which the past and the present might be put into meaningful dialogue with one another – is critical to the current study, and is one of the ways in which it refutes the assumptions of universalism. Human nature is not essentially always the same, regardless of time, place or political circumstance. How would *Romeo and Juliet* resonate when performed at Stratford in 2004, compared to its reception in London in 1595, for example? What about a performance in 2003 with a south Asian cast playing the Capulet family, and opening in Birmingham, UK, a city with a large Asian community? Most obviously, perhaps, Elizabethan theatregoers no doubt interpreted *The Merchant of Venice* (1596) very differently from audiences in Nazi Germany (where it was very popular in the 1930s), or audiences in Israel in 1972. As understandings of ourselves as men and women, as members of different racial, cultural or national groups, as human beings, evolve, so these texts take on new meanings for us.

The precise subject matter of this book was engendered, in part, by my own interest, as an academic and as a director of student drama, in the revenge tragedy genre, coupled with a long-standing fascination with screen violence, traceable back to horror movie double bills on BBC TV in the early 1980s. Since the early 1990s, I have found a number of critics noting, almost always in passing, that revenge tragedies have something in common with contemporary violent cinema, and suggesting an affinity between the frequently explicit and inventive violence of early modern tragedy (especially revenge tragedies) and the graphic violence that finds its way into a number of different genres of popular film.[7] At the same time, none of these writers seemed inclined to pursue the implications of the idea any further than idle speculation. Often, the connections seemed to be made in order to draw students and inexperienced readers of Renaissance texts into the works of Webster, Middleton or Shakespeare, suggesting to them that these texts may not be so very far removed from the entertainment of their own time, after all. An initiative to take these casual comparisons further resulted in the creation of a new undergraduate module, named 'Body Parts: Early Modern Tragedy and Millennium Cinema', which was designed to investigate the parallels more thoroughly. The module set out to discover what preoccupations, tropes or patterns could be traced, mapped or analysed in and between the two genres, and reflected on the discoveries those parallels revealed, regarding both the mysterious past and the often equally disorientating present.

One recurring issue in the design and delivery of the module has been delimiting the genres, and it might be useful at this point to offer some working definitions and provisional categories in order to explain the way in which selections and omissions have been made. The term 'revenge tragedy' has become something of a catch-all term for a large proportion of the tragic drama of the Jacobean period; a homogenising tendency has traditionally classed any play that either includes a vengeance-themed narrative thread or indulges in spectacular and multiple acts of violence as a revenge tragedy. A survey of some of the most familiar plays commonly included in anthologies illustrates the potential difficulties: Katharine Eisaman Maus's collection selects a progenitor (Thomas Kyd's *The Spanish Tragedy* [1584]), Middleton's fairly familiar *The Revenger's Tragedy* (1606), and two plays less frequently staged or studied, George Chapman's *The Revenge of Bussy D'Ambois* and Tourneur's *The Atheist's Tragedy* (both 1609–10).[8] Her choices are all readily classifiable as revenge tragedies, and all of them scrutinise issues of revenge and justice. Gamini Salgado's anthology, on the other hand, chooses a selection of plays that are more familiar in terms of stage history and of their status as study texts: *The Revenger's Tragedy*, *The Changeling* (1622) and *The White Devil* (1612).[9] In both *The Changeling* and *The White Devil*, though revenge plots are discernible, neither provides the extended meditations on justice and revenge that many of their predecessors do. The texts I have traditionally proscribed for the module, and which are studied in most depth in this book, are the more familiar (and, often, more ideologically conflicted) plays such as *The White Devil*, *The Changeling*, *The Revenger's Tragedy* and *Hamlet* (1601). While the revenge theme can be traced in most of them, they perhaps tend towards the looser classification that Fredson Bowers suggests with his term 'tragedy of blood'.[10]

In terms of the range of films chosen for the study, I have used the beginning of the 1970s as a starting point. It is generally agreed that there was a major shift in Hollywood's treatment of controversial issues, notably sex and violence, after the elimination of the Production Code in 1966. It may have taken a few years for the effects to filter through production into product, but within a couple of years, films were breaking new ground in terms of the graphic representation of violence: *Bonnie and Clyde* (1967), *Point Blank* (1967), *The Wild Bunch* (1969) and *Straw Dogs* (1971) were crucial in this transformation. As far as genre is concerned, I have been far more eclectic in my choice of films than in my selection of dramatic texts, where the category of revenge tragedy has provided a useful filter. Cinematic violence may have begun in the thriller genre, as the titles above suggest, but it was not long before it took a strong hold in other genres, notably the horror movie. The discussion in the book, in line with the shifting focus from justice and revenge, to gender, to representations of the damaged body, moves from groundbreaking violent thrillers of the early 1970s, to more recent entries in the thriller and horror genres. Inevitably, the possibilities have been endless, certainly far more open-ended than in the drama, where the proportion of extant texts narrows the field considerably, and the amount of readily available texts thins out the competition still further. My choice of films has generally been in line with the decision to consider texts representative of popular culture – a fraught classification that I shall consider more carefully in a moment. That aside, the aesthetic qualities of the films have been less of a concern than the ideological positions they propose, reflect, challenge or explore. For this reason, analysis ranges from an efficiently made horror movie with little imaginative flair (such as *Friday the 13th* [1980]) to the brilliantly made, but, for most feminists, deeply troubling, *Straw Dogs* (1971).

Pop goes the culture

The terrain this study covers is expansive, from early modern revenge tragedy to urban vigilante movies of the 1970s, slasher movies of the 1980s, teen horror of the late 1990s and early 2000s, and recent 'revenge' movies such as *Man on Fire* (2004) and *Kill Bill* (two parts,

2003 and 2004). Bringing such diverse texts into dialogue raises issues not only of historicity and specificity, but also engages debates about the relationship between popular culture and so-called high culture. Discussion about cultural status quickly becomes complex when either philosophical terms of reference, or paradigms imported from cultural studies, are deployed.[11]

Strictly speaking, mainstream film is an instance of mass culture, since it is produced 'for the people' rather than 'by the people', and it is disseminated globally. Early modern theatre evidently works on a scale (in terms of audience exposure) that is incommensurate with the Hollywood industry (although there are certainly workable parallels between the competing theatre companies of Elizabethan London and Hollywood studio rivalries). Nevertheless, it is probably true to say that, in many respects, the plays themselves would feel more at home in this popular, or mass culture context, given that the original audiences for these plays would undoubtedly have been much more socially hetero-geneous than the middle-class audiences that patronise subsidised theatre in Britain at the start of the twenty-first century, even bearing in mind the various audience demographics for the outdoor playhouses, private playhouses and regular performances at court. While the idea of Queen Elizabeth I attending a performance at the Curtain theatre in disguise – as she does in the climax to the hit film *Shakespeare in Love* (1998) – is fanciful, it does alert us to one very striking aspect of early modern drama: that they were created for both a common and an aristocratic audience, since the plays performed daily in the public playhouses were also presented, at certain times of the year, at Greenwich Palace.

This study is predicated on the idea that there is a direct, cyclical relationship between the structures and institutions of a society, the individuals that make up that society, and the culture they consume. The beliefs, values, political notions and material social relations of a society all inform and, in turn, are informed *by* its individual members. Producers of culture for that society (in particular, popular forms of culture and entertainment) are also part of that network of circulating ideas: they are influenced by it, and respond to it, and often possess a heightened awareness of current ideological shifts. As a part of these cycles of mutual interaction and change, cultural forms – for example, popular film or popular theatre – will be shaped by those ideologies and will in turn contribute to them, helping to mould the representations by which people make sense of themselves, their fellow human beings, and the world around them.

Michael Ryan and Douglas Kellner suggest a number of ways in which these ideological shifts may be processed in popular culture forms: sometimes they seem to offer 'idealize[d] solutions' to contemporary crises, while at other times they may project contemporary fears into 'metaphors that allow those fears to be absolved or played out'; and others offer only 'a nihilistic vision of a world without hope or remedy'.[12] They cite *Dirty Harry* (1971), *Jaws* (1976) and *Chinatown* (1974) as representative examples of each category in 1970s Hollywood. In the context of the other time period covered by this study, a list might include *Henry V* (1599) (idealised solution), Marlowe's *The Jew of Malta* (c.1589) (fears played out) and *King Lear* (1605) (nihilistic vision), while acknowledging that each choice is contentious, and could very easily provide three chapters of heated debate. In terms of methodology, the key focus for the study of the texts that follows is the impact they have had on the lives of those who consume them. The idea that mass culture can do nothing but endorse the dominant ideology remains current among a community of more high-minded media critics, even while the theoretical structures that underpin such a belief, epitomised by Theodor Adorno and Max Horkheimer's *Dialectic of Enlightenment* (1947), have been radically overhauled or abandoned. Mainstream popular film's detractors tend to dismiss these films as 'eye candy' and 'popcorn movies', assuming that audiences check in their brains at the box office and collect them again as they leave. According to these critics, high-cultural texts favour symbol, metaphor and indirection, while popular texts are direct, explicit and graphic; high culture is polysemic and multivalent, while popular culture deals with the surface and is monological; high culture appeals to our imaginations and extends the boundaries of thought and feeling, while the popular can tell us nothing we do not already know; high culture evokes emotions that are appropriate and proportionate, while the popular trades in the sentimental, and excesses of emotion; the popular text leaves us where we were when we began our encounter with it, but the high-cultural text transforms our notions of ourselves and the world around us.

Certainly, there is some truth in the charge most often laid at the door of popular culture; that is to say, it will tend to re-inscribe values that maintain social order and apparent harmony, rather than challenging the ideology of the status quo. The reasoning is almost tautological: a popular text, to win or maintain popularity, needs to be in line with, or at least convergent with, the dominant ideology. However, as the history of popular culture shows us, this is only half the story. There are many instances when the dominant pattern is disrupted by unexpected, radical eruptions, and the alarm these artefacts inspire in those whose interests they threaten can produce marked ruptures in the fabric of the culture, often scarred further by heavy-handed attempts at censorship. Michael Bristol, writing about early modern theatre, talks of the playhouse as a place where

> the audience has an experience that provides an alternative to regular social discipline: between periods of authorized activity an 'interlude' provides an escape from supervision and from surveillance of attitude, feeling and expression.[13]

Obvious examples of eruptions in the popular culture of the twentieth century include the *EC* horror comics of the late 1940s and early 1950s in the USA, and the 'video nasty' panic in the UK in the 1980s.

The encoding of political ideas and, more generally, notions about the way in which a society should operate, is, of necessity, a covert process. There are exceptions, of course: the films of Michael Moore in recent years are defined by their explicit engagement with politics and a specific agenda, whether it be confronting corporate capitalism (*Roger and Me*, 1989), gun control (*Bowling for Columbine*, 2002), or the bizarre mix of stupidity, shrewd gamesmanship and greed that constitutes the Republican party and the President of the United States in the early years of the new millennium (*Fahrenheit 9/11*, 2004). Moore's work, especially *Fahrenheit 9/11*, is a good example of a rare disruption of the status quo. The revival of interest in the documentary film, via Moore's work, and other surprise box office hits such as Morgan Spurlock's attack on McDonald's culture, *Supersize Me* (2003), along with other diverse documentaries such as *Touching the Void* (2003), and *Capturing the Friedmans* (2003) indicates one way in which cultural shifts can occur, with an innovative box office hit helping to set the agenda for a new fashion. Furthermore, a wider perspective on cultural change at the beginning of the new millennium reveals evidence that an audience had already been primed for the political depth charges of *Fahrenheit 9/11* and *Supersize Me* by the anti-globalisation trends epitomised by the likes of Melanie Klein's *No Logo* (2000) and Eric Schlosser's *Fast Food Nation* (2001), and widespread activism by environmentalist and like-minded groups, particularly the regular disruption of G8 conferences around the world. For the most part, however, ideology works through popular culture in much more subtle and complex ways than this, and the work of Michael Moore is, in terms of the current debate, anomalous precisely because of its documentary style and subject matter.

Robert Kolker draws our attention to the way in which American film has always 'attempted to hide itself, to make invisible the telling of its stories, and to downplay or deny the ways in which it supports, reinforces, and even sometimes subverts the major cultural, political and social attitudes that surround and penetrate it'.[14] Kolker reminds his reader that film is a fiction, a representation that processes 'reality': 'It substitutes images and sounds for "real" experience, and with those images and sounds communicates to us and manipulates particular feelings, ideas and perspectives on reality.'[15] At the same time, it is important to beware the totalising tendency of Foucauldian interpretations of culture that choose to depict societies as being devoid of agency. More recent social histories have emphasised the notion of 'individuals as active agents within their life-worlds, able to negotiate with conventions of their time and place by finessing the inherent contradictions of social hierarchy and arbitrating between competing expectations'.[16]

And what of drama and ideology in the early modern period? There is no doubt that theatre around 1600 was preoccupied with the tangled live wires of political tensions, most importantly the continuing oppression of Catholics, and internal Protestant struggles between the traditionalists and the Puritan factions. There was deep-seated anxiety about the future of the English throne as Elizabeth neared the end of her life, and the same concerns can be traced in Shakespeare's history plays, and many of the political tragedies of the era. Franco Moretti even suggests tragedy was at this point in history 'an unrivalled instrument of criticism and dissent'.[17] These critiques – if they were that – were inevitably covert: as Ben Jonson knew from personal experience, playwrights could be imprisoned for cutting too close to a political nerve; for his part in the authorship of *The Isle of Dogs*, and its 'very seditious and slanderous matter', he served time in prison in 1597, and ran into trouble again with *Sejanus: His Fall* in 1603. Historians and literary critics frequently cite the case of *Richard II*, revived for a performance at the Globe in February 1601 at the request of supporters of Robert Devereux, the Earl of Essex. The revival, Essex hoped, would stir up the people to support him in his attempt to seize the throne from Elizabeth. The fact that it failed miserably to rouse any rabble whatever is almost beside the point: what matters is that Essex believed the play had the *potential* to incite rebellion. C. L. Barber, considering the case of *The Spanish Tragedy*, finds it 'remarkable', at a time when there were constant fears of assassination attempts on Elizabeth I, that 'the public theatre was able to take the liberty to represent, over and over again in a smash hit, an author-actor arranging, by a play, to butcher an entire royal line'. He suggests that Kyd's later arrest, imprisonment and torture may well have had something to do with 'the seditious potential of [his] art'.[18] Of course, James I was also acutely aware of the political potential of the theatre, and moved swiftly to establish his control over it, ensuring that patronage of the playing companies was a right of royalty, not of the nobility, as it had been under Elizabeth.[19] It is worth bearing in mind the degree of self-censorship playwrights of the time might have felt obliged to exercise, since '[a]mong the 2,000 plays composed between 1590 and 1642,' Nigel Wheale writes, 'there is only evidence of censorship being exercised on about thirty occasions, and few of these were directly political interventions'.[20]

The notion that it is useful, important, or even vital to seek ways of understanding, decoding and critiquing the popular forms of entertainment that have such a massive impact on society and personal identity in the West is no longer seriously contested. The belief that students might be educated and empowered by the capacity to interpret (rather than simply consume) images on TV, the cinema screen and in other new media such as games consoles and the Internet has found widespread acceptance. Tony Bennett, writing in his introduction to the collection of essays on *Popular Fictions* (1990), claims that the best reason for studying popular fictions is 'that it matters', for 'popular fictions regulate our sense of ourselves and structure our daily lives'.[21] Proof of the extent to which our understanding of our world is refracted by popular culture is all around us. The perceptions of many people witnessing the destruction of the Twin Towers on 11 September 2001, either directly or via TV, that it seemed 'just like a movie', are familiar. Tom Shone notes how, within three days of the attack, bootleg DVDs were on sale in China that intercut images from the terrorist attack with 'the theme from *Jaws*, and clips from *Godzilla*, *Pearl Harbor*, and *The Rock*'.[22] Amid the horrifying accounts of death and survival in the reports emerging from the Asian tsunami disaster in December 2004, one had a hotel waiter running from the surging flood shouting, 'it's *The Day After Tomorrow*', a reference to the Hollywood disaster movie released earlier the same year that had New York City disappearing under a massive, globally-warmed tidal wave.[23] If a teacher chooses to explain a term such as 'hegemony' to her students via references to the Nora Ephron/Mel Gibson movie *What Women Want* (2000), or the concept of gender as a sliding scale via discussion of *Lara Croft: Tomb Raider* (2001), then this is not about being patronising, but rather employing strategies chosen precisely because hegemony or gender identity matter to those students first and foremost in terms of the way they relate to their own culture and society.

Texts constructed according to formulas, tailored as potential blockbuster material, concocted via painstaking distillation of box office figures, market surveys and test audiences, do not necessarily offer themselves up for straightforward analysis. As Gerald Graff puts it succinctly, 'what creates difficulty ... is not just the object of study but *the kind of question being asked about it*'.[24] The readings that follow – offering an analysis of *Titus Andronicus*, for example, or a study of a contemporary popular horror film – do not rely primarily on such notions as thematic, character or linguistic complexity, but rather on the effects on an audience. In the same way that, in film studies, a movie such as *Dirty Harry* may be of interest for the way in which it intervened in American culture, politics and society in the early 1970s, a play such as *The Changeling* can be analysed not primarily in aesthetic terms (which may, depending on taste and fashion, lead us to denigrate it), but in order to consider it primarily as a cultural artefact.[25] At the same time, of course, it would be foolish to assume that under-standing the specific ideological contours of a text's impact can be separated from its aesthetic form.

Between two worlds: *Doctor Faustus* (1588) and *Se7en* (1995)

In order to consider a 400-year gap in Western culture, separating, roughly, the centuries 1600 from 2000, religious belief can operate as a useful marker of historical difference. A Gallup International poll taken in 2000 yielded a global figure of 87 per cent responding that they considered themselves to belong to some kind of religion.[26] However, the survey also revealed that only 63 per cent felt that God was 'important in their life', and only 45 per cent of those expressing a belief in God claimed to have a concept of the divinity as a 'personal God' as opposed to some kind of life force (30 per cent). Naturally, the proportions change geographically: 49 per cent of Western Europeans considered God to be significant in their lives, compared with 97 per cent of West Africans. However, even in what are routinely referred to as the post-Christian societies of the developed world, the results of a Harris Poll in 2003 that revealed that 90 per cent of adult Americans believe in God, and 84 per cent believe in the survival of the soul after death, may come as a surprise.[27] A number of cultural critics have noted that, in the post-9/11 climate, some kind of revival of interest in and exploration of religion is not a total surprise: Mel Gibson's lurid account of *The Passion of the Christ* (2004) established itself rapidly as the highest-grossing R-rated[28] film of all time, courting controversy for its alleged anti-Semitism along the way. Even a film as unlikely as the remake of *Dawn of the Dead* (2004) took time out to make some capital out of its tag-line ('when there's no more room in hell, the dead will walk the earth'), with a TV evangelist ramming home the message of God's judgement on a people that allows drugs, drunkenness and sexual immorality to run rampant. Matt Zoller Seitz notes the post-9/11 touches and the 'end of days' feel of the movie, very different from the Romero film it is remodelling:

> The ruined America depicted in the new *Dead* still appears democratic, capitalist, secular. But an unknowable spiritual world lurks beneath the surface. When the spiritual world erupts and the horror show unfolds, we sense that characters who didn't think about the afterlife before are thinking about it now.[29]

Nevertheless, looked at more closely, the precise nature of contemporary belief in God, even within the Christian tradition specifically, is revealed as something that must be in many ways incommensurate with the God of the pre-Enlightenment era. Some extreme forms of fundamentalist Christianity aside (where science is exchanged for the superstitious conviction that mental illness can be explained by demonic possession and cured by exorcism), religious belief has altered drastically since the time rationalism and empiricism slowly drove a wedge between the material world and the spiritual dimension. In a society where the average life expectancy was little more than half of what it is now, when an eruption of the plague could wipe out almost a quarter of London's population, as it did in 1603, the line between this life and the next must have seemed much more apparent, and much more easily crossed, or tripped, over. Concepts of heaven and hell, damnation and salvation would presumably have been more concrete and immediate to a typical Elizabethan than they seem to many of us today. Christopher Marlowe's *Doctor Faustus*, for example, seems to be predicated on an understanding of existence that takes for granted the supernatural realm: indeed, physical reality and the spiritual cohabit the stage in a way that roots the play in the medieval tradition of mystery and morality drama. The controversial religious subject matter of *Faustus* certainly piqued the interest of the Master of the Revels in early performances of the play; he probably decided that it transgressed a law that banned the use of the name of God, Jesus Christ, the Holy Ghost, or the Trinity in stage plays, and censored it accordingly. Even in its cut version, however, the play remains remarkable for the way in which the immediate, imminent presence of the supernatural erupts, both in the direct representation of spiritual beings on stage, and in conversations between Faustus and Mephistopheles. Medieval drama is populated chiefly by virtues, vices, angels and devils (entities that would today be understood largely as mythical figures and abstract terms), and in these plays it is man who is the abstraction. The 'Everyman' figure (the play's closest approximation of a 'hero') is not an individual 'character', but an allegorical representation of sinful humankind. *Doctor Faustus* features devils and angels, as well as the seven deadly sins, and manifestations of mythical figures such as Helen of Troy. Faustus is attended by a Good Angel and an Evil Angel, who tempt him and warn him, respectively, of the implications of his pursuits at crucial moments. At the same time, while predicating its action and its significance on the reality of the supernatural, Marlowe's play can be seen, paradoxically, as being deeply sceptical. One of the enduring, puzzling fascinations of *Faustus* is the way in which it straddles a faultline in the ideology of Elizabethan England – the text plays with different notions of the relationship between human and God, conflicting ideas rooted in theological debates about free will and determinism that raged during the Reformation. One of the reasons why the play may have created so much critical controversy is because it seems to encompass two different cosmologies, one centred on the traditional church doctrine and the other tending towards scepticism, pondering a human-centred universe where no divine blood streams in the firmament.

David Fincher's movie *Se7en*, for its plot, its atmosphere, and its disturbing, philosophical undertow, relies very heavily on a Christian metaphysic. The serial killer John Doe (Kevin Spacey) sees himself as divinely inspired, on a mission from God to make an example of the sinful men and women that surround him by creating a murderous masterpiece that illustrates the seven deadly sins, judging and passing sentence on each of his victims (or, more accurately, forcing each of them to pass judgement on themselves). Doe's apartment features a huge neon cross above his bed, and a large crucifix at the bedside. His killing spree sends Detective Somerset (Morgan Freeman) hunting in the library for clues, where he pores over works by Chaucer, Dante, Thomas Aquinas and Milton; the camera lingers over images of the suffering of souls – depicted in grossly physical form – in the tortures of hell and purgatory. When Detectives Mills (Brad Pitt) and Somerset talk to the doctor attending the victim Sloth, who has spent a year tied to a bed while carefully kept barely alive by Doe, the doctor tells them, 'He's experienced about as much pain and suffering as anyone I've encountered, give or take; and he still has hell to look forward to'. The line walks a tightrope that the film negotiates throughout, for this is, in short, lamb dressed as mutton: a philosophical film masquerading as a buddy-cop-serial-killer movie. The delivery of the line, as well as the framing of the moment, is crucial: somewhat underplayed by the actor, the placement of the doctor in the centre, with Mills and Somerset either side, allows for Morgan Freeman's reaction of puzzled but weary shock at the doctor's curiously moralistic bias. As elsewhere in the film, some doubt clings to the question of just how alien *is* Doe's disgust at the world?

'Come,' says Faustus to the devil Mephistopheles. 'I think hell's a fable.' 'Ay,' replies the devil; 'think so still, till experience change thy mind' (2.1.127–8). As the detectives in *Se7en* close in on their quarry, Somerset tells Mills, 'If we catch John Doe and he turns out to be the devil, I mean, if he's Satan *himself*, that might live up to our expectations but . . . he's *not* the devil: he's just a man.' In Act 1, Scene 3 of *Faustus*, the hero questions the devil about the nature of heaven and hell: 'Where are you damned?' he asks him, and Mephistopheles replies: 'In hell.' Faustus pursues his questioning: 'How comes it then that thou art out of hell?' and the reply is: 'Why, this is hell, nor am I out of it' (1.3.74–7). If, as Christian teaching would have it, hell is simply the absence of God – the one place where God is not – then *Se7en*, in its closing moments, abandons Mills and Somerset to damnation. For over an hour and a half, we (and they) have been immersed in gloom and rain, the darkest scenes grimly smudged with colour where shafts of light attempted to pierce the blackness. It is easy to see the cityscape as a kind of hell or purgatory, a place of such frequent and brutal acts of violence that Somerset begins the film backing out of it: he is due to retire from the police force in seven days' time. For the final reel, he and Mills leave the city behind and drive out into a bleak, parched, dusty wasteland, towards a destination proscribed by Doe. Their progress is carefully watched over from above by helicopter throughout their trip: there are frequent cuts to a God's eye view from the helicopter, often specifically through the binoculars of the oddly monikered officer, California, barking orders, apparently keeping a firm hand on proceedings.

Figure 1.1 Damnation in a world without God: Brad Pitt as Mills in *Se7en* (dir. Fincher, 1995)
Source: Publicity still, Rex Features.

As the final scene unspools, however, and begins to slip away from the officers' control, their confidence, and the helicopter's seeming omniscience, slips too. When Mills (see Figure 1.1), after the revelation that Doe has killed and decapitated Mills' pregnant wife, fires the first shot into Doe's head, there is a brief cut to the helicopter itself, a blur of confused motion as California, incredulous, shouts, 'Oh fuck, he shot him.' Mills's face is seen in close-up as he empties his clip into Doe's body, and after a shot of Somerset turned away, head bowed, followed by a wider shot with Somerset behind and out of focus and Mills in the foreground, shaky, his eyes darting and seeing nothing, we return to the God's eye view from the helicopter. However, this time, there is no sense of control, only horror in the fallout of events that have moved too fast and too unexpectedly to be dealt with. From the helicopter, the three figures are seen picked out in the landscape, Doe prostrate, Somerset motionless, Mills striding away, and the voice over the helicopter headset, no longer issuing orders but as lost and bewildered as those stranded below: 'Holy Christ. Somebody call somebody. Call somebody.' It is perhaps the most pessimistic line of the entire film, a cry from a bottomless pit of despair: no one to make the call, and no one at the other end of the line.

This brief discussion of *Se7en* and *Doctor Faustus* suggests, in impressionistic fashion, some of the ways in which the contemporary and the early modern can be read in parallel. Although, in tonal terms, it anticipates some of what follows, the analysis that makes up the three key parts of this study by contrast proceeds more systematically, building from the cultural specificity of context-setting chapters to detailed parallel studies of the likes of *The Changeling* and *Straw Dogs*, and *The Revenger's Tragedy* and *Taxi Driver* (1976). The first part covers the issues of justice and revenge. The context-setting chapters introduce the concepts, first in early modern tragedy and then in contemporary film, with a focus in the latter on the urban vigilante movie of the early 1970s. The third chapter of this section proceeds with a parallel discussion of the early modern and contemporary texts that considers the political and moral dimensions of the revenger; and it ends with an extended coda that considers the revival of the revenge genre in Hollywood since the terrorist attacks of '9/11'. The second part considers gender and violence: the early modern context chapter takes a conceptual approach and references a wide range of play texts, while the cinema chapter adopts a different strategy and instead offers a shorter overview followed by contrasting treatments of the issue of spousal abuse in two popular movies, made about a decade apart: *Sleeping with the Enemy*

(1991) and *Enough* (2002) (Chapter 7). The final part, centred on representations of death and the damaged body, takes a further step towards more complete integration, treating the genres in parallel via an introduction, then a study of physical damage and destruction ('Spectacles of Death') and finally the idea of death, punishment and damnation ('Punishment and Redemption').

The final part and the conclusion, which closes the book with a return to a more impressionistic approach, assumes that the reading strategies have been developed to the point that cautious *caveats* about historical specificity are no longer necessary. The conclusion returns once more to the key element that will reveal itself as being fundamental to the study as a whole, and offers a brief reflection on the rare figure of the female revenger. In the mainstream movies of the second half of the twentieth century, women are fought over by men; they are punished, abused and mutilated for assertions of sexual autonomy; but just occasionally they turn, rise up and wreak vengeance on their male oppressors.

Part I
Justice and Revenge

1
Introduction: 'Don't Get Mad, Get Even'

On the afternoon of 22 December 1984, on a busy Manahattan subway train, four youths challenged Bernhard Goetz, a self-employed electronics expert; one of them reportedly asked him for five dollars. When Goetz asked the questioner, Troy Canty, to repeat himself, he was told to hand over his money. Goetz responded by standing up, drawing a concealed revolver, and shooting and wounding Canty and his three associates. When the train came to a stop after the conductor in the next carriage pulled the emergency cord, Goetz made his escape by slipping off the train and across the tracks, afterwards hiring a car and driving to Vermont. He finally surrendered himself to New Hampshire police on New Year's Eve. The trial that followed featured furious debate about urban crime, vigilantism and issues of race: Goetz was white, and all four of his victims were African-Americans. While the controversies raged, it became clear that there was a strong groundswell of public opinion in favour of Goetz's actions: all four youths had criminal records prior to the incident (and all except for Darryl Cabey, left paralysed after the shooting, have committed further serious crimes since Goetz's trial). Despite his confession and plea of self-defence, Goetz, dubbed 'the subway vigilante', was acquitted of all nine felony charges at his trial – including one charge of attempted murder and assault against each of the four victims, and an additional charge of reckless endangerment – but found guilty of illegal possession of a weapon. He served eight months in prison. In 1985, Cabey filed a civil suit against Goetz and, over ten years later, a jury found that Goetz had acted recklessly and deliberately inflicted emotional distress on Cabey, who was awarded US$43 million in damages. Goetz filed for bankruptcy and left New York City soon afterwards, telling one newspaper: 'Let's say this town won't have Bernie Goetz to kick around anymore.'[1]

The human desire to seek vengeance on those who wrong us is deeply rooted in human psychology, sociology and religious belief. Despite René Girard's contention that interfamily vendettas or blood feuds define 'the fundamental difference between primitive societies and our own',[2] the fantasy – if not the reality – of vengeance is not limited to so-called primitive societies, but recurs throughout the history of Western culture. *Hamlet* (1601), which has perhaps spawned a theatrical afterlife, and a critical and literary legacy, unmatched by any other dramatic work, is structured around a revenge narrative. The play has cast a particularly powerful spell over audiences down the centuries, and there is no doubt that this mysteriously elusive text has distinct features that mark it out from other revenge tragedies. It has provoked the widest possible range of different reinterpretations, from psychoanalytic to existentialist and deconstructionist studies, but when the haze of critical readings clears, it is the revenge plot that remains at the heart of the text – or, more accurately, *four* revenge plots: as well as Hamlet's own vendetta against Claudius for having killed Old Hamlet, Laertes seeks revenge on Hamlet for the death of his father Polonius, and, on the outskirts of the play, the Norwegian prince Fortinbras seeks revenge against Denmark for the death of his father; in addition, at Hamlet's request, an actor recounts the tale of Pyrrhus and Priam. All three revenge sub-plots are used to highlight Hamlet's own reluctance to move against Claudius – often by Hamlet himself.

Reports of acts of revenge, factual, fictional and mythical, have seeped deeply into Western culture. It is very much part of our common conceptual currency: an Internet news search engine, on any particular day, may turn up a dozen different revenge-related stories that have hit the electronic headlines within the hour, even if over half of them are likely to be items of sports news ('The Best Thing Ever: Red Sox Revenge'; 'Eagles Look for Revenge Against Blue Bears'; 'Venus [Williams, tennis pro] Gets Revenge'). During the course of the writing of this book, particularly notable issues and events have included the ongoing Arab–Israeli conflict, frequently reported in terms of reprisal and revenge ('Hamas Threatens with a Painful Revenge Attack'). The bombing of a nightclub in Bali in October 2002 was termed an act of revenge for the deaths of Muslims in Iraq, Palestine and Afghanistan by its architect, and the trial of one of the suspects, Amrozi, in a country that routinely enforces the death penalty, sparked a debate about vengeance and retribution. Most obviously – its scale eclipsing all other instances – the destruction of the World Trade Centre on 11 September 2001 has taken on a monumental significance in terms of reprisal and revenge, with ideas and debates about justice and retribution ramifying in ways that are impossible to record comprehensively. In Europe, the conflicts in the Balkan states of Albania, Serbia, Montenegro and Macedonia have generated a large body of historical and sociological work, as well as film, poetry and fiction, interpreting the wars and associated atrocities in terms of blood vengeance.[3]

If the popular arts supply a space for the dreams and fears of a culture, it should not surprise us to find revenge returning to haunt us like a recurring nightmare, or (to some, or in some circumstances) a reassuring, cathartic fantasy. John G. Cawelti notes that while the law of 'an eye for an eye' (or *lex talionis*) has been rejected by most civilised cultures, it has continued to flourish in popular literature: 'There, unlike in life, circumstances can be manipulated to insure a moral and poetic equivalence between the criminal act and the hero's vengeance.'[4] The protracted, graphic display of the plotting and enactment of revenge allows the audience a space in which they may indulge their own frustrations and fantasies, while allowing them to endorse the orthodox abhorrence of such base drives and emotions in the real world. Crucially, the transformation of revenge from reality to representation allows the artist the opportunity to ensure that the violence perpetrated by the revenger is in some way restorative. Richard Slotkin's analysis of violence in the Western genre argues that violence is justifiable when it is redemptive, or progressive – bringing about positive social change.[5] This works as a useful principle for the revenge genre too: the fantasy of revenge requires the neatly tailored fit of poetic justice in order to fulfil its function. More often than not, the revenge narrative establishes the revenger as a figure so profoundly wronged that the audience is coerced into feelings of sympathy and understanding that it will often find impossible to resist. Hamlet is deprived of a beloved father by his uncle, who not only steals the throne, but also the queen, Hamlet's mother. Titus Andronicus is confronted with the sight of his raped and mutilated daughter. Frank Castle in *The Punisher* (2004), Sean Vetter in *A Man Apart* (2003) and Paul Kersey in *Death Wish* (1974) suffer brutal assaults upon, or the slaughter of, their wives and children. Vinidice (*The Revenger's Tragedy*) is introduced to us bearing the skull of his beloved, poisoned by the lustful duke after she refused to surrender herself to him. In *The Spanish Tragedy*, Hieronimo and Isabella find their son butchered and left hanging in an arbour. In such instances, the audience is invited to relish, within safe, fictional boundaries, the acts of vengeance. However, as I will show, a number of the texts challenge, disrupt or attempt to subvert the concept of natural, or 'poetic' justice, and it is at these moments that the genre ignites some of its most potent and provocative flashpoints.

Art forms in both 'high' and 'popular' culture have over the centuries displayed, time and time again, the wide-ranging and powerful appeal of the notion of purifying violence. Terence Hawkes describes how, '[f]or a culture in crisis, the narrative structure of tragedy seemed to offer an effective form of shaping and control to set against the incoherence and confusion of the "tale told by an idiot" otherwise confronting it'.[6] Revenge narratives, with their self-immolating protagonists, have always provided useful source material for tragedians, although it is also worth noting that the same plot has, on a number of occasions, run itself into the sand, particularly within the urban vigilante genre. The revenge plot carries a powerful emotional punch, and almost always lends a narrative a terrific forward momentum. However, it can also descend into hackneyed formula, as a brief rundown of the *Death Wish* series shows. Charles Bronson played the quiet liberal turned gun-toting scourge of the streets, Paul Kersey, in five films between 1974 and 1994, and a sketch of the premise for each illustrates the collapse of the franchise: in *Death Wish* (1974), Kersey's wife is killed, his daughter left catatonic, and Kersey launches his vendetta against New York's muggers; in the cynically exploitative *Death Wish II* (1982), his daughter recovers, only to be raped and killed, along with Kersey's housekeeper; in *Death Wish 3* (1985), an old friend is beaten to death; in *Death Wish 4: The Crackdown* (1987), Kersey tackles America's drug problem; and in *Death Wish V: The Face of Death* (1994), the original plot is recycled again when the hero's fiancée is murdered.

Although Terence Hawkes' phrase 'culture in crisis' is open-ended enough to apply to many different societies, it is possible to identify specific aspects of particular cultures that constitute a seedbed for the cyclical revival of revenge narratives. In the early modern political climate, particularly following the succession of King James VI of Scotland to the English throne in 1603, strands of social and political development can be traced that may have 'primed' the theatre audiences of the time in this way. The revenge genre, of course, pre-dates the Jacobean period, but its full flowering, in the dark hues bestowed upon it by the likes of John Webster and Thomas Middleton, would come in the new century, and the specific contours the genre developed in the early 1600s – especially in relation to the protagonist's dilemma in confronting a corrupt justice system – take on a special significance after James I's succession.

The first of the three cultural moments under close consideration in this part of the book, then, is the Jacobean period, and the tragic drama of that era. The second period is the early 1970s, where the sudden proliferation of violent films preoccupied with revenge and, specifically, the close conceptual relative of revenge, vigilantism, is considered in relation to the political upheavals in America at that time. Although the cop action/thriller has been a staple of the Hollywood dream factory since the late 1940s, there are two noticeable 'spikes' along Hollywood's timeline when the vigilante sub-genre has come into favour: in the early 1970s, and in the first few years of the new millennium, the figure of the revenger seems to have gripped the collective consciousness of film-makers and audiences, especially in the USA. Although there is a danger of simply 'reading off' overt or subconscious 'messages' encoded in movies such as *Death Wish* (1974), *Dirty Harry* (1971) and, more recently, *Man on Fire* and *The Punisher* (both 2004), and *Kill Bill* (two parts, released 2003 and 2004), nevertheless, there are associations that are difficult to ignore. Both in contemporary reviews and with the benefit of hindsight (particularly in terms of the films of the 1970s), critics have habitually read the films as political texts that engage with contemporary issues, and some of the most popular thrillers of the respective eras – their aesthetic merits notwithstanding – are fascinating documents of the interaction of popular taste and political change at different points in history.

Via parallel treatments of texts such as *The Revenger's Tragedy* and *Dirty Harry*, I hope to provide some speculative answers to a number of key questions about the representation of revenge; for example, what does the exploration of this fundamental human drive in entertainment form reveal about the way we relate to one another, and to our wider social contexts? What can it tell us about oppositions and tensions between the state and its subjects? How are the dichotomies of state justice and personal vengeance worked through in texts from different historical periods? J. W. Lever's prescient, influential study, *The Tragedy of State* (1971), found in the tragedies of the Jacobean age something that corresponded to the insecurities of his own time:

The nihilism of our own age, sprung of a sense of helplessness in a world controlled by huge aggregations of power, has its affinities in folk attitudes in other times...The spectacle of the court, caricatured, degenerate, pullulating with intrigue, would mirror the secret attitude of the people down the ages towards the powers that be, recognizing in them qualities at once horrific, fascinating, and funny; an attitude which, out of a conviction of helplessness resembling our own, of necessity tempers hatred with laughter.[7]

The conflict between state justice and individual revenge is fundamental to very many early modern tragedies. Four hundred years later,
such conflicts reverberate in sub-genres of contemporary violent film.
Furthermore, their recurrence in mainstream movies can also be tied to
specific shifts in the social and political culture. By exploring possible
parallels and connections, as well as sharp distinctions between the two
periods, a fuller understanding may emerge of the human fascination with
revenge, and our apparently insatiable hunger for vicarious experience of
this most consuming of human passions.

As the short parallel study of *Doctor Faustus* and *Se7en* in the Introduction suggested, there are huge differences between the early modern
mindset and our understanding of society and the world today; the
respective cosmologies, our ways of understanding the universe in
metaphysical terms, are worlds apart. To put it simply, and to take just
one example, it would have been almost impossible for an Elizabethan
or a Jacobean citizen to consider the problem of revenge without an
awareness of what would now be labelled Reformation theology, and
specifically the prohibition of acts of vengeance on the basis of the
biblical warning in the Apostle Paul's letter to the Roman Church:
'Dearly beloved, avenge not yourselves, but rather give place unto
wrath: for it is written, Vengeance is mine; I will repay, saith the Lord.'[8]
This is only one example of historical difference, but, as I will show in
the next chapter, it is a critical one: seventeenth-century England was
not a place where revenge was condoned by law, and where men
commonly fought duels over matters of honour. However, it would
seem that it was a place where old traditions of vendetta still lingered in
the cultural memory, despite legal and ecclesiastical prohibitions. For
this reason, revenge tragedies engaged with and intervened in very
topical debate.

Despite cultural historical differences, revenge narratives spanning
the centuries play variations on key themes in fascinating and mutually
enlightening ways. This study will consider the ways in which these
preoccupations are reworked in a set of key texts including *Hamlet*, *Titus
Andronicus*, *The Revenger's Tragedy* and *The Spanish Tragedy*, and *Dirty
Harry*, *Death Wish*, *Taxi Driver*, and *Se7en*. Revenge is crystallised in
these texts in two related forms: first, the vigilante, an individual
(almost always male) who engages in a (usually lone) battle to carve out
a path for natural justice in the face of a ruling power that is profoundly
corrupt and a justice system that is often compromised, hopelessly
weak, and unable to right the wrongs perpetrated against victims of
crime; and second, the personal avenger, the individual victim of a

profound wrong, who compromises his own moral purity in order to redress the imbalance and punish the wrongdoer. After considering the political and cultural context for two periods (the Jacobean period and the early 1970s), the investigation will consider three key aspects: the revenger as political figure; the audience's engagement with the revenger; and the morality of revenge. The chapter will conclude with some reflections on the revival of the genre in the early years of the twenty-first century, in particular in the wake of the terrorist attack on the World Trade Center on 11 September 2001: a stark reminder of the continuing, terrifying relevance of these debates.

2
Revenge in Its Social Contexts: Early Modern Tragedy

'Where the offence is, there let the great axe fall': *early modern revenge*

Any attempt to understand the popularity of the revenge tragedy genre in Elizabethan and Jacobean drama must take into account not only the socio-political context, but also the cultural heritage: it is a commonplace that the early forays into the genre in the last years of the sixteenth century were influenced heavily by the Senecan tradition. From Seneca, the dramatists inherited the call to blood-revenge, often via the spirits of the dead or visions of the Furies, as well as a basic structure of exposition of a revenge plot, development, confrontation, delay and catastrophic action. However, as John Kerrigan points out in his study of representations of the execution of Charles I in relation to revenge tragedy conventions, '[t]he attractions of Seneca were always partial...and in themselves political', entwined as they were with concerns about counselling rulers against tyranny and poor government.[1] While it is important not to neglect the Senecan influence – particularly on the earliest experiments in early modern English revenge tragedy – the present study's main concern is with the relationship between cultural artefacts and their socio-political context; in other words, the cyclical action and reaction of the lived experience of a people and what be recovered of their popular culture.

History and anthropology reveal revenge to have been fundamental to the customs and practices of primitive societies. Fredson Bowers notes that 'the modern theory of crime presupposes the existence of a State', and in a society with no state, there could be no crime in this strict sense: the only recourse for the wronged party was direct revenge on the one who had inflicted the injury.[2] With the emergence of patriarchy as a determining force in society, the moral 'right' to revenge was formalised as a 'binding obligation', and the vendetta or blood-feud held sway in England until the notion of a central authority (the monarchy) took hold. René Girard writes, '[a]s long as there exists no sovereign and independent body capable of taking the place of the injured party and taking upon itself the responsibility for revenge, the danger of interminable escalation remains'.[3] In this respect, Bowers notes the increasing significance of the monarch in terms of the law and punishment, including evidence from as early as the seventh century that the king had an entitlement to damages in civil cases.[4] Murderers were still being given a choice of trial by jury or judicial combat during the reign of Edward II (AD 975–78), but the arrival of William the Conqueror hastened the establishment of centralised state justice in England.[5] Bowers notes the shift from the appeal system (whereby the widow of a murder victim, or his heirs, could prosecute the killer) to indictment (the accused put on trial on the presentation of evidence to the authorities) as crucial in the phasing out of blood revenge.[6] However, the appeal system had not been abandoned completely by the sixteenth century, and in this way the spirit of vendetta lived on in the culture in residual form.

The Church had already maintained this strong line, militating against revenge, for some time. The scriptural authority most often cited was the prohibition set out in Romans 12:19 ('Vengeance is mine; I will repay, saith the Lord'), along with similar verses in the book of Hebrews (10:30) and the Old Testament book of Deuteronomy (32:35). In *The Spanish Tragedy* (1584) Hieronimo makes reference to the Biblical injunction:

> *Vindicta mihi!*
> Ay, heaven will be reveng'd of every ill,
> Nor will they suffer murder unrepaid:
> Then stay, Hieronimo, attend their will,
> For mortal men may not appoint their time. (3.13.1–5)

However, the speech that follows proceeds to justify his case for seeking his own revenge, and ends with his resolve to do just that (3.13.20). For an unorthodox Elizabethan, such a decision might well have been interpreted as a route to eternal damnation. Both Prosser and Bowers quote a number of writers of the period who spell out the consequences of the decision to take revenge into one's own hands, including Bishop Hall's warning (published 1612) that it meant a double death, the death of body and soul.[7] Hamlet's suspicion that the ghost of his father might be 'the devil' in a 'pleasing shape' come to 'abuse...me to damn me', by tempting him to kill Claudius (2.2.588–92), can be read as a line in keeping with the orthodoxy about revenge and damnation. Furthermore, one who would seek vengeance was depicted by many of the same writers as damned to endure mental torture in this life, too: a clear precedent for the dramatists' convention of the madness of the revenger. Prosser concludes that, 'Elizabethan moralists condemned revenge as illegal, blasphemous, immoral, irrational, unnatural and unhealthy – not to mention unsafe'.[8] In this respect, then, the church's line is what might be expected at this time: its moral teaching maintains the political status quo, supporting the orthodox line with a series of warnings about the perils to the human soul for those who would ignore its teaching. The belief that God would distribute his own kind of justice, Kerrigan notes, led many to look around for evidence of his judgement on evil-doers and while some writers – notably Jonathan Dollimore – suggest that providentialist belief was falling away as early as 1600, Kerrigan believes there is little historical evidence to support this theory.[9] While *The Revenger's Tragedy* and even *The Atheist's Tragedy* can conceivably be read as parodying the idea of the 'theatre of God's judgements' (to steal a phrase from a popular collection of cautionary tales put together by Thomas Beard), the dramatisation of the Christian dilemma of justice and revenge in *Hamlet* and a number of other plays of the period offers much more serious engagements with providentialism.

In England, then, there seems to have been a gradual shift away from privately exacted revenge and the tradition of feud (wars between families) – with its roots in chivalric codes of honour and vengeance – towards a centrally-organised justice system, as the state became more firmly established, its hegemony underpinned by Christian doctrine. By the sixteenth century, a serious crime against any subject of the Crown is being interpreted as a crime against the monarch him- or herself, and the state is required to respond.[10] Plotted revenge is clearly regarded as 'murder with malice *prepense*' (premeditated), and as such was outlawed; the only possible exception was in the case of spontaneous response to an injury, which could be classed as manslaughter (and could therefore be pardoned by the monarch).[11] This distinction in Elizabethan law between premeditated murder and manslaughter is important: the murder of an individual as a spontaneous act of passion would have been considered far less serious than a premeditated act, and in the revenge tragedies of the period the dramatists frequently devote time and space to their revengers' meticulous plotting and keen anticipation of their actions. When this does not feature as a part of the drama's development, it is quite possible that the audiences would have been inclined to respond differently to the revengers. However, to all intents and purposes, it seems, the Elizabethan state refused to countenance acts of private revenge, and the research of a number of critics has uncovered a wealth of references in the writings of preachers, philosophers and moralists that condemn it in the strongest terms.[12]

However, what requires closer attention is the potential for tension between orthodox decrees about the immorality of revenge on the one hand, and the lived and felt reality of the Elizabethans themselves, on the other: what would the playhouse audiences have made of plays such as *The Spanish Tragedy*, *Hamlet* (1601) and *The Revenger's Tragedy* (1606) when they were first staged? The true dynamics of this tension are likely to remain largely a mystery and a matter for speculation, since recorded accounts of audience responses to specific plays are few and far between. However, it is easy to believe that many who had inherited a tradition in which families settled scores for themselves at a local level could have felt intense frustration at the introduction of a centralised legal bureaucracy and, under these conditions, it is quite feasible that revenge tragedies might have provided some kind of pressure valve release. Jong-Hwan Kim, recognising that some residual commitment to the old ethic of blood vengeance probably lingered in the cultural memory of the audience, speculates that, in writing *Hamlet*, Shakespeare might have 'hoped to appeal to audiences' instinct' by presenting an individual's 'struggle against ruthless revenge and his reluctance to be the conventional revenger'.[13] Jong-Hwan Kim believes that Shakespeare resolved the dilemma by allowing providence to reveal Claudius's villainy publicly, although it is still difficult to find a way around the fact that Hamlet gives providence a helping hand (or two) by stabbing Claudius with the poisoned sword, and finishing him off by pouring the dregs of the spiked drink down his throat, once Laertes has revealed the true extent of Claudius's treachery.

Lawrence Stone notes the exceptionally sharp rise in litigation between 1550 and 1625, and comments that '[s]ocieties being weaned from habits of private revenge always turn to the law with intemperate enthusiasm'.[14] There was enough flouting of prohibitions on revenge at this time to compel the authorities to pass specific laws against duelling towards the end of the sixteenth century, and the court of the Star Chamber addressed it again in 1615.[15] After all, one who feels compelled to enact private revenge is expressing, implicitly or explicitly, dissatisfaction with the state's ability to intervene in an effective manner. Consequently, 'Blood vengeance', as Katharine Maus remarks, 'almost automatically subverts the power of the crown.'[16] Peter Corbin has noted how James I clearly conceived of the law as an expression of the king's will.[17] Stone, considering the enforcement of law and order in Tudor England, believes that quarrels between individuals of the gentry were generally left to litigation in the courts of law. However, he continues, '[a]s soon as personal feuding looked like turning into treason...the Council acted promptly enough'.[18] If the revenger challenges the rule of law, and if the rule of law is so closely identified with the monarch, is it possible to interpret the revenger as a politically subversive figure in the drama?

Francis Bacon's now wearily familiar phrase, 'Revenge is a kind of wild justice' is probably a fairly reliable indicator of the attitudes of his own time. Less clichéd, but perhaps more significant in terms of the current discussion, Bacon's assertion that, 'as for the first wrong, it doth but offend the law; but the revenge of the wrong putteth the law out of office' is in keeping with the notion of revenge as a crime against the state.[19] In *The Revenge of Bussy D'Ambois*, Clermont repents of his vengeful ways, declaring:

> All worthy men should ever bring their blood
> To bear all ill, not to be wreaked with good.
> Do ill for no ill: never private cause
> Should take on it the part of public laws. (3.2.113–16)

Revenge is regarded as an act even more serious and transgressive than the wrong it seeks to redress: in *Bussy*, Clermont has remained within comparatively legitimate bounds by challenging his brother's murderer to a duel. Widening the search, Eleanor Prosser's study of twenty-one plays written between 1562 and 1607 takes account of around forty characters 'faced with the decision of whether or not to take revenge'. She counts 'six virtuous characters who explicitly reject revenge, five originally virtuous characters who turn villain when they embark on a course of vengeance, seventeen out-and-out villain-revengers, and many others whose threats or advice to pursue revenge are clearly judged as evil'.[20] However, the reality is not quite so simple. Not only do the difficulties in interpreting the interplay of dominant, emergent and residual ideologies need to be considered, there are a number of other variables that are very hard for us to pin down. Prosser's statistics are useful in some respects, but there are inherent dangers in the use of value judgements such as 'virtuous', 'out-and-out villain' and 'evil' in assessments of dramatic characters. It is impossible to know how many members of the audience at a performance of *The Taming of the Shrew* (c. 1596), for example, would have endorsed Petruchio's brutal treatment of his wife Katherine, or agreed with his notion that she is 'my goods, my chattels...my house,/My household stuff, my field, my barn,/My horse, my ox, my ass, my anything' (3.2.219–21). At performances of Christopher Marlowe's *The Jew of Malta* (c. 1590), how many members of the audience would have booed and hissed the pantomimic Jewish villain, Barabas, and how many would have been inclined to cheer his exposure of the hypocrisy of the Christian governor, Ferneze, and the clownish, lustful friars? Or, more pertinently, how many might have found the experience even more thrilling precisely because the performance provoked simultaneously such powerful and mutually contradictory reactions?

For similar reasons, it would be unwise to assume that the playwright or his audiences would have taken particular positions with regard to characters such as Hamlet, Vindice or Hieronimo. Close study of the revenge tragedy genre reveals a spectrum of different attitudes towards and representations of the revenger figure. If *The Atheist's Tragedy* (1607) neatly sets the active, villainous seeker of revenge D'Amville on the one hand, against the virtuous Charlemont, who resigns himself to accepting and waiting on divine providence on the other, D'Amville is by far the more vital character (there is a similar dichotomy in Marlowe's *The Jew of Malta*). René Girard reminds us, in his glancing consideration of Greek tragedy, '[t]o attempt to extract a coherent theory of vengeance from the drama is to miss the essence of tragedy', since 'each character passionately embraces or rejects vengeance depending on the position he occupies at any given moment in the scheme of the drama'.[21] Similarly, it would be dangerous to conclude that the Elizabethan or Jacobean revenger is to be regarded as, at worst, a villain (D'Amville) and, at best, misguided (Hamlet): in the thesis advanced by Eleanor Prosser, Hamlet's early speculations (2.2.587–92) that the Ghost of Hamlet's father is the devil come to tempt him to sinful revenge, are correct, and the Ghost does indeed represent a 'goblin damned' (1.4.19). Hamlet, of course, struggles with the morality of revenge throughout the action: it is only at the end of the play, in the mysterious calm he experiences as he approaches the eye of the storm, that he seems to accept his fate. His mind circles obsessively around the notion that, despite all current teaching about the immorality of revenge, it must be 'perfect conscience' to kill his villainous uncle (5.2.68). Perhaps it is the difference between his own failed schemes and his fortuitous return to Denmark that prompts his reflections on the 'special providence' in something as trivial as 'the fall of a sparrow' (166–7). Perhaps his speculation that 'There's a divinity that shapes our ends,/Rough-hew them how we will' (10–11) indicates a realisation that, after all, God has appointed him as 'scourge and minister', and has engineered circumstance accordingly. If this is the case, none of it is stated explicitly. Hamlet's anguish over the morality of his calling contrasts starkly with the words of Claudius, who reassures Laertes that his desire to 'cut [Hamlet's] throat i'th' church' is a legitimate one: 'No place indeed should murder sanctuarize;/Revenge should have no bounds' (4.7.102–4).

Trouble at the court of King James

According to Eileen Allman, 'Jacobean revenge tragedy spoke to the cultural moment...when James's struggles with Parliament over absolute authority made tyranny an inflammatory subject'.[22] In an interview with film-maker Alex Cox on the release of his film version of *The Revenger's Tragedy*, he discusses the technique familiar to Jacobean dramatists of using an apparently alien setting for their dramas (usually, in their case, the courts of Italian city-states) in order to offer a coded critique of their own society.[23] It has certainly become part of literary critical orthodoxy to see the customarily Italianate settings as analogues for the Jacobean court. J. W. Lever baldly states that the aim of the writers of revenge tragedies 'was not to re-create history, but to express contemporary anxieties by transposing them into a period and setting which had become the type and pattern of naked despotism';[24] that is to say, Italy of the fifteenth and sixteenth centuries. Lever sees in *The Revenger's Tragedy*, for example, a play 'acutely responsive to the contemporary scene ... a lurid picture of waste and corruption, in which wealth and fertility are being squandered away by spendthrift heirs, the new rich, and noblemen turned courtiers'.[25]

The representation of corrupt Italian courtly life is epitomised in the opening scene of *The Duchess of Malfi* (1614), which finds Antonio, newly returned from his travels, depicting for his friend Delio the harmonious state of the French court, and providing for the audience an image of the ideal state against which they will judge the Arragonian court of Ferdinand, the Cardinal and the Duchess:

> a prince's court
> Is like a common fountain, whence should flow

> Pure silver-drops in general. But if 't chance
> Some curs'd example poison't near the head,
> Death and diseases through the whole land spread. (1.1.11–15)

It is hard to imagine a Jacobean audience failing to connect Antonio's description of the French 'judicious king' who 'quits first his royal palace/Of flattering sycophants, of dissolute/And infamous persons' (1.1.8–10) with their own monarch. James I's tendency to surround himself with his favourites, upon whom he would lavish titles and wealth, was well known; the Scots who trailed after him in the wake of his coronation in London were the most obvious beneficiaries of his bounty. On Elizabeth's death, there were fifty-five peers; James added more than twenty in the first years of his reign, and tripled the number of knights within a year of his accession.[26] George Villiers, Duke of Buckingham, was one of James' particular favourites, of whom one visitor to court remarked, 'I never yet saw any fond husband make so much or so great a dalliance over his beautiful spouse as I have seen King James over his favourites, especially the Duke of Buckingham'.[27] The king himself said of Villiers that 'Christ had his John and I have my George'.[28] Unlike many who attained the precarious position of confidant to the king, whose falls from grace were often as spectacular as their rise to prominence, Buckingham retained his position even after James' death, and his role as a mediator between the king and those who would petition the monarch invested him with considerable power.

Although the 'play within a play' convention had already been established as a feature of revenge tragedy, the use of the masque in *The Revenger's Tragedy* is worth noting in view of James' famed fondness for lavish court masques celebrating his power, royalty and wealth. Alvin Kernan notes that £3,000 was spent on *The Masque of Blackness* in 1605, and by 1634, the cost of the annual masque had rocketed to £21,000.[29] Tales of the excesses of King James' court are legion, with varied accounts of events such as banquets and masques, and implications (or bald reports) of sexual excess and licence, drunkenness and debauchery.[30] One of the most frequently cited contemporary documents, a letter written by Sir John Harrington describing the visit of King Christian of Denmark to King James' court (1606), gives a vivid account of an assembly rendered helpless by excessive eating and drinking; 'I never did see such lack of good order, discretion, and sobriety, as I have now done,' he marvelled.[31] There are a number of references to James' tendency to fondle in public his male favourites. To add to the sense of licentiousness, according to the admittedly extremely partisan Sir Anthony Weldon, James was cursed with 'a tongue too large for his mouth, which ever made him speak full in the mouth, and made him drink very uncomely, as if eating his drink, which came out into the cup of each side of his mouth'.[32]

Court scandal, meanwhile, became a familiar feature of James I's rule. J. W. Lever suggests that audiences watching *The Duchess of Malfi* (1614) would most probably have been put in mind of the case of Lady Arabella Stuart, a cousin of King James who secretly married William Seymour against the king's wishes (both were of royal blood and so perceived as potential political threats). They were imprisoned, escaped, and fled separately, planning to rendezvous in Ostend, but Arabella was captured at sea and spent the rest of her life in prison.[33] Christina Malcolmson believes that the scandal over the death by poisoning of Sir Thomas Overbury, and the subsequent trial of Frances Howard and her new husband, the Earl of Somerset, in 1615, provided the source material for *The Changeling* (the trial revealed Howard to be the instigator of the crime; Overbury had been outspoken in his criticism of Howard's relationship with Somerset and her moves to annul her marriage to the Earl of Essex).[34] Whether or not the settings of plays such as *The Duchess of Malfi* and *The Revenger's Tragedy* are intended as covert attacks on the Jacobean state, it is certainly true that the societies depicted in the plays tend to be morally bankrupt and institutionally corrupt. The image of the king and his court as a place marked by its taste for excess, and its tendency to reward and favour a select few, clearly contradicted the early modern ideal of the state as a place where bounty flowed purely and freely from its fountainhead, the monarch.

Dissatisfaction with the Scottish king was no doubt exacerbated by a tendency to look back on Elizabeth's reign as a golden age of prosperity, harmony and consolidation of England's power on an international scale. It is likely that Middleton's choice for the name of Vindice's dead beloved, Gloriana, in *The Revenger's Tragedy* was invested with a special significance: Jennifer Woodward suggests that he probably intended it as a direct allusion to the dead Elizabeth I, and Gloriana was a name so frequently bestowed on the queen that it is hard to imagine members of the audience around 1606 *not* making the connection. Woodward claims that, in that same year, a funeral effigy of the queen (first fashioned immediately after her death in 1603) along with her tomb (which also included a lifelike sculpture), would have been on display together in Westminster Abbey. With the dressing of the dead

Gloriana, and the use of her skull to poison the Duke, Woodward concludes:

> At the moment of revenge…for some in the original audience at least, the skull in its flowing tires momentarily became Elizabeth-Gloriana, and the duke, profligate ruler of a corrupt court, became James, her successor, poisoned in the act of her violation.[35]

There is an interesting echo of the funeral effigy tradition in Cox's film adaptation of the play, although it uses Isabella rather than Gloriana: after Isabella's suicide, her body is displayed in public and, in a fashion that characterises the film as a whole, broadcast across the city-state, provoking national mourning that is a clear reference to the reaction to the death of Princess Diana in 1997 (which included a considerable degree of hostility towards the Windsor royal family, and their perceived inappropriate and inadequate response to the event).

Even more crucial, perhaps, was the recognition of the way in which corruption had spread into political office at the highest levels. Linda Levy Peck cites the charges of corruption filed in Star Chamber against the Lord Treasurer Thomas Howard, Earl of Suffolk, his wife and another official, Sir John Bingley, who were accused of '"bargaining, delaying, persuading, threatening etc. saying no door could be opened without a golden key"'.[36] The belief that the Jacobean justice system could be bought and sold may well have inspired the cynical representation of the trial of the Junior Brother in *The Revenger's Tragedy*, which depicts a society that seems irredeemably corrupt. Crucially, this is a world where judicial matters are decided on the whim of the Duke. Middleton's use of images of bodily disease to depict the corruption of the state reminds us of the ubiquity of the concept of the monarch's two bodies, the body natural (the physical body of the king or queen) and the body politic – the society over which s/he was sovereign.[37] Both Elizabeth in her ascension speech, and James in his first speech to Parliament, made specific references to this doctrine. Some time later, metaphors of bodily corruption became common currency in discussions of the state of James' court in the 1621 session of Parliament.[38] The revenger figure steps into these vicious worlds, usually alone, and takes on the role of scourge of a corrupt society and of a justice system that is systematically and irrevocably breaking down.

Speculation about audience responses to the figure of the revenger, then, leads us along routes parallel to the tension referred to earlier, between ancient traditions of vendetta and more recent attempts to control and codify such violence. On the one hand, the revenger is a figure whose complexity and dramatic potential is rooted in his moral dilemma: challenged by a sense of obligation to right a wrong, any legitimate paths to justice are thwarted, and he is faced with no alternative but to seek his own route to redress, and, in almost all cases, is forced into conduct that conflicts with orthodox morality. The revenger's determination to seek his own form of justice brings him into conflict with the ruling power, because of orthodox political doctrine (an offence against a subject is an offence against the state, which is the body of the monarch) and because, in most cases, the state's failure to deliver justice is a result of its own insidious corruption. The following chapter will consider how different but analogous social and political conditions may have contributed to the rise of the revenger in the Hollywood thriller of the 1970s, and its revival in the early years of the new millennium.

3
Revenge in Its Social Contexts: Late-Twentieth-Century Cinema

Vigilantism, USA: the revenger in 1970s Hollywood

A number of writers have noted that the concept of the vigilante is deeply rooted in American history and culture, especially in the South and the West in the nineteenth century: the gold rushes in Montana and California during this period were particular flashpoints for the custom of vigilante justice.[1] However, as John Cawelti points out, many of these historical vigilante traditions were 'a collective phenomenon, the result of mob action or of organizations like the Klan and the quasi-legal vigilante committees of some early western communities'. As such, they were '[as] frequently the expression of racial or social prejudice, as they were against criminal violence'.[2] Richard Kazis writes that, '[b]etween 1882 and 1951 over 4,700 Americans were killed by unorganized lynch mobs', and that 'well over 80 per cent of the victims were black'.[3] The vigilante tradition that concerns us is based on the concept of the 'lone wolf' avenger, figures that are more closely analogous to Middleton's Vindice or Kyd's Hieronimo. In this respect, one of the most significant icons is the enduring image of the Western lawman – the isolated, self-sufficient hero enforcing justice in a society on the border of wild anarchy. Nevertheless, there are aspects of the vigilante mindset that apply regardless of the way in which it is embodied – by a community or in individuals. Franklin E. Zimring suggests that two elements require special attention: first, that 'the celebration of private and community use of force implies some distrust of government'. He continues:

> The enthusiastic vigilante either distrusts the government's intentions or its capacity to keep the peace, or both. The vigilante tradition is

one which values the community's interests and those of the individual more highly than it values the prerogatives of government.

The second element, according to Zimring is that 'vigilante attitudes ... assume away the need for the investigation of crime and the proof of guilt', and dismiss the processes of investigation, proof and trial as 'costly and time-consuming enemies of justice'.[4] Popular representations of vigilantism serve to highlight distinctions between the concepts of revenge and retribution, and dramatise relations between the individual, society and the state.

There is a clear genealogical link between the urban vigilante movie of the 1970s and the 'lone wolf' of the Western tradition, epitomised by Marshal Will Kane in Fred Zinnemann's *High Noon* (1952), which found Gary Cooper's lawman abandoned by the townsfolk, standing alone against the outlaws. Indeed, the moment at the end of *Dirty Harry* when Harry Callahan flings his detective's badge in the river, having just shot dead the serial killer Scorpio, unashamedly mimics Kane's expression of disgust at the community of deserters when he throws his own badge in the dust. *High Noon* was itself seen as a political film, though, unlike *Dirty Harry*, a fiercely liberal one: it was intended in part as a response to the Red Scare witch-hunts of the McCarthy era and the blacklisting of Hollywood personnel by the House Un-American Activities Committee. Its politics consequently rendered it suspect in the eyes of many – John Wayne, disgusted by Kane's rejection of the community he has saved, famously described the film as the most un-American thing he had ever seen in his life. However, the tradition of the lone lawman (either within or outside the official role of sheriff or marshal) stretches back beyond *High Noon*, to Henry Fonda's Wyatt Earp in *My Darling Clementine* (1946), and continues via a populous tradition that includes *Shane* (1953), *Comanche Station* (1960) and *Death of a Gunfighter* (1969). Revenge was fundamental to many more Westerns of the 1950s and 1960s, notably *Winchester '73* (1950), *The Man from Laramie* (1955), *Man of the West* (1958), *Once Upon a Time in the West* (1968), and, most famously, *The Searchers* (1956), in which Ethan Edwards (John Wayne) embarks on a ferocious quest to avenge the deaths of his brother and his family, and retrieve his niece, seized in the Comanche attack. Ethan's status as avenging hero is rendered highly problematic, most significantly because of his racism.

Clint Eastwood's most famous persona before he starred in *Dirty Harry* was undoubtedly his 'Man with no Name' character in Sergio Leone's 'Spaghetti Westerns' of the late 1960s, and one way in which the

Western revenger crossed over into the contemporary urban setting was via Eastwood's career path (the *Dirty Harry* role was originally envisaged for Frank Sinatra, but it eventually went to Eastwood after Sinatra had to withdraw because of a hand injury, and a number of others including John Wayne and Paul Newman had also turned it down). The fact that Clint Eastwood would for some time be almost synonymous with the role is due in part to the sense of continuity between the Harry Callahan persona and his roles in Leone's *A Fistful of Dollars* (1964), *For a Few Dollars More* (1965) and *The Good, the Bad and the Ugly* (1966), along with a Leone-influenced US production, *Hang 'Em High* (1968); the *Dirty Harry* instalments would be interspersed by a variety of films, but again the Western remained a familiar touchstone: *Joe Kidd* (1972), *High Plains Drifter* (1973), *The Outlaw Josey Wales* (1976). Even in the 1980s, when the Western was considered to be a defunct genre, Eastwood made *Pale Rider* (1985). In many of these films, vigilantism is again central; Eastwood's characters are often represented as the lone defenders of what is right in corrupt, violent and unjust societies. Significantly, however, they frequently act within a context of social nihilism: endings are resolved not with any restoration of social harmony or affirmation of the status quo, but with the corrupt order in ruins, and with little or no apparent hope of reconstructing anything more just: 'the Man with No Name', J. Hoberman writes, 'is an anti-bourgeois loner with a gun, a Righteous Outlaw without cause'.[5] Harry, continuing this line of anti-heroes sketched out in the Leone Westerns, is a 'lone lawman' suggesting 'an updated, downgraded Gary Cooper in *High Noon*'.[6]

The Western is widely perceived as having gone into decline in the late 1960s, and was largely moribund in the 1970s and 1980s, despite a few spirited attempts at revival – some of the rare successes being Eastwood vehicles. The film often credited with ruining the United Artists studio and killing off the Western in the process, Michael Cimino's *Heaven's Gate* (1981), is in itself a complex treatment of ideas of justice and revenge, with Marshal James Averill (Kris Kristofferson) attempting to protect the European immigrants accused of rustling cattle from the wealthy landowners and their hired vigilante Nate Champion (Christopher Walken). There are also overtones of suspicions about the government protecting the land barons, contrasting with Averill's increasingly desperate attempts at even-handedness. However, even with the Western in decline, some of Hollywood's most memorable (and controversial) screen personae of the 1970s were still revengers, most often in a contemporary urban setting. The *Dirty Harry* and *Death Wish* films may have been the most notable, but there were many more thrillers structured around the revenger or vigilante figure, notably *Point Blank* (1967), *Joe* (1970), *Billy Jack* (1971), and *Walking Tall* (1973). Revenge was also fertile ground for numerous so-called 'exploitation' films such as *Ms. 45: Angel of Vengeance* (1981), *I Spit on Your Grave* (1977), *The Last House on the Left* (1972) and *Thriller: A Cruel Movie* (1973), all of which feature female revenger protagonists – something that distinguishes them from the male-dominated mainstream.[7] It is only recently that the female vigilante has found her way into the mass market, via Quentin Tarantino's *Kill Bill* films (2003 and 2004), and Tarantino has been very clear about the debt he owes to cult and exploitation films, notably *Thriller* (also known as *They Call Her One Eye*) and the Japanese film *Lady Snowblood* (1973). I shall return to the female vigilante in the book's conclusion, but it is enough to note here that the spectre of the violent woman seems to have remained until very recently essentially off-limits in mainstream entertainment. In the shadows of the cult and the underground, however, she was already a force that would refuse to be neglected.

The perception that, in the early 1970s, America was emerging from a social revolution has sometimes been illustrated in shorthand via the cultural shift evident in two infamous rock documentaries of the era – the fuzzy, 'turn on, tune in, drop out' optimism of *Woodstock* (festival staged August 1969, film released March 1970), with its already jaded talk of peace and love, was quickly supplanted by the spectacle of the death at the Rolling Stones' Altamont concert of a rock fan, stabbed and beaten by a number of Hell's Angels security guards, while Jagger pranced to the tune of 'Sympathy for the Devil' (staged in December 1969; the film *Gimme Shelter* was released in December 1970). The ideals of love and harmony were falling apart as whatever social cohesion had developed in 1960s youth culture fractured and splintered into different aspects of the 1970s counter-culture. Advances made in terms of liberal politics – feminism, sexuality, and black civil rights – had been scarred by the deaths of Martin Luther King and President Kennedy; there was increasing disillusionment with and resistance to a war being waged in a foreign country; and the ever-lurking American distrust of big government would, within a few years, find its self-fulfilling prophecy in the Watergate scandal. In this context, it is not far-fetched to interpret the popularity of cinematic vigilante anti-heroes such as Paul Kersey (*Death Wish*) and 'Dirty' Harry Callahan as part of a right-wing backlash against the counter-culture. Seth Cagin and Philip Dray note the way in which Richard Nixon and Spiro Agnew's re-election rhetoric associated their political opponents with the counter-culture, damning the anti-Vietnam movement and eliding it with a wider agenda that accused the liberals of being soft on crime (the same see-saw politics would still be dominating election campaigns thirty years later); in this way, the liberals were associated with the rising tide of activism and protest on student campuses, where the escalating violence culminated in the death of four students at Kent State University in May 1970.[8] In political terms, the right-wing backlash would be felt most keenly later in the decade, as the New Right championed conservative values in terms of economics, social policy and morality, reasserting, in league with Christian fundamentalist TV evangelists, the Church and traditional notions of the family. However, the seeds were clearly being sown in the 1970s by movies such as *Joe*, *Dirty Harry* and *Death Wish*, all of which expressed the sense of paranoia and frustration that seemed to be growing among what Nixon dubbed (in November 1969) America's silent majority.

Cagin and Dray see the low-budget movie *Joe* as an accurate barometer of the highly charged atmosphere of confrontation that dominated the turn of the decade. Depicting the alliance of the eponymous working-class bigot (Peter Boyle) with an upper-middle-class businessman, Bill (Dennis Patrick), it charts their search for Bill's daughter (Susan Sarandon) through the shady world of hippiedom, after she has gone on the run in the wake of the murder of her drug-addicted boyfriend – murdered by her own father in an uncharacteristic fit of rage. The alliance of so-called hard-hat, working-class Joe and liberal, affluent Bill can be understood as a snapshot of the fraught political state of the USA at this time, signalling an unusual consensus between social groups that traditionally are divided. What unites them is what Ryan and Kellner describe as American populism: 'a celebration of the virtue of the common man, resistance to large impersonal institutions, and a privileging of nature, rurality and simplicity over urban, cosmopolitan modernity'.[9] A similar set of prejudices is exploited in *Dirty Harry*, which lambasts a system seemingly paralysed by laws protecting the criminal rather than the victim, and presents a convenient hate-figure for conservatives in the form of Scorpio, a dishevelled long-hair with a prominent, distorted peace symbol on his belt buckle. More disturbingly, the day-to-day threats to social order Harry deals with (usually while drinking coffee or eating a burger) are routinely black or Hispanic. In *Death Wish*, the protagonist Paul Kersey is presented in schematic, clumsy fashion as (to quote his workmate Sam) a 'bleeding heart liberal'. Sam quotes street crimes at Kersey (fifteen murders the first week Kersey was away on holiday, twenty-one in the second week), and asserts that, 'The underprivileged are beating our goddamn brains out'; his solution is to 'stick 'em in concentration camps'. When he declares that, 'What this city needs is more cops than people', his boss points out that it wouldn't work, with another anti-big government jab: 'No-one could pay the taxes.'

'The law's crazy' – 1970s vigilantism

The screenwriters and directors of 1970s Hollywood had no need to disguise their critiques of what they saw as the failings of their own government and justice system in the way that the cautious Jacobean dramatists did. In *Dirty Harry*, the San Francisco police department is baldly represented as having been bled dry by bureaucracy, paranoia and wishy-washy liberalism. With the Supreme Court judgements in the cases of Escobido and Miranda (1964 and 1966, respectively), a number of key principles were established that had an impact on police procedures in terms of search and seizure, and informing a suspect of his/her rights. Harry Callahan and his .44 Magnum (which he famously introduces to hapless crooks as 'the most powerful handgun in the world') compose an iconic image of the period. Making his first appearance in the film of that name (1971), the *Dirty Harry* sequels were *Magnum Force* (1973) (the gun even supplanting Harry in both the title and the opening credits sequence), *The Enforcer* (1976), *Sudden Impact* (1983) and *The Dead Pool* (1988). In the anodyne 1990s, a rogue cop such as Mel Gibson's *Lethal Weapon* persona Martin Riggs (1987, 1989, 1992, 1998), or Bruce Willis's John McClane in the *Die Hard* franchise (1988, 1990, 1995) has little political resonance. In 1971, however, Don Siegel's *Dirty Harry* took a sledgehammer to liberal values, advocating vigilante justice and seemingly demanding the police officer's right to be jury, judge and executioner.

Dirty Harry represents Callahan as a hard-working cop whose efforts are frustrated repeatedly by a liberal criminal justice system, and who finds his own ways of dealing with the criminal element. While it was a box office hit, and lauded by many, some critics (notably Pauline Kael) hated it, remarking, 'The action genre has always had a fascist potential, and [in *Dirty Harry*] it has finally surfaced.'[10] Pat Dowell notes that, while liberal critics lambasted the film for its political crassness, the Philippines police wanted to use it as a training film.[11] It is not entirely surprising, perhaps, that Callahan's most famous line ('Go ahead, make my day' – in fact not spoken until the *Sudden Impact* instalment in

1983) was appropriated by the right-wing president Ronald Reagan (1981–9) as a threat against congressional Democrats; it is merely indicative of the kind of sympathies the films invoke: once again, the paradigm of tough, conservative Republicans against soft, liberal Democrats resurfaces.[12] As Reagan's presidency drew to a close, there was even talk of Eastwood himself running for office, and the *U.S. and World News Report* of 2 February 1987 ran the headline 'Dirty Harry for President', reporting that souvenir shops in Carmel, the town where Eastwood had been elected mayor the previous year, were doing brisk business selling t-shirts emblazoned with legends advocating his candidacy.[13] J. Hoberman also notes that the first President Bush would credit Ronald Reagan with turning America into a nation that appreciated *Dirty Harry* rather than *Easy Rider* (1969) – a stark example of the way in which these popular texts can be appropriated to support political agendas.[14]

Walking Tall is based on the true-life events of Buford Pusser, sheriff of McNairy County, who apparently waged a campaign of zero tolerance on illegal gambling and the manufacture of illegal whisky on the Mississippi–Tennessee border between 1964 and 1970. The 1974 film immortalised him as a modern-day vigilante lawman, waging a campaign virtually single-handedly against crime – a rural equivalent of Harry Callahan. The film has an undeniable power, and it undoubtedly tapped into the same kind of preoccupations as *Dirty Harry*, replacing the urban jungle with the unique vicissitudes of the small rural town, bringing the vigilante figure closer to his Western roots. On its initial release, with a marketing campaign based around its hard-headed violence, the movie bombed. However, re-released with a new tag-line ('Audiences are standing up and applauding'), it went on to out-gross major films such as *The Godfather*; J. Hoberman notes that *Rolling Stone* magazine hailed it as 'the best American movie so far this year'.[15] The film is a good example of the paradigm that pits the individual against the 'system', a nebulous term that is used not only to define the apparatus of the state – in terms of law and justice – but also big business, organised crime, and anything else that seems to take power out of the hands of the ordinary working man and the family he is struggling to provide for. As the film opens, Pusser arrives with his wife and children at the rural idyll of his parental home, having left behind his wrestling career and moved back home to escape that life, which he describes in dismissive, rueful terms as 'organised dishonesty – a system'. He sees his retirement as an escape from a world where 'other people [were] running my life their way' and he was forced to be 'a trained animal in someone else's circus'. After he is involved in a brawl at the Lucky Spot bar, provoked by an argument over loaded dice in the backroom casino, he is beaten unconscious and has his torso repeatedly slashed in sadistic fashion, before being dumped on the roadside and left for dead. Deciding to prosecute his own form of justice, he returns to the Lucky Spot with a wooden club, beating his attackers, claiming the money he believes he is owed, and insisting on a signature before he leaves. The subtext is clear: Pusser is claiming nothing more than what he believes is his due. After he is arrested, he defends himself at his trial; stripping to the waist to display the horrific scars on his torso, and with an appeal to the jury's sense of natural justice, he is found not guilty. 'I went in there to remind them that somewhere in this world there's still a little law and order left', he remarks afterwards. Once elected sheriff, his campaign against institutionalised crime and corruption steps up a gear. Armed with his club, recruiting a new raft of deputies, including his Black Power friend, Obra Eaker, he wages war on local hoodlums and criminals.

Pusser insists on two simple rules: to uphold the law equally, and to take no bribes. Via the figure of Judge Clarke – who attempts to convict Pusser, and later does all he can to hamstring Pusser's attempts to enforce law and order – the film pursues a line similar to both *Dirty Harry* and *Death Wish*, and in particular the critique of Miranda and Escobido rulings, and all they represent. When Clarke orders Pusser to set free the men whose moonshine whisky has poisoned and killed fourteen people, citing the sheriff's failure to obtain warrants and protect the accused's rights to silence and counsel, the confrontation recalls Harry Callahan's dispute with the D.A. and Judge in *Dirty Harry* (see p. 55 below). Pusser is told in no uncertain terms that what he sees as 'technicalities' would not be seen as such by the US Supreme Court: 'It's the law of the land', the judge pronounces. 'The law of the land shouldn't be for sale,' Pusser counters, in one of the film's many populist one-liners. In a later scene, the issue of Miranda rights is revisited with brutal irony, when Pusser comes across a prostitute suspected of working as an informer, whom the criminals have stripped naked, tied to a bed and beaten. As Pusser takes her attackers apart with his club, he punctuates the blows by reading them their rights. The film is blatant in its populism, and it situates Pusser within a lineage that stretches back to the lawmen of the classic Westerns, legitimating his vigilantism in the face of a deeply corrupt bureaucracy.

Dirty Harry and *Walking Tall* are both predicated on the failure of law and order, the apparent privileging of the criminal's rights over those of the victim, and the dangers of the urban jungle environment (an anxiety exploited with cold efficiency in *Death Wish*, discussed in more detail in the following chapter). The faceless, uncaring bureaucracy of the system is challenged by the individual, who meets the threat of lawlessness in two forms – the actions of the criminal and the lack of ability or lack of will on the part of the apparatus of law and order – and establishes his own form of natural justice. If a film such as *Dirty Harry* does indeed swim with the anti-liberal tide of 1970s America, a neo-conservatism born of a sense of growing anxiety about the counter-culture, it is also impossible to ignore its uncompromising vilification of bureaucracy, the suspicion that the law has distanced itself so far from justice that it is worthy only of contempt. The next chapter will consider further the significance of the revenger and the vigilante, and explore parallels between the revenger in his/her different historical contexts.

4
'When the Bad Bleed, then is the Tragedy Good': Politics, Morality and Revenge

The previous two chapters have identified ways in which a play such as *The Revenger's Tragedy* or a film such as *Dirty Harry* might be read to discover both how they *reflect* aspects of their immediate social contexts, and how they might have had an *impact* on that context: how did their contemporary audiences approach them, and how did they respond to them? If popular culture is a major contributor to the ways in which individuals, and society, construct their identities, what does the revenger figure, in its various forms, tell us about ourselves? Sam Peckinpah claimed that his film *Straw Dogs* was 'about the violence within all of us. The violence which is reflecting on the political condition of the world today.' In response to a letter from a viewer complaining that the level of violence made the film impossible to enjoy, Peckinpah responded, 'I didn't want you to enjoy the film, I wanted you to look very close at your own soul.'[1] Remarks such as these may give us pause, and provoke us to consider how the revenge narrative, which is after all one of the most ancient and powerful of all Western story structures, works on us. In her introduction to her collection of *Four Revenge Tragedies* (1995), Katharine Eisaman Maus suggests that 'the revenger's problem must be shared, albeit in an attenuated form, by the spectators to his tragedy...his dilemma must condense some more widely experienced anxiety into an artistically persuasive form'.[2] Maus's perspective highlights the tension between historical specificity and transhistoricism, a principle that is foundational to this book. This chapter is an attempt to read the figure of the revenger *across*, rather than simply *within*, his or her[3] different forms and histories. This is not simply a matter of understanding the revenger as a 'universal' figure, although that is one aspect of the investigation

48

that requires significant attention. By sketching parallels between, for example, Vindice and Travis Bickle or Harry Callahan, a picture may begin to emerge revealing how the revenger works, either as a potentially subversive or as a conservative figure in the popular culture of different periods.

I have already noted an important distinction between the revenger and the vigilante: revenge is generally understood to be motivated by a personal injury, often enacted when the state will not or cannot redress the imbalance via its own apparatus of conviction and punishment. The vigilante may be inspired by a personal injury, but the targets of retribution are not necessarily those involved in the initial wrong against him or her. The vigilante's aim is to right a criminal wrong by criminal means, in the service of a sense of 'real' or 'natural' justice. In their discussion of the vigilante figure of 1970s Hollywood, Seth Cagin and Philip Dray suggest, 'Whether he's a champion of the right, like Dirty Harry, or an avenging angel of the left, like Billy Jack, the vigilante obliterates coherent politics; resorting to violence, he undercuts the very social order he purports to defend.'[4] The tension between the state's legal apparatus on the one hand, and the notion of natural justice on the other is one of the most intriguing relationships in the genre, and it becomes even more sharply defined in the context of vigilantism, where the focus is not simply on righting a personal wrong, but on attempting to bring about what is perceived to be a more just society.

What I am calling natural justice has, perhaps necessarily, proved to be a somewhat nebulous concept: its elastic nature allows the authors of revenge narratives and their audiences plenty of room to legitimise the actions of the revenger. Ideas of justice have, it goes without saying, mutated over the period covered by this study. However, a useful working definition would understand it as maintaining what John Locke defines as the original state of nature – a state in which all individuals enjoyed equality and independence, lived lives of reason and tolerance, and abided by the dictum that no one had a right to harm another's 'life, health, liberty, or possessions'.[5] In situations where a society is unable to maintain this ideal state, and where the system is not simply inadequate but also corrupt, drunk on its own power, this 'breach of trust', according to Locke, means 'they forfeit the power the people had put into their hands ... and it devolves to the people who have a right to resume their original liberty, and by the establishment of a new legislative, such as they shall think fit, provide for their own safety and security, which is the end for which they are in society'.[6] Locke was writing towards the end of the seventeenth century, of course, in the context of a nation that had survived the Civil War. However, even though Locke was working with a more enlightened and democratic understanding of social relations than would have been conceivable a hundred years earlier, the notion that the vigilante might be justified in acting against the law of the land in order to enforce a higher form of justice is one that underpins the representation of Vindice, Hieronimo and other revenger figures. In this respect, the fictional vigilante has true subversive potential: both in the early modern and the contemporary setting, a decision to step outside the boundaries of legal action has to be perceived as a transgressive act, one that challenges the rule of law. However, it is also important to recognise that in many cases the actions of the vigilante are, ironically, intended to maintain the status quo, or at least a perceived ideal state of social stability that the current ruling power has been unable to maintain.

As we have seen, there are certain texts in which the categories of vigilante and revenger cross over, sometimes unexpectedly; for example, Paul Kersey in *Death Wish* is driven by the attack on his family to begin stalking New York City's urban jungle and shooting muggers dead at random, making no attempt to track down his wife's killers. The dilemma of the vigilante is rendered all the more acute in the early modern context in *The Spanish Tragedy*, and in contemporary film via *Robocop* (1987). Both Kyd's revenger Hieronimo and the eponymous hero of Paul Verhoeven's science fiction film are ostensibly representatives of the law, and both are forced, in different ways and for different reasons, to abandon legitimate, due process in order to prosecute their own revenge. It is at critical points such as these that the dilemma of justice and revenge is put into sharp relief. Most provocatively of all, when the enforcer of the law crosses the line between justice and personal revenge, the strain on such categories becomes more than the texts can bear, yielding moments in performance or on screen that challenge audiences to re-evaluate their own understanding of the relationship between natural and legal justice.

'The law is a ass' – the vigilante and the system

A common feature of the vigilante narrative is the revelation of the justice system as corrupt or impotent and inadequate, and the previous two chapters noted how very different social tensions – unrest under an unpopular king in the seventeenth century, and a clash of the forces of liberalism and conservatism in the early 1970s – may have led to a common preoccupation with the issues of social cohesion and justice in the popular culture of the time. Certainly there is an analogous anxiety crystallising in each period around the notion of centralised power: in the early seventeenth century, James I's very public insistence on his divine right to rule, published in *Basilikon Doron, Defence of the Right of Kings* and other works, seemed to signal an initiative to sap power from an aristocracy accustomed to a somewhat flatter (though hardly democractic) relationship with its monarch.[7] *Hamlet*, first staged in 1600 or 1601 for an audience aware of a looming political crisis as Elizabeth grew old and frail, raised the thorny issue of political insta-bility, and royal legitimacy and succession. In American politics, as the radicalism and optimism of the 1960s gave way to the cynical 1970s, the president was found to be trying to rabble-rouse a silent majority and clinging to power via the kind of illegal activities that were blown apart in the Watergate scandal of 1972.

This is not an attempt to make a case for a direct parallel between England under James I and the USA under Richard Nixon: no doubt a study of the history and culture of the intervening period would throw up other instances that would also work as analogous cases (although it is worth mentioning that the revenge genre itself seemed to have played itself out by the time the theatres were closed in 1642, and it never really resurfaced in the theatre at any point after the Restoration). However, it is true to say that these different films and plays share a preoccupation with a system that overpowers and then disempowers subjects of the state, and that this concern finds expressive form in the way the writers depict the society upon which they let loose their avengers. *The Revenger's Tragedy* is exemplary in this respect, showing the ruling power in all its inglorious corruption: the second scene stages the trial of the Duchess's youngest son (the Duke's stepson), known only as the Junior Brother, who has been charged with the rape of Antonio's wife. Despite the Duke's stern words as the company assem-bles ('His violent act has e'en drawn blood of honour/And stained our honours;' [1.2.2–3]), and his declared intention to let justice run its course ('I leave him to your sentence; doom him, lords –/The fact is great – whiles I sit by and sigh' [19–20]), he still reserves the right to intervene as sentence is passed. As the Duchess and Junior's brothers, Lussurioso and Ambitioso, plead for leniency, the Duke is silent, and the First Judge reaffirms the apparent determination to see justice done: 'Tis the duke's pleasure that impartial doom/Shall take fast hold of his unclean attempt' (41–2). By contrast, Junior is surprisingly flippant as he faces the court: asked what moved him to commit the act of rape, he lewdly and cynically replies, 'Why, flesh and blood, my lord./What should men move unto a woman else?' (47–8). The judges, both deeply shocked by the crime, hint that the punishment will be severe, but Junior can only shrug and suggest that, 'My fault being sport, let me but die in jest' (66). The Duchess interrupts to prevent the First Judge from passing sentence, and while he appeals to what is 'but the justice of the law', she retorts, bizarrely, that the law 'is grown more subtle than a woman should be' and rounds on her husband, equating his apparent unwillingness or inability to intervene as proof of impotence, political and, by implication, sexual: 'O what it is to have an old-cool duke,/ To be as slack in tongue as in performance!' (74–5). The Duke, clearly stung, prevents the judge from saying any more than 'Let that offender –...Be on a scaffold –' (79, 80), stopping the session in its tracks and declaring that 'We will defer the judgement till next sitting' (83). The judges do not speak again during the scene; Spurio, the bastard son of the Duke, who would rather see Junior dead, remarks grimly that 'if judgement have/Cold blood, flattery and bribes will kill it' (90), already convinced that Junior will escape punishment. The Duchess has a similar cynical view of the law, and how her son should stand in relation to it:

> One of his [the Duke's] single words
> Would quite have freed my youngest, dearest son,
> From death or durance, and have made him walk
> With a bold foot upon the thorny law,
> Whose prickles should bow under him. (101–5)

There is no doubt about the need for some kind of action to restore justice. The Duke's weak and corrupt rule, Vindice reveals, has a history: Vindice's key motive for revenge may have been signified at his first appearance, bearing the skull of the murdered Gloriana, but Vindice's family have suffered at the hands of the Duke long before this: there are early references to Vindice and Hippolito's father's death, precipitated, it would seem, by being rejected by the court. During the extended torture and murder of the Duke in Act 3, Scene 5, Vindice's brother and accomplice Hippolito confirms this when he tells the Duke that 'our lord and father/Fell sick upon the infection of thy frowns/And died in sadness' (166–8). However, the idea that Vindice or Hippolito might fit the archetype of the vengeful son seeking justice for a dead father – as in *Hamlet* and *Antonio's Revenge* (1602) – is not carried through with any conviction. The idea of blood vendetta is instead played out between the warring factions within the Duke's own family. The overriding motivation for revenge in *The Revenger's Tragedy* is the murder of Gloriana.

There are many reasons why Vindice might feel frustrated by the process of the law (or its failure), and Antonio also feels a very acute and furious sense of frustration at the law's subjection to the whim and will of the Duke. Displaying his dead wife (who has poisoned herself rather than live with the shame of rape) to 'certain lords', including Piero and Hippolito, the expectation, once again, is tough justice: 'what judgement follows the offender?', Piero asks (1.4.50); 'Faith, none, my lord; it cools and is deferred', is Antonio's grim reply. 'Judgement in this age is near kin to favour' (51, 55). Antonio, Piero and Hippolito subsequently swear a pact that in itself has a deep, radical resonance:

> *Hipp.* Strengthen my vow, that if at the next sitting
> Judgement speak all in gold, and spare the blood
> Of such a serpent, e'en before their seats
> To let his soul out, which long since was found
> Guilty in heaven.
> *All* We swear it and will act it. (1.4.60–4)

Hippolito, like Spurio, assumes that the law is for sale ('judgement speak all in gold'). It is in the alliance of avengers that the play begins to turn from personal revenge to something more like vigilantism. Vindice's aim, it seems, is not straightforward revenge; instead, he aims to cut down, root and branch, the corrupt regime in the hope that something healthier may be planted in its place.

In *The Spanish Tragedy*, Hieronimo is genuinely motivated by a desire for justice after the death of his son, and his position is complex in terms of this particular debate: he is outraged at the state's failure to redress the injustice of the murder of his son, a failing he feels all the more acutely on account of his own position as knight marshal, a civil servant 'charged in the English court with maintaining the peace within twelve miles of the royal presence'.[8] Seeking revenge for his son's death, he goes insane, driven to distraction in part by the conflicting principles represented by his public role (as one who doles out public justice) and his role as bereaved father (one desiring swift and direct retribution). He confronts the king, screaming for justice ('Justice, O justice, justice, gentle king!' [3.13.63]), and, in his distracted state, begins to dig at the ground:

> I'll rip the bowels of the earth,
> And ferry over to th' Elysian plains,
> And bring my son to show his deadly wounds. (71–3)

The Spanish Tragedy is also unusual in that it stages a public execution by hanging. Pedringano has carried out the murder of Serberine on Lorenzo's orders, and has received reassurances that Lorenzo will protect him from the law. However, in Act 3, Scene 5, the Page opens the box that should contain Pedringano's letter of pardon and finds it empty. Hieronimo hears the case against Pedringano, while reflecting grimly on his own predicament ('That only I to all men just must be,/ And neither gods nor men be just to me [3.6.9–10]), and passes sentence: 'For blood with blood shall, while I sit as judge,/Be satisfied, and the law discharged' (35–6). Driven to a fury by Pedringano's impudence (the servant remains convinced that his deliverance is at hand), and by the irony of his situation – a judge who can find no justice for himself – Hieronimo exclaims, 'Murder, O bloody monster, God forbid/ A fault so foul should 'scape unpunished' (95–6) and the stage direction for the executioner is *'turns him off'* (104 s.d.). James Shapiro notes the singularity of this specific manifestation of death in the drama of the period, arguing that, by showing the failure of the execution, judicially and politically, this specific representation of state violence 'undermines the authority of the state ... Rather than confirming state justice, Pedringano's death merely parodies and demystifies it'.[9] Hieronimo is not only denied justice himself, but his own attempts to enforce the law, effectively, come to naught; and worse, they aid the antagonist, Lorenzo, in his attempts to evade justice himself.

In the contemporary context, the scenario of the justice-seeking vigilante confronting the failure of the legal apparatus has become a standard convention: a hard-working, straight-talking detective bangs heads with his superior officer, or some representative of the judicial process, and finds all his efforts frustrated by a system that is too weak, or too corrupt, to facilitate natural justice. In *Dirty Harry*, Callahan's first meeting with authority draws distinct battle lines: ushered into the mayor's office, he is requested to give his report on the investigation of the shooting of the serial killer Scorpio's first victim. Asked what he has been doing, his laconic reply immediately sets the hard-working cop against the 'all talk and no trousers' bureaucrats: 'For the past three-quarters of an hour I've been sitting on my ass in your outer office, waiting on you.' When Callahan suggests they should allow him to meet with Scorpio instead of giving in to the ransom demand, the mayor and the police chief decline the offer, fearing a 'bloodbath'. They remind Harry of a recent example of his unique approach to law enforcement, to which Callahan responds: 'When an adult male is chasing a female with intent to commit rape, I shoot the bastard, that's my policy.' Asked how he determined intent, he replies, 'When a man is chasing a woman through an alley with a butcher's knife and a hard-on, I figure he's not out collecting for the Red Cross.'

The early confrontation – with its crowd-pleasing kiss-off line – sets the pattern for the narrative that follows, notably a scene between Callahan, the District Attorney and Judge Bannerman that is in many ways more riveting than Harry's face-to-face encounters with Scorpio himself. Having taken Scorpio into custody, after shooting him in the leg and torturing him to gather information on a hostage, Harry arrives at the D.A.'s office the next day clearly expecting to be congratulated on his successful capture of the serial killer. However, the D.A.'s initial apparent enthusiasm ('a very unusual piece of police work – really amazing'), to which Harry responds with pleased modesty ('Well, I had some luck') is soon revealed as veiled sarcasm. Callahan finds that he is lucky not to have been indicted for assault with intent to commit murder. 'That man had rights,' the D.A. storms, quoting Escobido and Miranda. Callahan, his anger growing, responds with another sarcastic, audience-recruiting quip: 'Well, I'm all broken up about that man's rights.' Told that the rifle he recovered from Scorpio's hovel is 'inadmissable as evidence...It's the law', Harry fires back with the most blatant challenge so far to the legal system: 'Well, then, the law's crazy.' The film cuts immediately to a medium close-up shot of the shocked expression on the face of the other occupant of the room, whom the D.A. introduces as Judge Bannerman. The judge proceeds to deliver a patronising account of the ways in which Callahan violated the suspect's rights. Harry's pleas for the real victim, Ann Mary Deacon ('What about her rights? Who speaks for her?'), fall on deaf ears, and Harry leaves convinced that he will have to find his own way to bring Scorpio to justice. Such depictions of a corrupt legal system are certainly distinct from the early modern examples, but they play to analogous audience prejudices and frustrations at the failure and inefficiency of state law, and those frustrations are a seedbed for the development of the relationship between the audience and the revenger.

'As kill a king?' – radical revengers

The extent to which any of these texts can be read as truly radical is debatable: when does railing at the system translate into subversive action, or even the potential for such action? An extreme contemporary example of the way popular culture can trigger anxieties in ruling powers concerns the censorship of the 2004 version of *The Punisher* on its release in Malaysia. A number of lines from Frank Castle's speech about justice and revenge were cut. At the end of the version of the film presumably released everywhere else worldwide, Castle is depicted surveying the city in *Dirty Harry* style, promising retribution to all criminals, setting up a sequel and underlining once more (as if it were needed) the legitimacy of his actions. In Malaysia, a subtitle tagged on to the end of the film informed the audience that, soon after, Frank Castle was arrested and sentenced to life in prison without parole. According to Malaysian Deputy Home Minister Datuk Chor Chee Heung (in this case discussing the ban on another Marvel vigilante movie, *Daredevil* [2003]), films were usually banned if they went against the board's guidelines for containing 'excessive violence and sexual material or elements which can create chaos in the community', and *The Punisher* clearly fell foul not only of the first guideline, but, more importantly, the third: as a potentially subversive text, it seems the authorities deemed it necessary to exercise a fairly radical form of censorship.[10]

The Revenger's Tragedy ends with the slaughter of the Duke and his progeny, and the installation of the righteous Antonio in his place. However, as a number of commentators have argued, both the death of the Duke in *The Revenger's Tragedy* and the execution of his heir by the masque of revengers are easily understood as being semi-comic and satirical. It is likely that the ending was not played as a tragic climax: certainly, in revivals of the play in recent decades, the final scene is more usually played out as farce, and, as Peter Corbin suggests, Antonio's naïve declaration of faith in heavenly justice – 'Just is the law above' (5.3.90) – is most likely to provoke laughter in the theatre.[11] The comedy may be double-edged – is the laughter intended at the expense of the Duke (and so potentially radical), or does the comic tone in fact contain, or neutralise, that radical impulse (by suggesting to the audience that none of this should be taken seriously)? Undoubtedly the use of the masque, while it might in one respect be interpreted as a direct reference to James' self-indulgent and extravagant habits, formalises and ritualises the slaughter. The metatheatrical dimension places a heavy emphasis on the 'play within a play' mode, and even though the staging of the deaths would probably have been on a par with the realistic representation of violence that most critics assume was common in the theatre of the period, the performative framing of the action once again weakens its potential for radical impact. Furthermore, despite the earlier alliance between Antonio and Hippolito, Antonio acts swiftly to consolidate power. When Vindice, unable to contain his glee at the sight of the slaughter, reveals his and Hippolito's part in the multiple murders, Antonio immediately gives the order for their arrest and execution: 'You that would murder him [the Duke] would murder me' (5.3.104). The play ends with his prayer that the blood of so many corpses 'may wash away all treason' (128), but, like his earlier declaration of belief in divine justice, it rings hollow.

It becomes increasingly difficult to cling on to the political thread of the revenge narrative as the drama unfolds. Any subversive potential *The Revenger's Tragedy* might have is largely defused by the motivations for the various interlocking revenge plots, since almost all of them are sexual rather than political. The opening scene introduces the Duke not as a tyrant but as a 'royal-lecher' (1.1.1). Vindice's motivation is not a will to power but is instead fuelled by an obsession with his dead fiancée, Gloriana: it is her skull that Vindice carries as the play opens and it becomes a totem of his revenge and even a macabre prop in the enactment of his retaliation. The play's two other key revenge narratives are both sexually motivated: Vindice pursues Lussurioso for attempting to seduce his sister, Castiza, and Antonio seeks retribution for the death of his wife, raped by yet another member of the ruling family. The revenge sub-plots are rooted in the tangled web of sexual licence that defines most of the nobility's behaviour. Although the play undoubtedly critiques the ruling power as one riddled with corruption and nepotism, its overriding preoccupation is, as Dieter Mehl writes, with a society 'poisoned by lust and sexual indulgence, [where] chastity becomes of very rare value... Virtue is unfashionable... a thing of the past and of the backward rural culture'.[12]

In the early stages of his plot, it is true to say that the sabotage Vindice engineers is indeed an assault on the integrity of the ruling family: he convinces the Duke's son Lussurioso that the Duchess is in bed with his father's bastard son, Spurio. Lussurioso, incensed, crashes into the bedroom, sword drawn, only to discover the Duke and Duchess in bed together. The family threatens to implode in the wake of the abortive attack, and the rival brothers Supervacuo and Ambitioso are quick to capitalise on their sibling's wrong-footed move. The Duke, however, almost immediately issues a pardon to Lussurioso, and the other plots quickly dissolve into farcical mismanagement. When the masque of revengers kill the newly installed Duke Lussurioso, Vindice makes his motivation explicit as Lussurioso dies and the thunder rolls:

No power is angry when the lustful die;
When thunder claps, heaven likes the tragedy. (5.3.47–8)

Vindice intentionally dissociates the assassination from the political, and, while thunder traditionally marks the passing of a politically significant figure, Vindice interprets the divine sign for the audience. To be more accurate, one should say he interprets the *stage effect*, since the artificial nature of that sign has already been foregrounded for us: in Act 4, Scene 2, Vindice parodies the roar of the thunder-sheet and the notion that it might signify something of great import (196–7). Here, according to Vindice, the thunder signifies not divine displeasure at the sight of a dead ruler, but satisfaction at the death of a lecher.

While *The Revenger's Tragedy* dissipates its political charge amidst a tangle of sexual impulse and intrigue, *The Spanish Tragedy* offers the possibility of something more radical. Kyd's play retains its serious register to the end, and is less prone to being dismissed in the way that *Revenger's* might when the latter collapses into farce in its closing moments. More importantly, if *The Spanish Tragedy* succeeds in enlisting and retaining audience engagement with Hieronimo, then it may be that this has something to do with the way the play exploits a tension between old codes of honour, and the more recent hegemony of *vindicta mihi*. According to Katharine Eisaman Maus, '[t]he insupportable situations in which revengers find themselves .... [t]end to reflect contradictions in which their entire society, or some large subsection of it, participates'.[13] It is quite possible that the end of the sixteenth century and the beginning of the seventeenth marks what Alan Sinfield would call an ideological 'faultline', where one set of beliefs and practices is giving way to a new one, triggering apparent instabilities and contradictions in the process.[14] If what is happening is a paradigm shift from a code that would approve of personal revenge, to one that accepts the biblical injunction that vengeance belongs to God, then it should not be very surprising that such tensions erupt into the popular culture of the time. Much more so than Vindice, Hieronimo represents the values and loyalties of the ancient social order, the world of blood-feud and vendetta, still grimly clinging to the consciousness of the people despite all attempts by Church and state to stamp it out. At the same time, as Katharine Maus points out, there is a clash between the meritocratic values of Hieronimo and the aristocratic system that forms the code of the upper classes, where birth and patronage overrule what one might 'deserve'.[15] In *Hamlet*, meanwhile, the obligations of the old code of honour are given physical form (admittedly of an ectoplasmic kind) by the Ghost of Old Hamlet, who gives his son the unequivocal order: 'If thou didst ever thy father love – ... Revenge his foul and most unnatural murder' (1.5.23, 25). The ties of blood are strong, but what makes Hamlet's case even more exceptional is the illegitimacy of Claudius as king. It would seem that he has not only committed fratricide (a heinous crime in itself, after the pattern of the Bible's first murder of Abel by his brother Cain) and married his sister-in-law (which is suggestive of incest), but he has seized the throne of Denmark, and in such cases, it is possible that the play's first audiences may well have been more willing to countenance the legitimacy of Hamlet's revenge.

Could it be that this appeal to an older paradigm, then, operates as a way of legitimising the actions of the revenger? In the contemporary context, an analogous process is at work. In the previous chapter, I discussed the debt the urban vigilante owes to the Western, a genre which, despite its fluctuating commercial fortunes, has retained its status as the quintessential American form, dramatising many of the values central to 'WASP Americanhood'. In a number of the urban vigilante movies, Western conventions, narrative tropes and elements of character presentation and development are only a little way beneath the updated surface: while it may be concealed in a holster beneath his jacket, Harry Callahan still wields his .44 Magnum like a six-shooter, most blatantly in the bank robbery scene near the beginning of *Dirty Harry*. The use of a wide frame, in combination with low-angle shots emphasising Callahan's commanding presence; the coffee bar clearly modelled on the saloon and the city block the urban equivalent of the Western town's main street, as Callahan strides through the mayhem he has unleashed (see Figure 4.1); his almost casual engagement with

Figure 4.1 The Western hero in an urban setting: Clint Eastwood as Harry Callahan in *Dirty Harry* (dir. Don Siegel, 1971)
Source: Screen capture.

the enemy and his monologue over the last robber left alive – all these elements clearly establish that lineage back to Eastwood's own roots in the Western tradition. His showdown with Scorpio in the quarry also evokes the same setting. As in the Western, there is a close association between a pistol and a man's virility: in *Magnum Force*, when Callahan's boss and nemesis Briggs informs Harry that he has never taken his pistol out of his holster, Harry replies, 'A good man always knows his limitations.' By contrast, Callahan's first meeting with the team who will turn out to be the vigilante force takes place at the shooting range, where the young men bond with the veteran over gun talk.

In *Death Wish*, the references are less subtle. In Kersey's pivotal exchange with his son-in-law on his return from Arizona, he rejects pacification and passivity: in a conversation with his son-in-law Jack (who is still grieving over his wife's retreat into a catatonic state), he challenges him with the notion of 'the old American custom of self-defence'. Jack is nonplussed. 'What do you call people who, when they are faced with a condition of fear, do nothing about it, they just run away and hide?' Kersey persists. 'Civilised?' Jack replies, perplexed by Kersey's attitude. Instead, he appeals (like the early modern revengers before him) to an old code: in his case, the ethics of the lawman of the Wild West. The conversation is directly related to Kersey's business trip to Tucson, which has functioned as a kind of epiphany: visiting a film set of a Western town where a bank robbery scene is played out for the entertainment of the tourists, Kersey watches intently as the scene progresses. As it is wrapping up, with the marshal defeating the outlaws, a moralistic voiceover is intoned by the tourist attraction's MC, which makes the connection even more explicit (as if it were necessary) between the criminals and the 'honest men with dreams... [inaudible] who would plant the roots that would grow into a nation'. As Kersey himself grows into his role of vigilante after his return to the mean streets of New York, the Western lawman seems to be a significant component in his new understanding of himself: the coffee shop scene during which Kersey flashes his wallet, presumably enticing the muggers he knows are watching him to follow him out on to the street, recalls clichéd saloon-style settings; in his final showdown with a gang, facing off against the last hood left standing, Kersey is wounded and about to pass out: as he sways, sweat lining his brow, struggling to focus, he mutters the single word, 'Draw!', to his opponent, before collapsing. When the cop investigating the vigilante case, Frank Ochoa (Vincent Gardenia), visits him in hospital and cuts him a deal (Ochoa will not arrest him, but Kersey must leave town), Kersey calls after him: 'Detective! By sundown?'

It is no surprise that *Death Wish*, like *Dirty Harry* before it, was lambasted by liberal critics as a 'poisonous incitement to do-it-yourself law enforcement'.[16] Pauline Kael dismissed it as a 'primitive, shallow work', while ruefully acknowledging that it gave the audience a 'primitive kick'.[17] The film satirises the impotent, bureaucratic law enforcement agency with a press conference which hints that the vigilante's activities have resulted in a dramatic drop in the rate of street muggings (the spokesmen have no comment to make, and one member of the press asks snidely, 'Would you tell us if it *were* true?'). When Frank Ochoa meets with the police commissioner and the District Attorney, he is told in no uncertain terms that he must not arrest Kersey, but instead 'scare him off'. After Kersey is hospitalised in his last showdown with a group of muggers, Frank makes a deal with cop on the scene not to report the vigilante's recovered gun, and promises to remember his name (another suggestion of the crooked means by which the system operates). Frank visits Kersey in his hospital room and offers to dispose of the evidence against him if he arranges to be transferred to another city. As Frank leaves the hospital, he informs the press that the vigilante is still on the loose: the authorities cannot allow Kersey to continue his one-man campaign to clear crime from New York's streets, but they cannot deny his effectiveness in solving a problem that has long since spiralled out of their control.

Harry Callahan is a figure analogous in some respects to Hieronimo – the issues of law and justice are put under intense scrutiny by the fact that the revengers are officers of the law, and so confusion and cross-over arises between upholding or enforcing the law, and punishing those who transgress it. Although, strictly speaking, Paul Verhoeven's *Robocop* (1987) falls outside the period under consideration, it is particularly provocative in terms of political critique, and in some ways can be seen as a satirical version of the right-wing fantasies embodied in *Dirty Harry* and *Death Wish*. Like those films, and like many of the early modern revenge tragedies, it represents another honourable individual pitted against a corrupt justice system. Robocop's connection back to the lineage of the Wild West is established by Murphy's quick-draw, pistol-spinning trick (itself copied from his son's favourite television programme), something that is carried over into Robocop's programming (and helps his old partner, a woman called Lewis, to deduce his true identity). Yvonne Tasker notes that, while the standard Hollywood formula routinely associated illegal substances with black people,

Robocop, along with a handful of other films of this era, associated drug abuse instead with wealthy white corruption.[18] *Robocop* presents a society on the brink of fascism: with the law enforcement agency privatised and in the ownership of the corporations developing the weaponry for that agency, this society is ripe for exploitation, and the OCP corporation is cashing in. The film's satirical streak runs a mile wide: one of the scriptwriters, Tim Miner, deliberately categorises the movie as social satire rather than science fiction,[19] and Verhoeven depicts with flash and wit a world where capitalism has shifted into sixth gear, with the privatisation of the police force a direct attack on Reaganite economic and social policy. In a money-obsessed world, there is no escape from Wall Street: even the offices' urinals have stock checkers fixed to the wall above them.

In *Robocop*'s distopian near-future, Detroit is run by gangs or criminals, and a robotic police force is in development, ostensibly to establish order and stamp out crime. The prototype cop goes spectacularly wrong at a boardroom demonstration, riddling a low-ranking executive with thousands of high calibre rounds ('just a glitch', the project manager, Dick Jones insists), and a new prototype gets the nod, a creature part organic but mostly machine: Murphy, literally shot to pieces by sadistic gang-members at the beginning of the movie, is 'resurrected' and turned into Robocop. His memory is erased and he is programmed with three directives: to serve the public trust, protect the innocent and uphold the law. A classified Directive Four has also been installed, although the audience (and Robocop) do not learn what it is until towards the end of the film. However, as the film has progressed, Robocop/Murphy has skirmished with members of the gang that destroyed his former human self, and flashes of memory and marks of humanity disrupt the machine logic of his behaviour. Eventually, Robocop tracks down those who 'killed' him, and traces the corruption back to near the top of OCP. It is only after he discovers that the insti-gator of the plot is the corrupt executive Dick Jones that the nature of Directive Four emerges: Robocop has been programmed in such a way that any attempt to arrest a senior officer of OCP results in shutdown. 'What did you think, that you were an ordinary officer?' Jones laughs, as Robocop moves to arrest him, but instead finds his cybernetic limbs locking up. 'No, you're our product. And we can't have our products turn against us, can we?' However, Murphy's humanity has already prevailed to such an extent that he has engaged in a fight to the death with Boddicker, the man charged with Jones' dirty work, and the leader of the gang who tortured and 'killed' Murphy at the beginning of the film: when Boddicker insists that Robocop must exercise restraint, he replies, 'I'm not arresting you any more', signalling the extent to which he has broken free of the constraint of the law, and is acting out of revenge (and with the memory of the violence done to him, or his former self, as a person) rather than his duty as a police officer (and as a machine). However, it would seem that Directive Four is something he is unable to override: the final execution of Jones can only take place when the head of OCP (referred to only as 'The Old Man' throughout the film) turns on him and roars, 'Dick – you're fired!' Murphy/Robocop quips, 'Thank you', before shooting Jones, blasting him out through the window of the high-rise office block.

Robocop raises interesting questions about the dividing line between justice and revenge, quite literally embodying the dilemma in a figure designed as the perfect law enforcement machine, but compromised by the few shreds of humanity that are left in him. As Murphy's humanity gradually returns (the removal of the helmet is crucial in this respect, revealing an eerily vulnerable head) (see Figure 4.2), he trades in the concept of upholding the law for a personal quest for revenge on those who stole his humanity in the first place. At the same time, the film interrogates the relationship between the ruling power and a supposedly impartial justice system: after all, when the agents of law enforcement

Figure 4.2 Part man, part robot: the dilemma of the human justice machine. Peter Weller as Murphy in *Robocop* (dir. Paul Verhoeven, 1987)
Source: Screen capture.

are controlled by those who have political power, and when such power is available to the highest bidder, true natural justice becomes impossible. In *The Revenger's Tragedy*, those in power assumed that they had the right to 'walk/With a bold foot upon the thorny law' (1.2.103–4). Dick Jones and Boddicker believe they possess the same immunity, and even though both of them are, eventually, on the receiving end of Robocop's violent justice (or revenge), the film's political outlook remains a bleak one: after all, it is The Old Man, head of OCP, who retains ultimate authority. The apparently perfect robotic cop is really not impartial at all: Murphy's final act of revenge is, at the same time, a reinscription of the status quo. As he tells his wounded partner in the wake of the violent showdown with Boddicker and his gang: 'They'll fix you. They fix everything.' It is a fittingly cynical epitaph for the political revenger.

5
'Taint Not Thy Mind': The Morality of Revenge

'You talkin' to me?' The revenger and the audience

A key issue in current debates about retribution and justice concerns the involvement of victims of crime in the process. The issue comes to the fore at particular historical moments, such as the arrangements made for relatives of the 168 victims of the bombing of the Federal Building in Oklahoma City in April 1995 to witness, via a closed-circuit television relay, the execution by fatal injection of the convicted bomber Timothy McVeigh. The growth of victims' rights support and lobby groups in recent years has been significant in spurring lawyers, philosophers, psychologists and sociologists to reconsider the prevalent assumption in Western culture that revenge is, in and of itself, necessarily evil. Writers such as Charles K. B. Barton, who argues an eloquent case in his study *Getting Even: Revenge as a Form of Justice* (1999), have suggested ways in which the justice system might be reconfigured to accommodate the deep-seated need, or (as he suggests we conceptualise it), the *right* to personal retribution as part of the process.[1] Peter A. French makes an analogous case when he argues for what he terms the 'tailored fit' of proportionality in determining punishments for criminals. The logic of his case leads him to consider what might be fit punishment for a rapist (death), and, bizarrely, imagining a scenario when, to avoid any emotional or moral fall-out, we might employ 'robots or androids' to carry out the 'appropriate nasty business ... taking the sting out of it for the human punisher'.[2] A case for OCP and a new breed of robocops, perhaps. The sometimes alarming conclusions that Barton, French and others draw may be shocking, but they do meditate upon, in a different context, the provocative questions that revenge narratives raise, and may make us think more carefully about the implications of audience engagement with revengers. The revenger becomes a powerful projection of society's frustration at times when it sees (or is led to imagine) spiralling crime and a weak or incompetent effort on the part of the government to enforce law and order. In recent years in the UK, a number of 'moral panics' have sparked off vigilante campaigns. Perhaps the most high-profile case was in the summer of 2000, when, following the murder of eight-year-old Sarah Payne, the tabloid paper *News of the World* published a list of convicted paedophiles, prompting protest marches, and attacks and acts of vandalism on the property of those 'named and shamed'. Inevitably, victims included a number mistakenly targeted, including a female doctor: it seems that the vigilante gang had confused the crime of paedophilia with the doctor's specialism of paediatrics.[3] One might well take issue with the fantasies of retributive justice that arise from the trains of thought set in motion by the likes of Barton and French, or their less reflective, more populist equivalents in mass circulation news media, but there are customarily hidden, unspoken currents of feeling that run deep in the popular subconscious, and their sudden eruptions to the surface, in public debate and action, can take us by surprise, and may force a re-evaluation of what we understand by the term 'civilised'.

Tony Scott's *Man on Fire* (2004) functions as a useful example of the way in which a revenge text can work on its audience to ensure it engages as fully as possible with the revenger's motives. Its subject matter is emotive, telling as it does the story of ex-CIA operative Creasy (Denzel Washington), washed up and struggling against alcoholism, employed as a bodyguard for a young girl in Mexico City, the 'kidnap capital of the world'. When the girl, Pita (Dakota Fanning), is kidnapped, with Creasy left severely wounded, he seeks his revenge on the perpetrators. A number of the film's reviews noted the audiences' responses, in particular cheers and applause for the protagonist's acts of vengeance. Most frequently noted (perhaps unsurprisingly) was the scene in which Creasy places a plastic explosive up a villain's rectum, and then sets off the timer as he begins the interrogation. Having extracted the information he requires, Creasy strides away, leaving his victim to count down the seconds to his own demise. The care, attention and screen time devoted to building the relationship between Pita and Creasy means that the second half of the film – Creasy as revenger – has a much better chance of carrying its audience with it. The more the audience feels for the kidnapped Pita, and the more it participates in Creasy's sense of guilt, rage and desire for revenge, the more likely it is to sanction, and even applaud, the acts of retribution. In the eyes of many members of the audience, perhaps, the worse the violence, the greater the sense of satisfaction: a retired CIA agent and friend (Christopher Walken) puts it succinctly when he tells the Mexican detective investigating the killings, 'Creasy's art is death. He's about to paint his masterpiece', and the acts of torture and murder Creasy commits are presented to the audience in just that form: as works of art to be marvelled at and applauded.

There are significant differences between what contemporary and early modern audiences have been prepared to accept in terms of acts of vengeance. In Chapter 2 I noted Eleanor Prosser's classification of straightforward villain-revengers in tragic drama from 1562 to 1607. 'By nature committed to evil, they would be loathed by the audience even if they did not attribute their crimes to vengeance,' she writes.[4] Fredson Bowers believes that a typical early modern audience would have 'sentimentally sympathized with the Kydian hero revenger, and hoped for his success, but only on condition that he did not survive'.[5] However, some of these judgements are debatable, and there are certainly plenty of ambivalent revenger figures in other plays of the period who are much more difficult to categorise. Robert C. Jones, in his study of four early modern stage villains, reflects on the process of forming attitudes towards the characters acting on stage, especially when they are on the one hand evil, and on the other positioned as the protagonists of their respective dramas. The frequent use of asides and soliloquies by characters such as Richard III in Shakespeare's history play (1593), Barabas in Marlowe's *The Jew of Malta* and Vindice in *The Revenger's Tragedy* identifies them as the audience's most likely point of entry into the world of the play, but their villainy means that they are inevitably more ambivalent figures: thus, he argues, while they may 'engage' the audience, such engagement is not necessarily synonymous with 'sympathy'.[6]

What is most important is the crossing of the line between what an audience is still willing to judge as acceptable behaviour by the revenger protagonist, and what is considered to be too violent, extreme or disproportionate in terms of the initial wrong. Clearly, as notions of what a society considers to be just evolve, so the boundaries shift. *The Spanish Tragedy* walks the line at a time when the horrors of divine judgement and punishment still seemed real and imminent to the majority of the population – both in terms of God's revenge on the unjust (all in His own good time), and in terms of the fate that awaited those who had the temerity to take the duties of revenge upon themselves. By contrast, *Man on Fire* plays to an audience in a post-9/11 context, and in an intellectual climate where, even if religious belief is still a significant factor, the specific injunctions about revenge seem much less immediate or relevant. *Man on Fire* is in part built around Creasy's personal journey from his own private hell to a version of a state of grace by the film's conclusion: the idea that he requires redemption for the unnamed, perhaps unspeakable, acts he has committed in the service of his government is underlined in his conversation with Walken's character: 'You think God'll forgive us for what we've done?' he asks him, but the question seems rhetorical, even before it is fully articulated. Creasy battles to give up the bottle, and much is made of his re-engagement with the Bible, though it is chiefly via his relationship with Pita that he stumbles towards redemption, and any divine implications are firmly rebutted. When, mid-rampage, it is suggested that there may be room for forgiveness, his response is bluntly secular: 'Forgiveness is between them and God – it's my job to arrange the meeting.' The line echoes a similar strategy in the contemporaneous movie *The Punisher*: as Frank Castle (the Punisher) parts from Candelaria, the man who has nursed him back to health after he has been left for dead following the massacre of his family, Candelaria wishes him well: 'Vaya con Dios, Castle; go with God.' 'God's going to sit this one out', Castle replies.

Viewers of *Man on Fire* seem willing to maintain their engagement with Creasy's anti-hero figure for a variety of reasons, chiefly because of the relationship between Creasy and Pita that is carefully built and deployed for maximum emotional impact when she is kidnapped and then assumed dead. In *Dirty Harry*, on the other hand, perhaps a line *is* crossed, in terms of audience response, during Callahan's torture of Scorpio on the football field. Although Harry's higher motives are obvious – his desperation as he races against the clock to save Ann Mary Deacon – the film refuses to soft-pedal the depiction of Callahan's brutality. With Scorpio trapped in the stadium like an animal, a tiny figure picked out in the glare of the floodlights, Harry takes aim and fires as his quarry raises his hands in surrender. The camera angle emphasises and elongates the barrel of Harry's pistol, and there is a brief insert shot of Harry's point of view as he takes aim and shoots at Scorpio. In long shot, the bad guy goes down. Despite the glee Scorpio has expressed in wanton killing, he still strikes a pathetic figure, inspiring something akin to the sympathy one might feel for a dumb animal (the chief of police actually warns Harry not to treat Scorpio like an animal as he examines Harry's choice of rifle to hunt him down; in addition, Scorpio squeals like a stuck pig when stabbed in the leg by Harry's switchblade in an earlier scene). As Harry approaches him, the audience hears Scorpio's frantic, high-pitched, garbled pleading ('I want a lawyer, I have a right for [*sic*] a lawyer, I have rights!'). Harry, his face contorted in rage, tortures him by standing on his wounded leg. As the sequence ends, the scene is shot from the extreme high angle of a helicopter-mounted camera, and as the stadium recedes from view, it is shrouded by mist, drawing a veil over the torture scene. However, the film is careful to ensure a watertight case for Harry's violence. Scorpio is a monstrous creation – a sniper, a rapist, a man who kidnaps not just one child but a bus full of schoolchildren. Almost all his victims are women and children (at one point, as he seeks out his next random victim, his sights settle on one member of a gay couple). With his long hair, effeminate manner and build, his vaguely hippy clothing, and with a large peace symbol on his belt buckle, Scorpio is clearly set up as a figure for a large proportion of the audience to hate and despise. Scorpio is so comprehensively demonised that it becomes difficult to take issue with Harry's unorthodox, off-the-record methods of dealing with him. Eastwood himself claimed that Harry 'listens to a higher morality above the law',[7] and, speaking at the time he was directing the fourth film in the franchise, *Sudden Impact* (1983), he mused:

> I think that Harry stands out because of what he represents...especially now that the pendulum seems to be swinging in a more conservative direction. People are a little edgy about the rights of criminals taking precedent over the rights of victims. They are more impatient with courtroom procedures and legal delays. I think the public is interested in justice, and that's what Harry stands for. He's unique because he stood for the same principles from the beginning, when it wasn't terribly fashionable.[8]

Eastwood has, over time, backtracked away from the *Dirty Harry* persona, probably due in part to his decision to enter politics in the real world in the late 1980s. A revisionist opinion he expressed in 1989 sought to set some distance between himself and Harry Callahan, but retains the notion of a man alienated by the justice system: 'Harry is a bitter man, a roughneck, who in effect has no choice [but] to rebel against the rules he considers unfair.'[9] At the end of *Dirty Harry*, having shot dead the serial killer Scorpio, Callahan discards his police badge: a very deliberate and (apparently) final rejection of the legal machine. Susan Jeffords writes, 'Harry's heroism has a nihilistic edge to it that cannot reassure audiences that any of his actions have mattered or have changed the social order in any way.'[10]

In early modern England, while Bowers and Prosser both argue that the case against revenge was made so strongly by the dominant culture – governmental, judicial and religious – that audiences watching figures such as Hieronimo and Vindice would have effectively had no choice but to condemn their actions, there is nevertheless some evidence that the case may not have been quite so simple. Part of the fascination the revenger figure held for those audiences was precisely his ambivalence, and one way in which that ambivalence could be explored was in the depiction of a spiritual, emotional or mental transformation that took place as the desire for revenge grew. The revenger protagonist's tragic journey often involves a gradual descent into moral confusion and mental disorder. The measured, stately demeanour Hieronimo displays at the beginning of *The Spanish Tragedy* is exchanged for a desperate, frantic insanity that finds him tearing at the earth with his dagger in an attempt to clear a path to the underworld, in order to show the king and his followers his son's wounds. Hamlet's madness, of course, whether real, feigned or a combination of the two, is the topic of countless studies and dissertations. Often, a descent into madness is concomitant with a multiplication of revenge plots, or else a rapidly increasing body count that includes innocent victims. In *The Revenger's Tragedy*, the opening scene depicts Vindice casting himself as revenger for the death of Gloriana, and in the next scene, the Duchess vows revenge on her husband the Duke for failing to secure her youngest son's release, while the bastard Spurio wants his revenge for being denied his inheritance because of his illegitimate birth. We are still in Act 1 when we hear Antonio vowing revenge for the rape of his wife via a pact sworn with Piero and Hippolito; and it is Piero, not Antonio, who ends the scene with talk of becoming 'more familiar with revenge' (1.4.73). As the play gathers momentum, Vindice surrenders to the joy of the violence he perpetrates in the name of justice. His brother Hippolito acts as a useful index to Vindice's mental state and, by Act 3, Scene 5, Vindice's erratic mood swings are clearly unnerving him. When the macabre nature of Vindice's plot is revealed – and in performance the revelation would need to come just about simultaneously for Hippolito and the audience – it becomes clear that Vindice's thirst for revenge has driven him mad. Just as ghosts frequently return from the grave to incite their kinfolk to revenge, so Vindice has engineered Gloriana's return: her poisoned skull, veiled, is perched atop a figure dressed in robes, and Vindice will present her to the duke as a prostitute, so that she may, as Vindice says, 'bear a part e'en in it own revenge', and 'kiss his lips to death' (3.5.100–4). Again, at the beginning of Act 5, Scene 1, Hippolito makes desperate attempts to calm the over-excited Vindice as they prepare for the final stage of their plot. This is most obvious at the two climactic moments of the play – the murder of the Duke, and the multiple deaths at the performance of the masque in the final scene. He becomes fanatically committed to the aptness of his revenge, planning and executing his plot against the duke with minute attention to detail, and he insists on a polished performance in the final masque.

This kind of transformation is not always signalled by insanity. It can also be explored via a fundamental change in a character that strips him of his original beliefs and values, often deeply held, and refits him as a revenger or vigilante. For example, the opening few scenes of *Death Wish* carefully construct Kersey as a loving husband and a peaceful, law-abiding and liberal citizen. After the rape and assault of his wife and daughter, Kersey travels to visit clients of his architect's firm in Arizona. During his time away, during a visit to a shooting range with his Tucson associate, Aimes Jainchill, Kersey reveals that he was a conscientious objector during the Korean war, sworn off guns when his father was shot dead in a hunting accident. Kersey is, in fact, an expert shot and when he returns to New York, he takes with him a pistol – an unexpected gift from Aimes, who has already offered his own ideas about how to deal with crime: 'Muggers out here they just plain get their asses blown off.' Kersey's first act of retaliation against a mugger has tipped him over the edge into a fit of rage and self-loathing, followed by heavy drinking. Now, armed with a pistol, Kersey begins to warm to his task: although after his first armed foray he returns home and throws up, it is not long before he becomes immured to the emotional or moral consequences of killing: he saves a man from three hoodlums and shoots all three, even chasing after the one that tries to escape, to finish him off. For Kersey, there is a direct parallel between his daughter's mental collapse ('She had an experience she can't face and she's running away from it', his son-in-law Jack has told him) and the choices on offer to him. As he steps up his campaign, he is transformed. While Jack slumps into despair over Carol's worsening condition, Kersey, welcoming Jack into the apartment, bombards him with loud jazz, plies him with drink, and proudly displays the vibrant colours of his newly repainted apartment.

Vindice seems to become enraptured, as the play proceeds, with the concept of revenge, and is fanatically preoccupied with its timing, its aptness and its ferocity. When it is done, he cannot contain himself, and his desire for the world to know of his ingenuity and the perfect execution of his revenge ultimately leads to his downfall. In *Death Wish*, Kersey seems to grow into his vigilante role as the narrative unfolds, though it is difficult to determine whether his transition from nausea at the memory of killing to stony impassivity represents character development or simply a failure on the part of the film, its makers and Bronson himself to convey anything more complex. In *Hamlet*, the convention of delayed revenge becomes not, as it is in many examples of the genre, a problem for the author (how does one maintain tension and plausibility over the necessary time lag between exposition and motivation for the revenge plot, and the prosecution of the revenger's natural justice?), but instead moves to the centre of the play. Hamlet puzzles over the ethics of revenge, puzzles over his prevarication, and puzzles over his puzzlement in a series of ever-decreasing intellectual circles. Old Hamlet's injunction that the prince must avenge his 'foul and most unnatural murder' comes with a significant rider: 'Taint not thy mind' (1.5.85). What results is an at times exhausting exercise in inertia. Hamlet meditates on the call to revenge and thinks himself to a standstill, occasionally roused from his inaction by interventions such as the First Player's Pyrrhus speech which he sees as exposing himself as 'pigeon-livered' (2.2.565) for his failure to move against Claudius. Characteristically, having worked himself up into a lather once more, he defuses his resolve again by hatching a new plot to try to determine whether the spirit he has seen is honest, or is instead the devil in 'a pleasing shape' that 'abuses me to damn me' (2.2.589, 592). Even when he seems to have the final, definitive proof he has been waiting for after the success of the Mouse Trap, he offers another masterclass in letting himself off the hook:

> 'Tis now the very witching time of night,
> When churchyards yawn, and hell itself breathes out
> Contagion to this world. Now could I drink hot blood,
> And do such bitter business as the day
> Would quake to look on. (3.2.371–5)

This is a powerful, grandstanding soliloquy that speaks of a resolve more bloody than might have seemed possible since he first promised to 'sweep' to his revenge some 1,400 lines earlier. But what completes this line is not further resolve, but the almost comically bathetic 'Soft, now to my mother' (375). When, unseen, he comes across Claudius alone and vulnerable, he has the perfect opportunity to stage his much longed for act of vengeance, but the idea that he might dispatch the villain to heaven gives him pause: 'And so he goes to heaven;/And so am I revenged. That would be scanned' (3.3.74–5). His decision to delay revenge until he can be sure of sending his uncle's soul to hell probably shocked many members of the play's first audiences, bearing in mind what I have already established in terms of opinions about premeditated, as opposed to spontaneous, acts of vengeance (see pp. 30–1). It has certainly disturbed readers and playgoers down the ages: his justification was described by Samuel Johnson as 'too horrible to be read or to be uttered', and the Christian-inflected opinion of G. Wilson Knight contrasts Hamlet at this moment, 'his eye a-glitter with the intoxication of conquest, vengeance in his mind', with his potential victim, whose prayer he interprets as 'the fine flower of a human soul in anguish'.[11] However, in the light of all the procrastinations that have already gone before, it is as easy to interpret this new chance to 'scan' his options as yet another delay, and further evidence of his profound unease with the role of revenger.

'Taint not thy mind': the moral avenger

One notable feature of many of the revenger and vigilante figures under discussion is their preoccupation with moral purity, and their disgust at human failings, especially in terms of sexual immorality. Hamlet is a figure morbidly obsessed with human flaws, corruptibility and immorality; while he peppers much of his 'antic disposition' dialogue with such talk (notably in his humiliation of Polonius in Act 2, Scene 2), the obsession runs deep; his 'habitual feeling', as A. C. Bradley writes, is 'one of disgust at life and everything in it, himself included'.[12] His disappointment in mankind ('this quintessence of dust' [2.2.305–6]) expressed to his former friends Rosencrantz and Guildenstern matches his suicidal despair elsewhere ('To be or not to be' [3.1.57–89]). In his showdown with Gertrude, he shows her pictures of Claudius and Old Hamlet, pointing out for her 'your husband, like a mildewed ear/ Blasting his wholesome brother' (3.4.64–5). Hamlet's misanthropy has a marked misogynist slant to it, in keeping with the attitudes towards women that were common at the time. He rejects his former beloved Ophelia in a scene that seems to begin as another sequel in his antic disposition franchise, but soon takes on an authentic tone that speaks eloquently of his fastidiousness. 'Why wouldst thou be a breeder of sinners?' he demands of her (3.1.122–3); Hamlet accuses Ophelia not only of hypocrisy ('God has given you one face, and you make yourselves another' [144–5]) but also believes, like all women, she cannot help but prove to be unfaithful (as Gertrude has): 'wise men know well enough what monsters you make of them', he spits (139–41). His sense of betrayal is aggravated by his suspicion that she is working for Claudius and Polonius; in the theatre, this is sometimes made clear by stage business that signals Hamlet realises he is being watched. However, as far as Hamlet is concerned, the corruption runs much deeper: he is horrified not only by her potential for spiritual and sexual immorality, but also by the vision that opens up to him of his own baseness: 'What should such fellows as I do crawling beneath heaven and earth? We are arrant knaves all' (128–30). The misogyny erupts again in the scene with Gertrude (3.4), as he vents his disgust at her; his fury seems to provoke the sudden return of his father's ghost, who reminds him of his earlier injunctions not to harm Gertrude, and brings back to the centre Hamlet's 'almost blunted purpose' (103).

I have already suggested that *The Revenger's Tragedy* is built on a number of revenge plots, all of them essentially rooted in sexual intrigue and competing claims among men over female sexuality. Vindice is deeply preoccupied with sexual impurity, and he plots an elaborate plan to test the sexual probity of his sister and mother. In his opening soliloquy, he marvels over the Duke's lechery:

> O, that marrowless age
> Would stuff the hollow bones with damned desires,
> And 'stead of heat kindle infernal fires
> Within the spendthrift veins of a dry duke,
> A parched and juiceless luxury. O God! One
> That has scare blood enough to live upon,
> And he to riot it like a son and heir? (1.1.5–11)

His rhetoric is shot through with the kind of misogyny associated with malcontents such as De Flores (*The Duchess of Malfi*), Flamineo (*The White Devil*) and Iago (*Othello* [1603]). 'Their sex is easy in belief,' he tells his brother Hippolito (1.1.107); and in soliloquy he philosophises, 'Were't not for gold and women there would be no damnation' (2.1.250). His disguise as the pimp Piato suits him well, giving him plenty of opportunities to marvel ironically over the monstrous nature of women. While much of what he speaks when in disguise is moulded to his deeper purposes, his quip to Lussurioso that 'Tell but some woman a secret overnight,/Your doctor may find it in the urinal i' the morning' could just as easily be interpreted as Vinidice's heartfelt opinion (1.3.82–3). However, while Gratiana certainly conforms to Vindice's stereotype ('Men know, that know us,/We are so weak their words can overthrow us', she confides to the audience [2.2.104–5]),

Castiza, as her name would suggest, does not. When Vindice, in disguise, tests her chastity (2.1), he finds that she defends her honour vigorously, despite their mother's attempts to persuade her to sell her virginity. Vindice is relieved at Castiza's behaviour and horrified by his mother, and only her abject pleading, and Hippolito's cajoling, persuade him to forgive her. Even here, however, he cannot resist the temptation of another jibe against womankind: 'For honest women are so seld and rare,' he concludes, 'Tis good to cherish those poor few that are' (4.4.60–1). Vindice is driven to extreme actions by a sense of injustice, but the fuel that feeds the fire of his revenge is, more than anything else, distaste for the immoral behaviour that he sees infecting not only his enemies, but his own family too.

In some of the revenger films of the 1970s, there is an analogous preoccupation with immorality. Michael Ryan and Douglas Kellner suggest that films with a conservative perspective on social problems have traditionally seen crime as being a result of evil human nature rather than as a result of social conditions.[13] There are suggestions in *Dirty Harry* that Callahan may have voyeuristic tendencies;[14] however, in one early scene, Callahan drives through the red light district at night, observing the pimps, prostitutes and sex shows. He mutters to his partner, 'These loonies, they oughta throw a net over the whole bunch of 'em', and Sanchez murmurs in agreement. In *Death Wish*, out at night to lure muggers, Kersey eyes the prostitutes in the coffee shop with a similar, albeit unspoken, disdain. However, of all the vigilante movies of the 1970s, it is Martin Scorsese's *Taxi Driver* (1976) that most obviously shares with the revenge tragedies an odd combination of dread, disgust and fascination with human corruption. Interestingly, its angle is fairly determinedly apolitical. Travis Bickle, the psychically damaged, Nam Vet misfit spending his nights driving taxis and spinning out the days in front of the TV set, or gazing blankly at the screen in porn cinemas, is an enigma, the targets of his violence, once it erupts, seemingly diffuse and random. The trigger for Bickle's breakdown seems to be the collapse of his fragile relationship with Betsy (Cybill Shepherd), a campaign worker at the offices of Palantine, a candidate for election to the senate. After Betsy has rejected Travis (who has committed the excruciating faux pas of taking her to a porn movie on a date), his transformation begins. He equips himself with an array of guns and the scene with the weapons dealer, Andy, is played out as a pornographic fantasy; Andy purrs and coos over the guns as he offers them up for Bickle's inspection ('Look at that, that's a beauty...That's a beautiful little gun; isn't that a little honey?'). Travis toughens his body through a regime of exercise, a strict diet, and more extreme measures, including burning his hands over the lit stove in his kitchen, declaring in the voice-over, 'I gotta get in shape now' and prescribing a routine of push-ups and pull-ups – 'no more pills, no more bad food, no more destroyers of my body'. Travis is purifying himself physically and psychically of pollutants as he struggles to focus upon a new task, a new mission. Of course, with the nature of that mission hopelessly out of focus, Travis's mental trajectory is spinning without a centre, and cannot hold. Briefly, the film seems to connect with paranoia-fuelled political thrillers such as *The Parallax View* (1974) and *Executive Action* (1973), when Travis stalks Palantine, but he bungles the assassination attempt. It is not even clear why Travis plots the assassination in the first place, although a conversation he has with Palantine when the politician rides in his cab suggests it may be an expression of frustrated disappointment in the system (anthropomorphised in Palantine) and its failure to deal with the squalor he detests: 'I think someone should just take this city', he tells Palantine in a Vindice-like invective, 'and just...just flush it down the fuckin' toilet'. Subsequently, Travis becomes more and more fixated on the character of Iris, a child prostitute (Jodie Foster). Travis sees himself as the violent redeemer of an America that has dissolved into a cesspool of pimps, hookers and drug dealers. Gazing at human corruption night after night from the driver's seat of his cab, Travis is rendered almost inarticulate by his bottled up fury, his disgust emerging in blurted conversations with others (such as the child prostitute Iris) and, more often, with himself, strings of expletives that peter out into incoherence.

Travis's view of the street is accompanied by his soliloquy, his voice-over: 'All the animals come out at night, whores, skunk pussies, buggers, queens, fairies, dopers, junkies.' As Kolker argues, this is not necessarily a reflection of the 'reality' of New York City. The pimps, prostitutes, drunks and drug addicts 'constitute the only things he [Travis] perceives and, since the viewer's perceptions in the film are so restricted to his own, the only things the viewer is permitted to perceive as well.' Kolker continues: '*Taxi Driver* is not a documentary of the squalor of New York City but the documentation of a squalid mind driven mad by its perception.'[15] In one of his many voice-overs, Travis thanks God for the rain, for one day, he imagines, a 'real rain' will 'wash all this scum off the streets'. In the meantime, he is left to wipe the blood and semen off the back seat of his cab at the end of each shift. He sees a way out of his private hell in the form of two very different women. The campaign worker Betsy is represented as a cliché of the

Hollywood dream blonde (Travis describes her as being 'like an angel' appearing 'out of this filthy mess'), although the audience is made aware of a widening gap between Travis's idealisation and the reality of Betsy, who turns out to be a 'perfectly mediocre personality',[16] flirting idly with her co-worker and toying curiously with Travis, perhaps flattered by his image of her, and with a rather detached interest in his odd personality. The second female – the twelve-year-old prostitute, Iris – is, for Travis, another route to salvation. If Betsy cannot pull him out of the filth in which he seems to be drowning, then he will find a route to redemption by saving Iris from herself. Kolker interprets the film as a parody of *The Searchers* (and Scorsese and Schrader acknowledge it as an influence), in which Travis corresponds to John Wayne's Ethan, on an obsessive mission to save his niece (Natalie Wood's Debbie, corresponding to Iris) from the Indians (their chief, Scar [Henry Brandon], is mirrored in Harvey Keitel's pimp Sport), and many of the parallels work, even if in many respects Travis and Ethan are poles apart.

Joan Mellen dismisses *Taxi Driver* as another misogynistic and misanthropic invective, identifying Travis's ostensible mission to rescue the child prostitute Iris as a premise for 'Martin Scorsese and screenwriter Paul Schrader to wallow in one more neofascist depiction of the poor and disadvantaged as vermin'.[17] The history of film criticism has been kinder to the film, however. Other examples of the genre have not stood the test of time so well, notably *Death Wish*, which retains our interest principally as an historical curiosity, being one of the most unashamed exploitations of a genre that had clearly set a trend by the time it was released in 1974. At the same time, its demagogic power in its own time is difficult to deny. *Dirty Harry* offers something more complex in the way it explores the issue of justice, vigilantism, and the place of the principled law enforcement agent in a system that has tied itself in bureaucratic knots. But what all these texts share is an obsession with the tension between idealism and reality. Frequently, the female becomes the key symbol of that tension, either as a signifier of purity (Betsy and Iris in *Taxi Driver*, Gloriana in *The Revenger's Tragedy*, Tracy in *Se7en*, even the only briefly glimpsed Ann Mary Deacon in *Dirty Harry*) or of corruption (Ophelia and Gertrude in *Hamlet*, Beatrice-Joanna in *The Changeling*, Gratiana in *The Revenger's Tragedy*, the Pride and Lust victims in *Se7en*). More importantly, the revenger, in the grip of his obsession with corruption, frequently turns a piercing eye upon his own soul. The essential dilemma of the vigilante and, very often, the revenger, is this: how can a man who is driven to take action outside the law in a quest to rebalance the scales of justice remain pure? Must he inevitably be tainted by the actions he is forced to take? It is here, where the revenger is seen *in extremis*, that the final parallels and differences can be traced.

Reflections from the abyss: the revenger and his double

The moral status of the avenger has always been a preoccupation for the writers of revenge dramas. John Cawelti notes the importance of the superhero in American popular culture, embodying 'an inevitable nemesis or transcendent force that automatically responds to criminal activity with perfect justice'.[18] Unfortunately, the consummation of 'perfect justice' is rarely within the reach of the revenger in the thriller genre, who is often very clearly exposed as being all too human and morally compromised in some form, either before, or as a result of, the acts he is called upon to perform. Terry Eagleton goes so far as to propose that revengers such as Vindice 'turn by some fateful logic into the image of those they hunt down, growing less and less distinguishable from them'.[19] I am sure I am neither the first nor the last to include this quotation from Nietzsche in a production programme when directing *Hamlet*:

> He who fights with monsters should look to it that he himself does not become a monster. And when you gaze long into an abyss, the abyss gazes also into you.[20]

Michael Ryan and Douglas Kellner see a similar principle at work in the representation of Harry Callahan, as well as his close conceptual relative Popeye Doyle (Gene Hackman) in *The French Connection* (1971), casting them and their criminal antagonists as mirror images of each other:

> Mirrors can only give back what is projected, and what right-wing conservatives project is the motivating energy of their own social ideal – force, violence and a disregard for law. Both Harry and Popeye are characterized by a rather resentful attitude toward legal restraint which makes them mirror images of their opponents.[21]

The idea of the revenger and the target of his fury as reflections of each other has been a familiar trope in both early modern and contemporary popular forms.

Magnum Force confronts Harry with what could be interpreted as a distorted – but still recognisable – mirror image of himself in the form of a pack of vigilante cops. The 'perverts' Harry watches from his car after dark in *Dirty Harry*, and whom he thinks should be rounded up, find their corollary in *Magnum Force* in the swingers at the outdoor swimming pool, mown down by the four apocalyptic, leather-clad figures. It is only the death of Harry's old friend, Charlie McCoy, at the hands of one of the group that tips the scales against the vigilante cops. When the pack attempts to recruit Harry, making it clear that he must decide whether he is for them or against them, his reply is a simple, 'I'm afraid you've misjudged me.' Nevertheless, the distinction is likely to remain a pretty fine one for many members of the audience who were by then quite accustomed to Harry's unorthodox methods, and may have had trouble detailing the differences between his actions and those of the vigilantes. In the case of Travis Bickle, the metaphor of the revenger and his double is given its most literal expression in the famous scene where Travis struts in front of the mirror in his apartment, repeatedly drawing his weapon on himself, and challenging his reflection: 'You talking to me? You talking to me? Well, then who the hell else are you talking to? . . . You talking to me? . . . Well, I'm the only one here. Who the fuck do you think you're talking to?' The motif of Travis and the mirror – the frequent, insistent shots of his eyes darting to his rear-view mirror as he works the streets, as well as the more obvious 'you talking to me' scene – serve to heighten the sense of isolation and solipsism: Travis's chief target, though he is oblivious to it, is his own morally and spiritually bankrupt self. This deeper mystery remains hidden not only from Travis but also from Iris's parents, who write him a stumbling letter of thanks. Meanwhile, the New York media hail him as a hero of the people.

If Hamlet is torn between duty to his father and misgivings about the morality, even the logic, of revenge, then his mirror must be Laertes. Hamlet himself seems to recognise as much: 'For by the image of my cause I see/The portraiture of his', he tells Horatio (5.2.78–9). Goethe writes that, 'Shakespeare wished to describe the effects of a great action laid upon a soul that was unequal to it',[22] and Laertes is crucial in showing how this works. *Hamlet* establishes parallel tracks for the two young men: one forced to return home as the play begins, the other departing; one already deprived of a mother as the play opens, the other of a father, but both inspired to revenge in acts of filial loyalty. Laertes, it seems, is the kind of man who would 'sweep to his revenge' with wings as swift as thought. He still operates by the ancient, chivalric code which demands that he protect his family's honour. As he tells Claudius,

> That drop of blood that's calm proclaims me bastard,
> Cries cuckold to my father, brands the harlot
> Even here between the chaste unsmirched brows
> Of my true mother. (4.5.114–17)

The one line he aims at Hamlet when the prince appears at Ophelia's funeral, 'The devil take thy soul' (5.1.248), implies that he probably flies at him, and many editors have chosen to imply via interpolated stage directions a fight between the two at this point. In the theatre, it is often used as an opportunity to indulge the production's fight choreographer. Hamlet obviously admires Laertes; he tells Horatio he is 'a very noble youth' (5.1.214) and after their confrontation over Ophelia's grave, tells Laertes, 'I loved you ever' (280). While Hamlet frets over the implications of vengeance, Laertes plots with Claudius to avenge the death of Polonius. When Claudius challenges him, asking him what he would do 'To show yourself your father's son in deed/More than in words', Laertes' reply is blunt and uncompromising, untroubled by moral niceties: 'To cut his throat i' th' church' (4.7.101–2).

The playwright Charles Marowitz recognised the Hamlet/Laertes binary, and much of his *Collage Hamlet* is built around it. For Marowitz, Hamlet represents 'the supreme prototype of the conscience-stricken but paralysed liberal: one of the most lethal and obnoxious characters in modern times'.[23] The collage, first performed in the late 1960s, in this respect connects with the political groundswell I have identified elsewhere, the impatience and frustration with the perceived failures of liberal politics. Marowitz ridicules Hamlet repeatedly, often via the contrasts he sets up with Laertes' character, staged in amusingly slapstick fashion. The duel comes halfway through the play: after some perfunctory clack-clacking with wooden swords, the real combat begins, with each of them declaiming choice lines from their passionate speeches. For every one of Hamlet's ('The play's the thing/Wherein I'll catch the conscience of the king'), booed and hissed by the on-stage audience, Laertes counters with an angry, flamboyant retort ('I have a speech of fire that would fain blaze'), which inspires the audience to frantic applause.[24] Shakespeare's Hamlet, of course, finally discovers the power to act, but only when Laertes has taken revenge on him for the death of Polonius and Ophelia's suicide. When he does move against Claudius, it is in the heat of the moment, and it is not so very far removed from his crazed stabbing of a concealed Polonius. Ironically, having spent many long scenes and speeches puzzling over the grounds, implications and methodology of his revenge, the act itself reminds us of the definition of manslaughter, which included spontaneous response to an injury (and was, hypothetically, a pardonable offence).[25]

Perhaps the most complex exploration of the idea of the revenger and his double comes in *Se7en*. In this trend-setting serial killer movie, director David Fincher and screenwriter Andrew Kevin Walker set up a fascinating configuration between the three key characters: Mills is young, impulsive, not an inexperienced detective, but still naïve in many ways, and a man who operates by instinct and emotion rather than intellect. Somerset, on the verge of retirement, is analytical, methodical, and an officer whose length of service and depth of experience command the respect, and sometimes the envy, of his peers (the captain makes a semi-ironic reference to his 'great brain'). As he and Mills pursue their own lines of research, Mills pores over incident and mortuary photographs while the TV blares; Somerset works in the library to the strains of Bach's 'Air on a G String'. Somerset works his way through *The Canterbury Tales* and Dante's *Inferno*; Mills assigns a cop to buy him copies of Cliff Notes (student guides) on the same texts. Their histories are very different too, even in details that seem extraneous to the plot: Mills and his wife, Tracy, are high school sweethearts, whereas Somerset seems to have a sad, dark romantic history, and is now very much alone. The contrasts run very deep, but emerge at the surface, too: the young white detective, lean and hyperactive, constantly on edge, and the older, black detective, slower and more measured, his calm features care-worn and his eyes full of a deep sadness at all the cruelty of humankind that he has had to watch and endure.

So far, so formulaic: although we can admire the skill and care with which the Mills/Somerset binary is built, it is also true to say that, in this respect, it works within a well-established convention in the cop movie of the mismatched partners, which runs all the way from TV shows such as *Starsky and Hutch* (1975–9) via movies such as *48 Hours* (1982), *Point Break* (1991) and the *Lethal Weapon* series (1987–98), to more knowing manipulations in films such as *Copycat* (1995). However, *Se7en* is more innovative in its use of the mirror effect in that it includes Mills and Somerset's quarry John Doe (Kevin Spacey), setting up a dazzlingly complex relationship between the three of them. The opening credit sequence, although a first-time audience cannot know it, features Doe working on his books, the journals that Somerset and Mills discover later, which open up a perspective on his insanity. In retrospect, there is a clear connection between Doe's meticulous recordings of his interior monologues, and Somerset's careful scholarship. Both of them are painstaking and intellectual in their approach, educated and widely read (although it is important to mark the difference in the sound-tracks, with the opening credits' industrial noise rock, courtesy of Nine Inch Nails, set against Somerset's beautiful, mournful Bach). More disturbingly, as Somerset himself seems to realise when he and Mills drive Doe out into the desert for the final showdown, there are close parallels between his pessimistic humanism and Doe's nihilistic theism. The early sequences establish reasons why Somerset is taking early retirement. Recounting the story of a recent crime during which a mugger knocked a man out and robbed him before stabbing him in both eyes, Somerset concludes, 'I have no understanding of this place anymore.' Later, as he argues with the idealist Mills, who refuses to countenance the idea that anything they do finally matters very little, he declares, 'I just don't think I can continue to live and work in a place that embraces and nurtures apathy as if it was a virtue.' Doe speaks of his disgust at the world around him, epitomised in his victims, each of them guilty of one of the seven deadly sins, and when they are described as 'innocent', his response is chillingly close to Somerset's perspective on a world he has grown tired of:

> Only in a world this shitty could you even try to say these were innocent people and keep a straight face . . . But that's the point. We see a deadly sin on every street corner, in every home, and we tolerate it. We tolerate it because it's common, it's . . . it's trivial, and we tolerate it morning, noon and night. Well, not anymore. I'm setting the example, and what I've done is going to be puzzled over and studied and followed, forever.

The film's greatest achievement, in the end, may not be the way it allows Doe to finish his masterpiece. Certainly, there is something more than mechanical clever-cleverness in the way it is worked through: Doe is Envy, and has tried to live Mills' life, and taken a 'souvenir' of Mills' wife's 'pretty head' after his attempt to play the husband 'didn't work out'; Mills becomes Wrath, kills Doe and destroys himself in the process. The satisfaction the audience experiences in being permitted to witness swift retribution in action as Mills shoots Doe is problematised by a recognition that Doe has, by provoking Mills to commit the final deadly sin (Wrath), brought his murderous 'work of art' to completion. However, more significant is the film's acknowledgement of almost unbearably confused and blurred distinctions between morality and immorality, and the terrifying nature of the choices we confront or flee. Mills' position is analogous to Hieronimo's as a justice figure forced to spurn due process. As Doe kneels, convinced that Mills will shoot him when it is confirmed that the package delivered to them in the desert, opened by Somerset, is Tracy's severed head, he tells Mills: 'Become vengeance, David. Become...wrath.' Doe the vigilante, disgusted, like Somerset, at the sin of the world, is destroyed by Mills the revenger, while Somerset watches, helpless, staring into the abyss.

Revenge revisited: kicking ass, 2004

In 2002, Pathé Pictures released Alex Cox's film version of Thomas Middleton's *The Revenger's Tragedy*. In Cox's version, the action takes place in a near-future, post-apocalyptic, dystopic Liverpool, after a comet has wiped out France and the South of England. In an interview conducted in January 2003, he talked about the original ending of the film, which was altered before release under pressure from the film's financiers:

> We ended *Revenger's Tragedy* with a montage of the World Trade Center being blown up. Since we are now embarked on phase two of an endless war of revenge against all other countries, it seemed like a very, very appropriate ending for *Revenger's Tragedy*.[26]

As well as making us ponder the meaning of revenge in this context, Cox's remarks raise a number of provocative issues; how does a population process catastrophe? What is the relationship between the facts of history and their representation? What is the artist's responsibility in terms of entertainment, on the one hand, and communication and instruction on the other? How do the sometimes mutually antagonistic forces of taste, censorship and artistic expression interact in specific instances? And, most pertinently for the current study, what can be learnt from the juxtaposition of events, ideas and cultural artefacts from different historical periods?

If the period between the early 1970s and 2004 was considered in any depth, a succession of paradigms would reveal itself, gradually moving away from the Harry Callahan and Paul Kersey model. In a fascinating argument that suffers only from a tendency to totalise and homogenise, Susan Jeffords considers in detail the rise of the 'hard-bodied' hero and connects it with the presidency of Ronald Reagan, his government's aggressive foreign policy and its ruthlessly anti-liberal domestic agenda.

In the 1990s there is evidence, again, of the shifting dynamics of the political scene, with the election in 1992 of the Democrat Bill Clinton. A swing back towards a more liberal and pluralist agenda, one might speculate, is reflected, for example, in the rise of the female action heroine, in both film and on television (see Chapter 7, below). In considering a related genre, Leighton Grist considers the emergence of the 'revisionist' Western in the early 1990s, films willing to problematise the traditional heroic narratives, such as *Unforgiven* (1992), *Tombstone* (1993), *The Ballad of Little Jo* (1993), *Posse* (1993) and *Wyatt Earp* (1994).[27]

The Marvel Comics' character, Frank Castle, The Punisher, first appeared in *Spiderman* stories in 1974, and as such is contemporaneous with the loner, fine-line-of-the-law figures Harry Callahan and Paul Kersey. The Punisher had made his first celluloid appearance in a by-numbers action movie starring Dolph Lundgren in 1989. By 2004, both politically (in the wake of 9/11) and culturally (following a number of hugely successful superhero films such as *Spider-Man* [2002] and the *X-Men* movies [2000, 2003]), it seemed clear that Hollywood audiences were ready for a big budget update on Frank Castle. The screenplay adjusted the original story's motive for revenge (Castle's wife and child killed in Central Park when they witnessed a mob hit) to something far more brutal: the planned, deliberate slaughter of Castle's entire extended family, including the cruelly protracted pursuit and murder of his wife and son. Marvel CEO Avi Arad remarked, 'Like movies, comics are reflective of the time in which they are being published...The Punisher is a by-product of 70's anxieties about crime and social breakdown.'[28] The director of the 2004 version, Jonathan Hensleigh, clearly saw the relevance of the figure to post-9/11 audiences: 'I think he's a character of the times we live in. I think that questions of justice and the morality of acts of revenge or retribution are certainly on people's minds these days.' At the same time, Hensleigh insisted that he was careful to ensure Castle worked within his own set of 'hard and fast rules...He's not wanton in his vengeance'.[29] During the film, Castle comments that five months after the slaughter of his family, the FBI has not arrested one person; and it is this that acts as the film's justification for vigilantism. Castle is given a long, voice-over speech in which he intones:

> In certain...'extreme' situations, the law is inadequate. In order to shame its inadequacy, it is necessary to act outside the law. To pursue...natural justice. This is not vengeance. Revenge is not a valid motive, it's an emotional response. No. Not vengeance. This is punishment.

The voice-over is heard as the audience watches him prepare for his final assault on the fortress of the man responsible for the slaughter of his family, the ironically named Howard Saint, and it works to prepare the audience for the very deliberate, targeted revenge that will follow.

Between 2003 and 2004 a welter of new movies were released that centred explicitly on the brutal actions of revengers frustrated by the failures of the justice system. At the beginning of May 2004, three of the top four slots of the US box office were occupied by films based around a revenge narrative: *Man on Fire*, *Kill Bill Vol. 2* and *The Punisher*. Richard A. Clarke, in his inside account of life in the White House during and after 9/11, recalls a discussion at the birth of the 'war on terror' rhetoric that would dominate US (and world) politics for years to come. When Donald Rumsfeld questioned the use of pre-emptive force, noting that 'international law allowed the use of force only to prevent future attacks and not for retribution', Clarke reports that '[George W.] Bush nearly bit his head off'. '"No", the President yelled in the narrow conference room, "I don't care what the international lawyers say, we are going to kick some ass."'[30] Such attitudes are reflected even in the realm of official discourse. The United States' military response to the destruction of the World Trade Center was originally given the title 'Operation Infinite Justice'; but in the wake of Muslim protests (since, according to their religious teachings, only Allah can deliver such a thing), it was given the less immediately provocative title 'Operation Enduring Freedom' on 25 September 2001. Bush's preference for force of arms over negotiation characterized the United States' dealings with both the Taliban and with Saddam Hussein, and his rhetoric (such as his insistence to all other nations that 'you are either with us or with the terrorists') served to polarise debate and allow nothing but supposedly clear-cut morality, and a Hollywoodesque world of good guys and bad guys.[31]

It is not difficult to see a connection between an apparent revival of interest in the revenger figure and the recent, devastating national psychic trauma of the destruction of the World Trade Center. The revenger is someone prepared to go to any lengths in pursuit of 'natural' justice once the legal system breaks down, and the appeal of the man of action on the cinema screen (and, in this genre, the protagonist is almost invariably male), unencumbered by the obstacles, inconveniences and moral shackles of reality, is unmistakable. These films' tag-lines, posters and titles all emphasise the idea of the solitary male hero engaged with a task that is necessary and monumental: the man *apart*, the *man on fire . . . walking tall*; posters for the remake of the latter depict the star striding purposefully towards the viewer with club in hand, declaring, 'One man will stand up for what's right'; and *A Man Apart*'s publicity had Diesel in a strikingly similar pose, a shotgun replacing the club, and with his DEA badge on its chain dangling from his other hand. The *Man on Fire* poster depicts Denzel Washington, in suit and shades, stepping forward while laying a protecting hand on the little blonde girl he guards. For the Bush Administration, especially in the face of negative global opinion of the second war against Iraq, the icon of the lonely prosecutor of natural justice is a profoundly comforting myth. In an article for the *Wall Street Journal* in February 2002, former CIA director James Woolsey compared America to Marshal Will Kane in *High Noon*, who dismisses the last deputy and tells him to return to his family. Woolsey ended the article with a direct reference to the film, and Kane's final act of rejection of the society he saved from ruin after it abandoned him: 'Go on home to your kids, Europeans. Go on home to your kids. And then start praying that when it's over we won't drop our badge in the dirt.'[32]

An article in the *Washington Times* in April 2004 suggested that hearing news reports of 'charred American bodies dragged through the streets of Iraq is one way of experiencing the rawest and most honest of human emotions: the desire for revenge'; the author recommended a visit to the local Cineplex as a way of 'deal[ing] with the pent-up hostility', noting the near-simultaneous release of *Kill Bill*, *Walking Tall* and *The Punisher*.[33] *Man on Fire* received similar attention: Salon.com critic Jesse Walker made direct connections between the vicarious thrills of Denzel Washington's trail of revenge and the abuse of Iraqi prisoners in Abu Ghraib;[34] and Jay Boyar, namechecking the same films, wrote in the *Orlando Sentinel* that 'Ever since Sept. 11, 2001, America has been in a hurry to get even. If we're not getting there fast enough in the real world, we certainly are at the movies.'[35] The certainties that these films offer are many and varied: in *A Man Apart*, *Man on Fire* and *The Punisher* there are key scenes in which the revenger figure penetrates the villains' hiding-place and wreaks havoc, perhaps venting the rage felt by those frustrated at the failure of US forces to track down and punish Osama bin Laden; it is worth noting that when Saddam Hussein was captured in Iraq in December 2003, much of the rhetoric ('captured like a rat')[36] recalled the discourse used during the hunt for bin Laden in Afghanistan. It is also worth noting the South American setting for *Man on Fire*, which is instrumental in establishing the large margin of extra-legal activity Creasy enjoys; the lawlessness of the country endorses his own rejection of due process. The villains are corrupt, brutal and barbaric non-Americans, and the casting of Dakota Fanning as the abducted girl suggests the film's sub-text is about the threat to the all-American representative by kidnappers as swarthy, filthy and ruthless as the imagined al-Quaeda terrorist.

Of course, all these texts – both films and plays – need to be situated socially, politically and historically, and the contexts are going to be different in each case: the disturbingly fascistic overtones of the first two movies in the *Dirty Harry* series reflect an era of social crisis in the USA, and a politically conservative agenda. *Se7en*, exhibiting a moral complexity that is mirrored by its dark, oblique visual style, belongs to an era where the desperate grasping at ethical imperatives has given way to relativism and a surrender of the supposed certainties of the old order. Early modern revenge tragedies emerged from a culture very different from our own. As I have already shown, changes in the legal system may well have caused frustration and dissatisfaction in some social fractions, where individuals were more accustomed to bloodying their own hands in the pursuit of justice. Robert Watson notes that the Senecan model of revenge tragedy 'could hardly have proliferated so rapidly unless there were tensions in Elizabethan society to which it answered'.[37] It is also significant that, in almost every one of these revenge narratives, the revenger protagonist is male. The same can be said of many of the 1970s vigilante movies: J. Hoberman suggests that *Dirty Harry* 'offers an extreme definition of masculine behaviour and a pathological loathing of everything else'.[38] If Joan Mellen is correct when she concludes that *Death Wish*, *Taxi Driver* and *Dirty Harry* all posit the argument that, 'If we know what is good for us ... we will place our trust, and our very selves, in the hands of the angry avenger, the authoritarian, ever-violent male',[39] then there is one final set of texts that still require our attention. The book's conclusion will consider the curious anomaly of the female revenger.

Part II
Gender and Violence

6
Women Dipped in Blood: Gender, Violence and Control in Early Modern Tragedy

'And if there's a beast in men, it meets its match in women too.'
(*The Company of Wolves*: dir. Neil Jordan, 1988)

This entire section, made up of two contextual studies and two case studies, considers the complex network of sexual politics in early modern revenge tragedy and contemporary violent film. A number of recent studies of early modern representations of rape and sexual violence have made connections between these cultural forms and late-twentieth-century attitudes, laws and fictional representations (most frequently in popular film): Jean E. Howard and Phyllis Rackin describe rape as 'the gatekeeper for the gender hierarchy' and draw parallels between early modern representations and the systematic rape of women as a tool of ethnic oppression in Bosnia and other conflicts around the globe in the late twentieth century.[1] Jocelyn Catty discusses the courtroom drama *The Accused* (1988) in her conclusion to *Writing Rape, Writing Women in Early Modern England* (1999); Marion Wynne-Davis opens her study of rape in *Titus Andronicus* with a reference to the judge's summing-up of a 1986 rape trial;[2] and Karen Bamford's study of *Sexual Violence on the Jacobean Stage* (2000) begins with changing notions of rape in the 1970s informed by feminist critiques, concluding with a direct connection between the modern backlash against feminism and what she interprets as an analogous cultural reaction in the early seventeenth century.

Following an overview of the plays and films within their own specific cultural contexts in the first two chapters of this book, here we build towards an investigation bringing these apparently disparate sets of texts together in two parallel studies. The discussion will focus almost entirely on representations of female sexuality: how it is expressed and repressed, and how it is commodified by men and used in processes of exchange and theft, assault and retribution. Female sexuality, it would seem, is precious when intact and unsullied; when lost, damaged or impure, it is the cause of violent, usually fatal, cycles of action and reaction. While taking full account of all cultural specificity and difference, I will explore how the anxieties generated by uncontrolled female sexuality remain central in these texts, produced 400 years apart.

The key film texts that comprise the case studies are Sam Peckinpah's *Straw Dogs* (1971) and Paul Verhoeven's *Basic Instinct* (1992), films that feature characters and situations that seem to provoke similar male anxieties, and consequent violent reactions of suppression and control. These films have been chosen for a number of reasons: each can be seen as, in certain respects, being representative of the sexual politics of their period, depicting sexual liberation and a simultaneous backlash – male sensibilities both aroused and unnerved by active female sexuality. *Straw Dogs* can be taken, retrospectively, as a reference point for reiterative and mutating representations of gender, violence and sexuality in mainstream Hollywood since the 1970s. In *Basic Instinct*, the figure of Catherine Tramell can be viewed as an apotheosis of an evolving image of the 'dangerous woman', and as a marker of new boundaries. *Straw Dogs* forced a reconsideration of what was permissible in terms of graphic nudity and sexual violence in the early 1970s, and, twenty years later, *Basic Instinct* was widely touted as the most sexually explicit film ever to feature an A-list actor (although, significantly, this applied to Michael Douglas; for Sharon Stone, the film was her ladder out of B- and C-movie hell). Finally, both films are the work of skilled filmmakers presenting their audiences with texts that provoke contradictory and ambivalent responses within and between viewers.

The characters of Beatrice-Joanna in Middleton and Rowley's 1622 play *The Changeling* and Amy in *Straw Dogs* will be considered in terms of the gender, power and violence nexus that is at the heart of this section. In ways analogous to Amy's predicament in *Straw Dogs*, Beatrice-Joanna's sexuality is flaunted, guarded, commodified, and violated. Furthermore, both characters become sites of struggle rooted in crises of social class and attempts to assert dominance in 'homosocial' negotiations – conflicts between men. Beatrice-Joanna and Amy are deeply ambivalent figures, both for audiences of their own time and for contemporary audiences. Set against the Amy/Beatrice-Joanna discussion is a reconsideration of the stereotype of the *femme fatale*. Although the figure of the *femme fatale* is synonymous with a strain of Hollywood *noir* crime thrillers of the 1940s, the mythotype of the dangerous, seductive woman is one that recurs in Western culture, rising to prominence at certain critical ideological junctures; my comparison seeks to explore the resonances between the character of Vittoria in Webster's *The White Devil* (1612) and Catherine Tramell (Sharon Stone) in *Basic Instinct*. In conclusion, the section will anticipate a consideration of the 'slasher' movie genre that begins with *Halloween* (1978) and *Friday the 13th* (1980) and culminates in the so-called postmodern, ironic horror of the *Scream* trilogy (1996, 1997, 2000), *Cherry Falls* (2000), *Valentine* (2001), and others. In these films, expressions of female sexuality are almost without exception represented as transgressive and punishable. Male attempts to control and enact retribution are violent and frequently frenzied. The significance of the female body in 'body horror' movies, in particular the crossover between the body and control of sexuality, will be examined in Part III ('Death and the Damaged Body').

Gender and early modern tragedy

One of the most striking aspects of the revenge tragedy genre, noted by a number of critics with a variety of agendas and critical perspectives, is the rise of the tragic heroine. Broadly speaking, early modern tragedy had been preoccupied with royalty and figures of political significance – the dramas of semi-mythical kings such as Gorboduc, Macbeth and Lear, and the international conflicts of plays such as *The Spanish Tragedy* (1584). Exceptions can be found – *Arden of Faversham* (1592), for example, and *A Woman Killed with Kindness* – first performed in the year of Elizabeth I's death (1603) – are both domestic tragedies – but they are deviations from the norm. During the Jacobean years, domestic and intimate settings began to feature much more prominently. While the tragedies continue to move in courtly (or at least aristocratic) circles, since the tragic register is necessarily the domain of the elite in the early modern period, the focus is increasingly on personal, rather than state, politics. Celia R. Daileader's survey of Alfred Harbage's *Annals of English Drama* (revised edition, 1964) calculates that, of 216 plays surveyed between 1595 and 1621, all but ten works included what she defines as 'erotic activity'.[3] So, while *The Duchess of Malfi* is concerned with Italian court life, and the corrupt workings of state power, the central preoccupations of the play are sexual jealousy and intrigue, an affair between a lady and her servant, hints of incestuous desire between brother and sister, a sexually corrupt priest, sexually-motivated revenge and so on. While there are brief mentions of wider political concerns – inheritance and succession – they are peripheral: Ferdinand's claim that he had hoped 'to have gained/An infinite mass of treasure' by his sister's death (4.2.284) seems almost arbitrary amid the tangle of incestuous sexual jealousy that ensnares both him and the Duchess, and which leads to their deaths, and the slaughter of almost everyone closely connected to them through ties of blood or love. And while pomp and circumstance do grace the stage when the Duchess and Antonio are formally banished by the Cardinal in a strikingly ritualistic dumbshow (3.3), the play is concerned primarily with one woman's sexual desire set against her family's expectations for her in terms of love and marriage. Middleton and Rowley's *The Changeling* finds Beatrice-Joanna in a similar predicament, and Webster's *The White Devil* portrays the tragic fall-out of one woman's determination to be with the man she loves, whatever the cost. *The Maid's Tragedy* (1610) and *The Maiden's Tragedy* (1611) both founded their tragic plots on rulers whose sexual appetites lead them into conflict with their subjects, but the political ramifications of their fates are left largely unexplored.

The increased prominence of female characters in the drama's serious, tragic register is concurrent with the increased focus on sexual politics in the plays. For the most part, women figure as minor players in dramas about affairs of state, since their roles at court tended to be limited (the irony of a female monarch around this time notwithstanding). However, with interest moving towards the private, domestic sphere, women begin to take centre stage, so that it is in the tragedies of Webster, Middleton, Fletcher and Ford that some of the most fascinating, morally complex and ideologically conflicted heroines of early modern drama can be found. The emergence of sexuality as a frequent, central issue in the drama can also be associated with the move into the private and domestic sphere. There is a shift from debates around patriarchal power in matters of state politics to the exercise of patriarchal power in personal sexual politics, and the way that power is threatened and subverted or reinforced.

'God or a wolf' – gendered archetypes

One of the most readily identifiable conventions of the slasher movie – a cliché so familiar that screenwriter Kevin Williamson and director Wes Craven played with it quite self-consciously and unashamedly in the *Scream* series – is that the sexually promiscuous teens become the killer's prime targets, usually immediately after sexual indulgence; accordingly, as Carol Clover postulates in her seminal study of the 'Final Girl', it is the chaste, usually virginal, often defeminised, figure

that survives.[4] The idea that women are to be identified, either desexu-
alized or sexualized, as pure, chaste and faithful on the one hand or
impure, loose and deceitful on the other, has been identified by Joan
Mellen as a cornerstone of modern Hollywood cinema.[5] It is central to
the construction of the archetypal *femme fatale*, from Phyllis Diet-
richson (Barbara Stanwyck) in *Double Indemnity* (1944) to Laure Ash
(Rebecca Romijn-Stamos) in Brian De Palma's all-too-self-conscious
Femme Fatale (2002). However, what could be termed the virgin/whore
binary can in fact be traced back to the roots of Western Christian
culture. Kathleen McLuskie remarks how 'Misogynists from the Church
fathers onwards insisted on woman's direct descent from Eve which
gave her the attributes of lust and duplicity.'[6]

It is clear that, at certain points in history, such cultural constructions
take on a greater significance and prominence, and there is a marked
revival of the stereotypes evident in the drama staged in England at the
end of the sixteenth and the beginning of the seventeenth centuries. In
her study of rape in early modern literature, Jocelyn Catty reminds us
that there is a crucial difference between representation and historical
fact, and due caution should be exercised when making extrapolations
from cultural forms to social practices.[7] However, the concentration and
marked increase of depictions of violence against women in Jacobean
drama demands consideration, and the gender crisis that began to
stretch and tear the social fabric around the year 1600 has been noted by
many social historians and literary critics. Theresia de Vroom points to the
proliferation of plays with titles named after women during this period,
and quotes D. E. Underdown's reflection on cultural artefacts of the time:

> The flood of Jacobean anti-feminist literature and the concurrent
> public obsession with the scolding women, domineering and
> unfaithful wives, clearly suggests that the patriarchy could no longer
> be taken for granted.[8]

Underdown specifies the period 1600–40 as one preoccupied with
women as a threat to the social order (and also notes the concomitant
rise of prosecutions for witchcraft).[9] Texts such as Joseph Swetnam's
The Arraignment of lewd, idle, froward and unconstant women (1615) and
John Knox's *The First Blast of the Trumpet against the Monstrous Regiment
of Women* (1558) are the most familiar, but they are accompanied
by a huge supporting cast of sermons and homilies from the same
period. Steven Mullaney writes that, in sixteenth-century culture,
'Misogyny . . . is everywhere, unabashed in its articulation and so

overdetermined in its cultural roots that individual instances sometimes seem emotionally under-determined, rote and uninflected expressions of what would go without saying if it weren't said so often.'[10]

The virgin/whore binary is buried deep at the heart of many Jacobean
tragedies: in *The White Devil* (the play's oxymoronic title speaks for
itself), Bracciano declares that, 'Woman to man is either a god or a wolf'
(4.2.88–9), and a nineteenth-century reviewer's description of Vittoria
as 'startling by her beauty and wickedness' shows how the idea
persists.[11] The three key early modern characters discussed in this
chapter all work as provocative examples, in very different ways, of the
virgin/whore archetype, from the representation of Vittoria (the 'White
Devil' herself), to the extraordinary metamorphosis of Beatrice-Joanna
in *The Changeling*; *The Duchess of Malfi* finds Ferdinand musing that his
sister's 'fault and beauty,/Blended together, show like leprosy,/The
whiter the fouler' (3.3.62–4). At the same time, women such as the
Duchess and Vittoria can be read as being deeply ambivalent: one issue
that should recur with obstinate persistence whenever these plays are
studied, rehearsed or watched is the distinction between the way the
women are represented *by* the plays, and the way they are represented
by other dramatic characters *within* the plays. Although there are
certainly places where misogyny is embedded in the working assumptions of the texts, at other points the representations may be intended
as satirical critiques of the male characters or dominant patriarchal
structures. Lack of evidence and the complexities of historical difference
make it impossible to reconstruct the responses of the audiences that
first attended these plays with any degree of accuracy. However, in the
case of Vittoria, for example, it is conceivable to interpret the play as an
attack on the rhetoric the Cardinal mobilises against her rather than a
damning critique of Vittoria herself, and I shall explore this in more detail
in the case study to follow. The fascination of Vittoria, the Duchess or
Beatrice-Joanna is inherent in the volatile ideological potential of the texts.

In *The Changeling*, just as Beatrice-Joanna is a holy vision for Alsemero
(see pp. 124–5), so is the Duchess introduced in similar terms, repeatedly
represented in a way that sets purity and chastity against unbridled sexuality.
The audience is first introduced to her by the steward of her household,
Antonio, overheard in conversation with his friend Delio; his speech
stretches taut the tension between her alluring beauty and her chastity:

> She throws upon a man so sweet a look
> That it were able raise one to a galliard
> That lay in a dead palsy, and to dote

> On that sweet countenance. But in that look
> There speaketh so divine a continence
> As cuts off all lascivious and vain hope. (1.1.195–200)

Set against Antonio's idealised picture, however, is the very different image presented by her brothers, Duke Ferdinand and the Cardinal, whose own expectations are more in line with commonplace stereotypes of widowhood circulating in early modern culture. Once again, there is a clash of archetypes – the beautiful but chaste figure on the one hand, and the outwardly attractive but morally corrupt and sexually degenerate figure on the other. Despite her physical appearance (and her location, as the play opens, in a 'holy place'), Beatrice-Joanna is, in moral terms, closer to Vittoria than she is to the Duchess of Malfi. She attempts to caution a swooning Alsemero early in their relationship, warning him that our eyes sometimes 'tell us wonders/Of common things' (1.1.75–6). An actor today would probably choose to interpret this as either false modesty or a rare moment of self-awareness. However, putting aside character psychology, it is also possible to see the line being planted as an early, ironic commentary on the relationship between the real and imagined that causes Alsemero such anguish once he begins to discover Beatrice's terrible secret. At the end of the play, shamed and dying, Beatrice herself echoes these words when she prays that 'the common sewer' should take her blood away from public view (5.3.153).

'A giddy turning' – gender, autonomy and control

Time and again, these dramas of sexual intrigue and tragedy emphasise the male's need to dominate and control, and the female's urge to escape and assert autonomy. Several critics have interpreted the White Devil Vittoria's striving for independence in gendered terms. Gayle Greene describes her as 'the very antithesis of the Renaissance ideal of woman: disobedient, defiant of convention, sexual, subversive, she displays the assertion rather than the subordination of self'.[12] Mary Beth Rose interprets the Duchess of Malfi's determination to assert sexual autonomy as an object lesson in what she terms 'the heroics of marriage'.[13] These different kinds of responses to transgressive women alert us to the cultural difference that separates contemporary readers and audiences from early modern ones. While modern theatre critics (and literary critics, for that matter) have often interpreted the wilfulness of these plays' women favourably, representing them as feisty heroines, it is quite possible that contemporary Jacobean audiences would have seen the same behaviour as being at best dubious, and at worst monstrous. It is worth remembering that William Painter's *House of Pleasure* (1567), Webster's key source for *The Duchess of Malfi*, featured a much more sceptical and condemnatory representation of the Duchess. In all three cases – *The White Devil*, *The Duchess of Malfi* and *The Changeling* – the woman's attempt to assert her autonomy – most acutely in the area of sexuality – provokes swift and sharp responses from the patriarchy.

Female striving for sexual autonomy often triggers extreme, obsessive desires and the need for control and possession among the male characters. Deborah Burks has shown how the idea of the female as property – belonging to her father before marriage, passed over to her husband on her wedding day – can be traced back from cultural forms such as drama into civic law.[14] Female sexuality is strictly policed by the patriarchy: Ferdinand and the Cardinal watch their sister, the Duchess of Malfi, like hawks; Beatrice-Joanna in *The Changeling* is similarly watched by her father and her intended husband. The use of potions in order to test whether or not Joanna is still a virgin is perhaps the most striking manifestation of this male obsession with women's sexuality. In the subplot, Alibius, expecting to be cuckolded, locks up his young, attractive wife. Meanwhile, in *'Tis Pity She's a Whore* (1630), Annabella is caught between her violent husband and the plottings of her jealous brother, who is also her lover. When her suitor, Soranzo, is granted an audience with Annabella to try to woo her (3.2), Giovanni watches, delivering asides to the audience as the scene is played out. At first he is anxious, and before the wooing begins he warns Annabella, 'Sister, be not all woman; think on me' (3.2.11), with the clear implication that, as a female, she is likely to prove faithless. However, as he spies on the conversation, he reacts with increasing amusement as Annabella wittily rebuffs Soranzo's advances. Even here, while his confidence in his sister–lover's fidelity is confirmed, misogyny is detectable in the undertow: when she declares her intention 'To live and die a maid' (21), Giovanni smugly remarks, 'Here's one can say that's but a woman's note' – in other words, a 'false' note, deceitful and hypocritical (22). When Annabella is forced into marriage, Giovanni sulks and skulks his way around the edge of the social gathering, hardly able to endure 'this sight, to see my love/Clipped by another' (4.1.17–18), and he flouts decorum when he refuses Soranzo's invitation to drink a toast to the marriage. Finally, unable to bear the knowledge that she has become another's property, he kills her and stakes his claim of ownership by cutting out her heart and parading it in front of his father, Annabella's husband, and a host of others at Soranzo's birthday celebrations.

In *The White Devil* the audience learns that Flamineo has sworn a pact with Bracciano that neither he nor Vittoria should outlive their lord's death by any more than four hours. Although the apparent suicide pact turns out to be a sham, the audience has no reason to doubt that Bracciano suffered what Flamineo terms the 'deadly jealousy,/Lest any should enjoy thee after him,/That urg'd him vow me to it' (5.6.35–7). And while Bracciano insists on total possession (if not control) of Vittoria, he shares the familiar assumption that he himself has complete autonomy: confronted with accusations by his wife and her family that he is having an affair with Vittoria, he outfaces them all, and demands a divorce (2.1). Isabella, unable to persuade him to return to her, only asks that he allow her to declare publicly the divorce to be her own request, thus avoiding open conflict between him and her brother, Duke Francisco. For Isabella, there is no room for righteous anger, only the humiliation of witnessing her pleas fall on Bracciano's deaf ears. When she does let rip, it is, crucially, a *performance* of jealous rage (2.1.232–76), a performance that in fact rehearses the lines spoken by Bracciano in his demand for a divorce moments earlier. The woman has no recourse in this situation, and only saves herself from further embarrassment and shame by speaking lines that have, effectively, been scripted for her by the patriarchy. In Middleton's *The Maiden's Tragedy*, such obsession finds similarly morbid and extreme expression in the story of the Tyrant's desire for the similarly, oddly anonymous Lady: when she kills herself in order to avoid the shame of being taken from her betrothed (the deposed King Govianus) and turned into the sexual possession of the Tyrant, the latter disinters her body. Her ghost returns to Govianus to tell him that her body now rests in the Tyrant's 'own private chamber':

> There he woos me
> And plies his suit to me with as serious pains
> As if the short flame of mortality
> Were lighted up again in my cold breast,
> Folds me within his arms and often sets
> A sinful kiss upon my senseless lip. (4.5.67–72)

In the climactic final scene (5.2), the Tyrant has the Lady's body dressed in black velvet and placed on a chair, and he employs an artist (Govianus, in disguise, setting about the compulsory duties of revenge) to paint life back into the 'too-constant paleness of [her] cheek' (5.2.27).

At the end of *The Changeling*, Tomazo de Piracquo, brother of the murdered Alonso – Joanna's original intended husband – pre-empts the final slaughter with a demand that is drawn up in starkly economic terms:

> Give me a brother alive or dead:
> Alive, a wife with him; if dead, for both
> A recompense, for murder and adultery. (5.3.136–8)

The idea of women as tokens of economic exchange was first formalised by Gayle Rubin in her essay on 'The Traffic in Women' in 1975, and has been a working assumption of most feminist critics writing about representations of women in early modern drama since the 1980s.[15] Karen Bamford suggests that 'in Jacobean drama sexual violence is always represented within a web of male–male relationships', and that '[t]ypically the sexual aggression against women *matters* primarily as it affects these privileged male bonds, both enabling and disrupting homosocial solidarity'.[16] This is especially evident in *The Revenger's Tragedy*, which features three victims of predatory male attitudes: the dead Gloriana, Antonio's wife, and Castiza (Vindice's sister). There are also traces of it in the remarkable scene in *The White Devil* that stages a showdown between Bracciano and Francisco, who is outraged at Bracciano's semi-public affair with Vittoria and rejection of his wife (Francisco's sister), Isabella (2.1). Bracciano's spurning of his wife is perceived as a direct insult by Francisco and, when Bracciano refuses to alter his behaviour, the conference erupts in bragging, 'my cannon's bigger than yours' threats. In *The Duchess of Malfi* the Duchess's brother Ferdinand is tortured by raging, jealous, erotic fantasies of his sister and her lover. Here and elsewhere, the threat of the autonomous sexual female, compounded by the constant lurking danger of the jealous male, results in the narrative structures that define one of the most significant aspects of the revenge tragedy genre. The predominance of the virgin/whore stereotype, and the exploration of the significance of autonomy and control, leads us to another early modern preoccupation: female sexual desire.

'Sure the devil/Hath sowed his itch within her' – gender and sexuality

Despite everything we might have reasonably expected, the myth that a woman might be 'saying no, but meaning yes' when under threat of sexual violence has persisted in our culture. Joan Smith quotes Judge David Wild, summing up a 1986 rape trial and declaring:

> Women who say no do not always mean no. It is not just a question of saying no. It is a question of how she says it, how she shows it and makes it clear. If she doesn't want it, she only has to keep her legs shut and there would be marks of force being used.[17]

The same assumption can be seen in many representations of women in Hollywood cinema: it is crucial to any interpretation of the character of Amy in *Straw Dogs*. In the 1980s, it was foregrounded and scrutinised in the courtroom drama *The Accused* (1988), in which the character of Sarah Tobias (Jodie Foster) is presumed by the patriarchy to have 'asked for' the brutal gang rape that the film depicts by dancing provocatively, inviting the attention of the men at the bar. Women are expected to be sexually passive, and any assertiveness in terms of their sexuality is interpreted as an invitation. In *The Changeling*'s sub-plot, Isabella ruefully notes:

> Would a woman stray,
> She need not gad abroad to seek her sin,
> It would be brought home one ways or other.
> The needle's point will to the fixed north;
> Such drawing arctics women's beauties are. (3.3.215–19)

It is important to note how the woman's role in this process is represented: their beauties are 'arctics' relentlessly drawing men's 'needle's point[s]' (the lewd pun is present in the original), and the weight of guilt (or, at least, responsibility) hangs on them, not on the men. When Volpone prepares to assault Celia, she implores him to 'flay my face,/Or poison it with ointments for seducing/Your blood to this rebellion' (3.7.251–3): she believes that the weight of responsibility lies not with his lechery, but with her beauty, 'that unhappy crime of nature' (3.7.250).

In early modern tragedy, moreover, women are themselves repeatedly represented by the plays, or perceived by other characters in the drama, as being sexually insatiable. Beatrice-Joanna is an obvious example: De Flores chooses to interpret her interest in Alsemero and rejection of the husband intended for her as a basis for his own hopes of sexual conquest. Because, if a woman proves unfaithful once, he muses, 'She spreads and mounts then like arithmetic,/One, ten, a hundred, a thousand, ten thousand' (2.2.63–4). In *The Changeling*'s sub-plot, Lollio makes the same assumption: if Isabella is responsive to the attentions of Antonio, surely she will service his needs too: 'Nay, if thou giv'st thy mind to fool's flesh, have at thee!' he cries, before trying to kiss her (3.3.225). 'Let me feel how thy pulses beat;' he continues, 'Thou hast a thing about thee would do a man pleasure, I'll lay my hand on't' (237–9). As Beatrice-Joanna and De Flores await the outcome of the bed trick – Joanna's servant Diaphanta takes her place in the bridal bed in order to prevent Alsemero from discovering his wife is not a virgin – both of them comment on Diaphanta's sexual indulgence: Joanna fumes that 'This strumpet serves her own ends…Devours the pleasure with a greedy appetite', (5.1.2–3); 'Sure the devil/Hath sowed his itch within her', De Flores remarks (5.1.13–14); 'This whore forgets herself', spits Beatrice-Joanna (5.1.23), apparently blind to the hypocritical dimension of her fury.

The text of the play *The Insatiate Countess* may be uneven (it was left unfinished by John Marston and completed around 1610 by Lewis Machin and William Barksted), but it is nevertheless a fascinating document that has at its centre another, more extreme (near-parodic) representation of female sensuality in the form of Isabella, the unambiguously named countess of the title. Isabella clearly has little or no control over her own sexual desires. 'My blood,' she tells the audience (and the sexual connotation of the word is clearly in play), 'like to a troubled ocean/Cuffed with the winds, incertain where to rest,/Butts at the utmost shore of every limb' (2.3.42–4). Her seduction of Rogero in this scene brings to mind the Duchess of Malfi's wooing of Antonio ('Courting is not befitting to our sex,' she blushes, in what seems like a performance of coy modesty [2.3.80]); both the Duchess and Isabella are recently widowed and in search of new partners. But Isabella's dialogue with Rogero has none of Webster's sweetness or tenderness. Isabella has sexual relationships with four men before her career is cut short, and she is beheaded by a vengeful patriarchy. 'She died deservedly,' the Duke of Medina concludes; 'and may like fate/Attend all women so insatiate' (5.1.228–9).

In *The Changeling*, De Flores' misogynist attitude reminds us of similar tirades by Flamineo (*The White Devil*) and Bosola (*The Duchess of Malfi*), and it figures as another standard constituent of the malcontent's *persona*. Nevertheless, it is impossible to explain it away as a mere quirk of characterisation. The frequency with which the plot mechanism of female infidelity recurs in early modern drama (comedy as well as tragedy), is symptomatic of something embedded deeply in society, and also emerges in other kinds of cultural artefacts, such as ballads, sermons and treatises, as I have already noted. Joseph Swetnam's *The arraignment of lewde, idle, froward and unconstant women* (1615) rehearses familiar (though not uncontested) myths about the uxorious nature of women (and widows in particular). In the drama, the representation of the virgin/whore binary in contrasting figures may, as Jocelyn Catty notes, 'serve ... to heighten the glory of the plays' heroines. However, it also establishes promiscuity as normative female behaviour.'[18] Gail Kern Paster argues that 'Representations of the female body as a leaking vessel display that body as beyond the control of the female subject, and thus as threatening the acquisitive goals of the family and its maintenance of status and power.'[19] According to Paster, menstrual blood in early modern society was one of a series of signifiers that apparently 'proved' that women were naturally predisposed to 'leak'. And this series of signs together 'proved' that women did not have control over the workings of their own bodies. The logical next step, of course, was the assumption that women, in the absence of adequate self-control, needed men to monitor them for their own good.

In *The Duchess of Malfi*, warning their recently widowed sister against taking a second husband, Ferdinand notes how 'women like that part which, like the lamprey,/Hath ne'er a bone in't' (1.1.327–8). The brothers clearly have low expectations of her: while the Cardinal remarks that 'your own discretion/Must now be your director' (1.1.292–3), the Duke has already assumed that she will be unable to control her own sexual nature, and employed Bosola to keep a close eye on her. To them, any suggestion that she might wish to marry again would be a sign of 'luxurious[ness]' (1.1.297). When she offers a witty, presumably mischievous rather than genuine riposte – 'Diamonds are of most value,/ They say, that have passed through most jewellers' hands' (1.1.299–300) – Ferdinand snaps back: 'Whores, by that rule, are precious' (301). Just as De Flores reasons that when a woman strays, 'She spreads and mounts then like arithmetic' (2.2.63), so the Cardinal speculates that a widow's resolve to remain unmarried after her husband's death 'commonly ... lasts no longer/Than the turning of an hour-glass' (303–4). Once Ferdinand discovers that the Duchess has given birth to a child, he descends into a jealous hell of nightmarish visions centring on his apparently licentious sister:

> Talk to me somewhat, quickly,
> Or my imagination will carry me
> To see her in the shameful act of sin ...
> Happily with some strong-thighed bargeman,

> Or one o' th' woodyard, that can quoit the sledge
> Or toss the bar, or else some lovely squire
> That carries coals up to her privy lodgings. (2.5.39–45)

Theodora Jankowski points out how vital it is to Ferdinand and the Cardinal that the Duchess's body is kept pure, as an unpolluted vessel for reproducing her husband's and her father's bloodlines.[20] Jankowski interprets Ferdinand's obsession as both implying 'the demand (and desire) for more intimate sexual knowledge', and as indicative of Ferdinand's technique of 'asserting his power over his sister by symbolically dismembering her body'.[21] There is certainly a disturbing, but not unfamiliar, twisting of sexuality and violence in the text and sub-text of his speeches. Here, as in so many early modern tragedies, control and physical punishment are seldom very far apart, and the threat of sexualised violence hovers menacingly, reinscribing the power of the patriarchy.

Women's bodies are seen in terms of property in these negotations between men – whether it be in terms of purchase, exchange, theft or damage. Perhaps the starkest symbol of this kind of commodification is Gloriana's skull in *The Revenger's Tragedy*: Vindice's plot to wreak revenge on the lustful Duke who murdered Vindice's fiancée, Gloriana (murdered for spurning his sexual advances), is inspired by (and makes good use of) Gloriana's skull. The skull works as emblem and motive of revenge (much as the head in a box does in David Fincher's film *Se7en*). In *Titus Andronicus*, the display of Lavinia's body after her rape, her tongue cut out, her hands cut off, is one of the most gratuitous stagings of mutilation in a genre that often gives the impression that playwrights strove to outdo each other in devising such spectacles for their audiences. The object of the female body has rich connotations in both genres. The male fascination with, and fear of, female physiology is very evident in early modern tragedy and, as I will show, it is a preoccupation verging on obsession in contemporary violent film. More often than not, in both genres, such anxieties give rise to representations of the invasion, destruction and opening up of the woman's body – a theme explored further in Part III of this book.

It is certainly true to say that women take on more prominent roles in the tragedies of the Jacobean period. However, it is also the case that they never really manage to escape male power and containment: the white devil, Vittoria, for all her vitality, finally falls victim to the avengers of those she has wronged. The Duchess defies her brothers, marries the man she loves, and is brutally punished for her temerity. Beatrice-Joanna pursues her desire for Alsemero, is strangely and irresistibly drawn to De Flores, pursues both desires and finally dies shamed, understanding herself as one who has defiled her father, praying that the sewer take away her infected blood. However, to dismiss these women as nothing more than stereotypes of transgressive women, appropriately punished, would be to do the texts a disservice. All three of these women show qualities and vitalities that demand closer attention, and, in some cases, invite an audience's intense interest and identification. Some feminist critics may have (inadvertently) participated in the marginalisation of these heroines by insisting that male authors are unable to write female interiority with any degree of insight or sympathy.[22] In opposition to this is Stephen Orgel's contention that, since early modern theatres relied on the patronage of both men *and* women, 'the success of any play required the receptiveness of women'.[23] Alison Findlay similarly insists that, '[t]he tastes of female spectators had to be acknowledged and catered for by the companies whose productions they paid to see'.[24] The notion that male writers are incapable of representing female interiority with any degree of success is contentious, and something to which I shall return in the case studies that follow. As I hope to show, there exists in many of these texts the potential for interpretations that challenge the assumptions of the patriarchy I have outlined in this chapter. Even in the teeth of such fierce repression, there may still be ways to discern, or amplify, the dissenting female voice.

7
A Thin Red Line: Gender, Violence and Contemporary Cinema

Molly Haskell, assessing the place of women in Hollywood in the mid-1970s, concluded her study *From Reverence to Rape* in the pessimistic tone set by the book's title:

> Whether in the European or the American film, whether seen as sociological artefact or artistic creation, women, by the logistics of film production and the laws of Western society, generally emerge as the projections of male values. Whether as the product of one *auteur* or of the system...women are the vehicle of men's fantasies, the 'anima' of the collective male unconscious, and the scapegoat of men's fears.[1]

Although this is not the place for a full survey of the shifting position of women – as actors and representations – in Hollywood film, some stocktaking is necessary, and the different ways in which critics (especially feminist critics) have recorded that history is crucial. In the same way, the discussion of early modern drama in this study concentrates almost exclusively on the tragic genre, so the parallel analysis of cinema will be largely restricted to violent film, a wide-ranging categorisation that has to incorporate the diverse genres of action, adventure and horror. Since the subject matter of this section will include a number of films where fear, fantasy and gender intersect (mirroring the preoccupations of the early modern tragedies discussed above), the work of Mulvey, Haskell and Kuhn is particularly relevant to the discussion that follows.

The writings of feminist film critics of the 1970s, whether in the pyschoanalytically-inflected work of Laura Mulvey, the structuralist study by Claire Johnston, or the more materialist Marxism of Annette Kuhn, brought to light the ubiquity of Hollywood misogyny. Although the specifically psychoanalytic perspectives are less crucial to my own methodology, Mulvey's ideas of the active/passive binary, male anxiety, and fetishisation are crucial: they are elements that, as I have argued in the preceding chapter, are foundational to early modern revenge tragedy. In her essay 'Defacing the Feminine in Renaissance Tragedy', Sara Eaton attempts to implement Mulvey's ideas directly, suggesting that 'in the plays [of the period] most widely read, anthologised, staged and subsequently taught, women, acted by boys, are fetishized and represent constructs of desire'.[2] There might be suspicions about Mulvey's totalising approach – what allowance is made for resistance on the part of the female spectator? What about a feminist-inflected male gaze, or the non-heterosexual gaze? – but it remains nevertheless a vital critical paradigm. The emergence of the female action hero/-ine in the 1990s has complicated the debate still further, but despite these wider cultural shifts the misogyny identified by the feminists of the 1970s persists in many contemporary representations of women in Hollywood today. While taking into account historical differences and the different media (with the crucial absence, in the theatre, of the camera to direct the spectator's gaze), there are a number of cross-currents between contemporary violent film and early modern tragedy that allow consolidation and expansion of the tentative connections Eaton has suggested.

In the early years of the new millennium, we are undoubtedly in an era of much greater and more widespread female emancipation – in many ways, *Straw Dogs* is, like the plays I have discussed, of another era. However, a report by Amnesty International, published in 2004 and spearheading a campaign to stop violence against women, unveiled often deeply shocking statistics that warn us of the dangers of complacency: one in three women worldwide has been beaten, coerced into sex or otherwise abused in her lifetime; domestic violence remains the major cause of death or disability for women aged 16–44; in the USA, women accounted for 85 per cent of victims of domestic violence in 1999; and in the UK one incident of domestic violence is reported to the police every minute.[3] In the year 2000, the UN Population Fund estimated that there are 5,000 so-called 'honour killings' each year – instances of a woman being killed for her actual or perceived immoral behaviour, often involving marriage to a partner deemed unsuitable (often for religious reasons) by her family.[4] Amnesty argues that gender-based violence is neither 'natural' nor 'inevitable' but is rather 'an expression of historically and culturally specific values and standards', based on historically unequal power relations and cultural ideology.[5]

It is not very far from the way that sexual assault can be seen as reinforcing patriarchy in early modern drama. In view of this, the act of uncovering embedded connections between texts that are historically distant but, in terms of their encoded meanings, sometimes strikingly consistent, can be understood as an intervention into those processes. Such interventions are, perhaps, even more urgently necessary in our time: many have seen in contemporary culture a kind of backlash against the women's movement. Certainly, in discussions where feminism is touched upon, many of the female students I teach now rush to disavow any allegiance to it, with such disclaimers as 'I'm not a feminist, but...'. In such debates, situating myself as a heterosexual male pro-feminist strikes many of them as incongruous, and it is in the light of this that I wish to consider the changing representations of women in violent film.

Sisters doing it for themselves

To begin at a point of significant difference: it is not difficult to check off a fairly lengthy list of examples of active female protagonists in the action and thriller genres in the 1990s and the new millennium, and it is clear that such figures have only the most remote analogues in early modern drama. While there may be some striking instances – there is, for example, a remarkable precedent for the murderous Catherine Tramell from *Basic Instinct* in *The Maid's Tragedy* in which Evadne ties the King to his bed before frenziedly stabbing him to death – they are very much the exception. However, while they are becoming increasingly common, and while it is possible to celebrate a kind of progress in the emergence of the powerful female protagonist, equalling and often bettering her male counterparts, such representations are rarely straightforward. More often, they are compromised, conflicted or in some way defused of their explosive potential, or else they are demonised as examples of a new breed of *femme fatale*.

One remarkable phenomenon of recent years has been a recognisable fashion for what Marc O'Day terms 'action babe cinema':[6] the more high-profile examples include Angelina Jolie's embodiment of an adolescent male video game fantasy figure in *Lara Croft: Tomb Raider* (2001) and the clumsily titled *Lara Croft Tomb Raider: The Cradle of Life* (2003); Milla Jovovich as Alice and Michelle Rodriguez as Rain kicking zombie ass in *Resident Evil* (2002) and *Resident Evil: Apocalypse* (2004) (in which Rodriguez is replaced by the distinctly Lara-esque Jill Valentine [Sienna Guillory]); the high camp of the *Charlie's Angels* movies (2000 and 2003), which subvert the 1970s TV series by simultaneously challenging and playing up to the original's status as 'jiggle TV'; and television equivalents of the action babe in *Buffy the Vampire Slayer*, *Dark Angel*, *Witchblade* and *Xena Warrior Princess*. However, these movies and TV shows remain almost exclusively firmly located within variations of the fantasy genre. Although their significance is not to be underestimated (and there is evidence to suggest that icons such as Buffy have achieved a remarkable depth of impact in their culture, especially among young females), nevertheless their radical potential tends to be contained by their fantasy context. In this sense, they are in line with their most obvious precedents, Sarah Connor in *Terminator 2: Judgment Day* (1991) and Ellen Ripley in the four *Alien* movies (1979, 1986, 1992, 1997). Meanwhile, attempts to construct more powerful and active representations of women in more reality-based modes of the action genre – on TV via *Alias* and *La Femme Nikita* and in the cinema in a welter of different crime drama films (discussed below) – have tended to be compromised in one way or another, chiefly via the spectres of residual 'femininity' and conflicted sexuality.

The recent serial killer movie *Twisted* (2004) is a useful test case. Philip Kaufmann's film tells the story of homicide detective Jessica Shepherd (Ashley Judd) who appears to her colleagues to be physically and mentally tough, but who is privately tormented by the childhood memory of her father, another cop, who went on a killing spree that ended with the killing of his wife and his suicide. Jess drowns out her pain via rough sex with strangers, followed by drinking binges that render her unconscious. Her troubles really begin, however, when the men she has slept with start turning up dead. Meanwhile, her alcohol-precipitated blackouts leave her terrified that she is unwittingly committing the murders herself. Although the convoluted and implausible narrative gradually establishes her innocence (innocence that the audience never really doubts), the inescapable subtext is that Jess's unusual sex life is deviant, and she must be punished for it. Moreover, the film clearly sees a connection between her aggressive sexuality and her taste for violence, which gets her into trouble when she takes down a dangerous stalker in the opening sequence with excessive force, and, later, breaks her ex-boyfriend's nose in an explosion of uncontrolled self-defence-turned-aggression.

Twisted is one of a number of recent attempts to present more hard-edged heroines in crime dramas, building on the example of Jodie Foster's portrayal of Clarice Starling in *The Silence of the Lambs* (1991). Interestingly, Starling largely avoids the kinds of snares that would be set for her successors: as Carole Dole notes, 'Clarice refuses to act as a sex object, a role in which almost every male character tries to cast her, and so refuses to fall into the limiting categories of womanhood held by the men all around her.'[7] Even if the main line of the narrative (as Elizabeth Young points out) is profoundly misogynistic, with sexually insecure men targeting women and punishing them for their sexuality,[8] *The Silence of the Lambs*, for the most part, is much less compromising in its representation of the strong female protagonist in the crime genre than many of the films that followed in its wake.

Other, more recent, examples of an active female protagonist in the context of the violent thriller include the Sandra Bullock character Cassie Mayweather in *Murder by Numbers* (2002), a tough-talking, hard-drinking and sexually autonomous and dominant woman comparable to *Twisted*'s Jess Shepherd. However, like Jess, Cassie is damaged and tortured by memories of abuse, and her tough persona, it is implied, is neither natural nor necessarily positive (she is nicknamed 'The Hyena' by colleagues). The film may ostensibly be a murder mystery, but its real concern is Cassie's own psychosexual melodrama. Renny Harlin's *The Long Kiss Goodnight* (1996) featured Geena Davis as Samantha Caine/Charly, a contented wife and mother who gradually discovers her former life as a government operative and assassin. Alongside the surface narrative runs a more interesting parallel story charting Sam/ Charly's struggle to reconcile her former self (cold-blooded killer) with her new reality (wife and mother). However, not one of these films seems prepared to show a woman uncompromised by her role as an active/aggressive protagonist. More often than not, this is expressed via sexuality, either explicitly (as in *Twisted*) or symbolically (Tasker neatly encapsulates Clarice Starling's status as a 'cross-class cross-dresser').[9]

Gender, violence, control

I have already considered how the representations of female sexuality in early modern tragedy may be interpreted as signs of a crisis in gender relations that erupted in England around 1600. Within the imagined worlds of early modern tragedy, the Duchess of Malfi drives her brother mad with visions of her sexual adventures, and he devises elaborate tortures, imagined and real, to punish her, and eventually engraves those punishments on her body; Beatrice-Joanna is a heavenly vision that copulates with a monster; Annabella a woman who breaks the incest taboo and whose body is ripped open to reveal the secrets her heart wished to keep hidden. It could be argued that the years since the

1970s have witnessed ever more radical and widespread renegotiation of the status of women in society in relation to the workforce, marriage and the family, sexuality, and elsewhere, and I shall consider the way in which such ructions might be traced in popular film of the period, before considering in more detail two specific cases.

Graphic depictions of sexual violence have remained confined largely to the margins of the film industry, where the rape revenge genre has established quasi-canonical status in cult circles, and while incidents of rape have occasionally been foundational in plots of mainstream thrillers such as *The Accused* (1988), *Sudden Impact* (1983) and *An Eye for An Eye* (1995), none of these movies, for obvious reasons, are as crude and brutal in their depiction of rape as the exploitation films such as *Last House on the Left* (1972), *I Spit on Your Grave* (1977) or *Ms.45 Angel of Vengeance* (1981). Gender and violence can be traced through the mainstream in a number of other genres, however, notably the 'woman in peril' movie; the slasher genre (considered in Part IV); the new *femme fatale* movies; and films based around spousal abuse. One of the few films to feature rape prominently, and which as a result has been at the centre of much debate about the need for censorship, is *Straw Dogs*, which is considered in some detail in the case study that follows.

The 'woman in peril' film is a staple of the TV movie industry, and there is frequent crossover between this genre and the slasher movie: Sean S. Cunningham directed *Friday the 13th* two years before he made an early example of the woman in peril genre, *A Stranger is Watching* (1982); *When a Stranger Calls* (1979) is notable for having supplied the inspiration for the genuinely shocking opening sequence of *Scream* (1996); Brian De Palma, steeped in Hitchcockian themes and tricks, made a particularly nasty film out of the template with *Dressed to Kill* (1980); *Dead Calm* (1989) added a twist by setting the action on a yacht; *Hear No Evil* (1993), *Mute Witness* and *Blink* (both 1994) provided their own high concept twists with their heroines being assigned respective disabilities; the Sharon Stone vehicle *Sliver* (1993) was a potentially fascinating, sadly botched, extended meditation on voyeurism and control. In the new millennium, David Fincher's *Panic Room* (2002) upgraded the genre with a very modern heroine: the threat or enactment of sexual violence that usually underlies these films was excised, and Jodie Foster's Meg is a tough single mother battling for her own life and that of her daughter, against a group of burglars who have broken into her home.

However, the analysis that follows considers a pair of films that dramatise tension and conflict between men and women in a context that is roughly analogous to the plays discussed in the preceding chapter. *The Changeling*, *The Duchess of Malfi*, *'Tis Pity She's a Whore* and *The White Devil* are all concerned with the status of woman as wife and/or sexual partner. They focus on attempts by men to control female sexuality at a time when sociological and cultural evidence suggested that there was a growing sense of unease about female autonomy. Four hundred years later, of course, things are very different. The status of women in the West in the late-twentieth and early-twenty-first centuries has changed so radically as to be almost unrecognisable. Correspondingly, representations of women in popular film have also evolved and diversified. At the same time, however, in the popular media for example, sexuality remains very clearly and stubbornly at the centre of representations of women, from television, through advertising and magazine culture to popular film.

The idea of male control of the female is brought into focus most clearly in a strand of drama or melodrama that depicts spousal abuse, and women's attempts to endure, escape or even take their revenge on their abusers. Consideration of two contributions to the genre, eleven years apart, make for an interesting comparative study:[10] in *Sleeping with the Enemy* (1991) Julia Roberts' character, Laura, attempts to escape an obsessive-compulsive, physically abusive husband, Martin (Patrick Bergin). She fakes her own death by drowning and begins a new life in a new town with a new partner, Ben (Kevin Anderson), only to be tracked down by her violent, vengeful husband. In *Enough* (2002), Jennifer Lopez's character, Slim, finds that the rich man she married (Mitch, played by Bill Campbell) is having an affair, and when she confronts him he becomes violent. Slim escapes (with daughter Gracie in tow), but Mitch is relentless in his pursuit. Deciding that she can run no more, Slim trains in martial arts and sets up a final showdown with Mitch in which she kills him, making it look as though he attacked her and she retaliated only in self-defence. The structural parallels and contrasts between these two films are self-evident. However, while each film seems intent on projecting some kind of pro-feminist message – with varying degrees of subtlety and success – a closer study of each reveals much about changing Hollywood representations of gender and power.

'She's only my wife' – *Sleeping with the Enemy* (1991)

Sleeping with the Enemy and *Enough* work within a formula, and have some common structural features. They both begin with public and private scenes emphasising an apparently mutual and happy relationship.

In *Sleeping with the Enemy*, Martin and Laura leave a social event early and return home, and as Laura takes a bowl of strawberries from the fridge, Martin grabs her from behind and begins kissing and fondling her. To the melodramatic strains of Berlioz's 'Symphonie Fantastique', they proceed to have Hollywood-style, inventive but tasteful sex on the kitchen counter, moving around the kitchen, and ending up against the wall. The fetishising process is very much in evidence during the scene: the camera's preoccupations throughout are Julia Roberts' body, notably her fabled long legs. The camera zooms in on her orgasmic expressions, eyes closed, head thrown back, while Bergin, by contrast, remains masked. His character is neither sexualised nor shown in any way as being vulnerable: no bare male flesh is exposed, and as they climax, the camera frames only Roberts' face, leaving Bergin's buried on the other side of her face and neck.

However, a sense that 'all is not well' is also suggested from the very beginning of the movie. In the opening scene, the audience sees Martin before Laura does, and watches him watching her, unaware. Similarly, during the scene that follows, at a party, Martin observes Laura from a balcony, and it takes a moment for Laura to realise she is being watched. Throughout these opening scenes, there is a palpable sense of Laura feeling on her guard, and there are menacing signs: when Martin finds a set of towels incorrectly aligned on their rail in the bathroom, he fetches Laura and makes her adjust them to his satisfaction; Laura is also obsessive about the arrangements of items in the kitchen cupboard, clearly signalling deeper anxieties about Martin's expectations. Although these details are 'planted' early in the film for a pay-off at the film's climax (when they inform Laura, and the audience, that Martin has broken into her house), they can also be interpreted as signifiers of Martin's psychopathology: Jessica Farb and Felice Cherry have explored the film specifically in terms of its representation of domestic violence, and although they are critical of certain aspects of the film in terms of realism, they do suggest that Martin's obsessive-compulsive tendencies can be seen as symptoms of his fear of lack of control over his wife.[11] As in the revenge tragedies discussed above, much of the drama in the film revolves around the male's desperate, obsessive need to exert his power over the female.

It is not long before the first violent incident occurs: Martin meets Fleishman, a neighbour out with his yacht, who compliments Martin on his beautiful house. This provokes the pathologically jealous Martin to launch a verbal and physical assault on Laura. The moment is worth closer attention for the way in which it manipulates the gaze of the audience: when he hits her, there is a sequence of fast cuts from a medium close-up of the strike, to a medium shot of Laura collapsing, to a close-up of Laura weeping in a heap on the floor, before Martin kicks her in the stomach. The camera focuses on her anguished, bleeding face and, after Martin leaves, a high angle shot of Laura humiliated, half naked, picking up the pieces of the broken vase, is a disturbing one, falling into a familiar conventional male fantasy of the beautiful, suffering woman. Shortly afterwards, a cryptic conversation between the couple reveals an established history of abuse, and the puzzle of Laura's guardedness is solved. The film then proceeds with its narrative of Laura's escape, Martin tracking her down, and the climactic fight when Martin invades her new home.

Another common key structural element in this genre comes in the form of the protagonist's aide or aides, sometimes one specific character, and sometimes a series or group of different characters. In *Sleeping with the Enemy*, the role is taken on by the college professor Ben Woodward, established at once as a gentle and fun-loving guy (Laura spies on him from her bedroom window as he waters the lawn, singing a song from 'West Side Story'). Their first meeting is, unusually, lent a slightly ambiguous air by Ben's mock confrontational attitude over the apples Laura is picking up from the ground, and there is a provocative juxtaposition in the way the following scene is edited: Ben's rather presumptuous encroachment on Laura's territory as he follows her back to her house is spliced against a scene depicting Martin brutally ransacking Laura's possessions as his suspicions that she may have faked her death begin to take hold. For the most part, the neat binary opposition between Ben and Martin is maintained throughout. The controlled, fearful environment of Laura's married life is set against the relaxed, warm and funny relationship with Ben, most evident during the scene set in Ben's drama department wardrobe, where Laura dresses up in a variety of amusing costumes. Painfully overdone though it is, the point is well taken that Ben is giving Laura free rein to explore and express her identity via the dressing-up game. However, even here, Ben's watchfulness is apparent, as, for example, when the audience sees him gazing at her as she removes a top over her head (her body hidden behind a screen). The sense of discomfort is reawakened towards the end of the scene. At the beginning of the film the audience watched as Martin put on music before initiating sex with Laura. Now, Ben puts on a tape (the presumably ironic 'Runaround Sue' replacing Berlioz) and begins dancing with Laura, and while the atmosphere remains light (their dancing is dynamic and energetic, not slow and sensual), there are clear echoes of the matching sequence, including a point-of-view (PoV) shot at the beginning of the sequence as Ben approaches Laura from behind. The scene cuts to Laura and Ben returning to Laura's house, and it is then that Ben makes his move, their kissing growing more passionate until Ben lays her down on the staircase and bears down upon her. When Laura shows signs that she doesn't want to make love, Ben ignores her at first, and it is not until she becomes more forceful, both physically and verbally, that he desists. Even the most romantic and gentle of men, the film seems to suggest, may have difficulty in controlling their 'natural' instincts. When Laura asks Ben to leave, however, Ben places the blame on Martin – 'God, what did he do to you?' – thus entrenching the movie's safe binaries. Despite the menacing hints noted above, the film maintains that the violent control freak Martin is not a 'natural' or 'normal' image of heterosexual masculinity. Jacinda Read suggests that Ben, by contrast, is associated with criteria established by Steve Neale as signifiers of 'old-fashioned' romance, including his vintage car and a propensity for poetry and poetic speech.[12] The audience is led to assume that Martin identifies Ben as his rival when we, with Martin, watch Ben's sensitive performance to his class of a speech by Chekhov's Treplev.

Martin's jealousy is irrational and, like Ferdinand when he hears of his sister's relationship with Antonio, his imagination is plagued with wild sexual imagining: from the first violent scene when he assumes Laura has slept with Fleishman, to a gay professor he first assumes to be Laura's lover ('My wife, she's only my wife, wonderful fuck, isn't she?'). As Martin watches Laura and Ben at the funfair, slow-motion camerawork heightens the sense of jealousy fury; he observes them on the Ferris wheel; Laura's screams of pleasure are picked out for his ear, and he watches them kiss. Like so many films depicting this kind of violence between husband and wife, the portrayal of the abusive husband as monstrous eventually weakens the film's impact. Not only is Martin irrational and brutally violent, he also attempts to kill Laura's blind and infirm mother. Attempts to imply that Martin feels conflicted about his treatment of Laura are weak, reserved for a moment early in the movie when he returns to the house, believing Laura has drowned in a storm. He picks up the statue that was his honeymoon gift to her; catching his own eye in the mirror, he hurls the statute and shatters his own image. This strikingly Lacanian moment, however, is too fleeting, and too isolated, to signify anything of import.

Ironically, the climax to the film is brought about by Ben's insistence on playing the non-aggressive role. On the night that Martin stalks them, Ben contents himself with a high-school-sweetheart-style kiss on the doorstep, before leaving Laura to return to her house alone, while Martin watches from the bushes. Just as Martin invaded Laura's private space in their beachside home, ransacking her belongings to discover the hidden truth of what happened that night in the storm, so he invades her new home too, preparing it for her return, after her night out with Ben. He overflows the bath, lines the towels up straight, and rearranges the contents of her kitchen cupboards, terrifying and disorientating her, and making the space his own. When they meet again, it is to the melodramatic strains of Berlioz once more, and the audience catches sight of him over Laura's shoulder, as she stares in terror at the booming stereo. Martin steps forward to reclaim his 'princess', and the focus is on repossession of the object of his desire: 'The first touch after so long apart – have you been thinking of it, too?' he asks, as he buries his face in her hair, before being rudely interrupted by Ben's knock at the door. When Ben breaks in and is knocked unconscious by Martin, Martin insists that Laura disowns and disavows her new boyfriend ('He doesn't have anything to do with us, princess, does he?'), and reclaims her by reliving their honeymoon night, and re-presenting her with the wedding ring she had thrown away ('We are one, we will always be one, nothing can keep us apart'). Laura's decision to shoot Martin when she gains the upper hand in the struggle that ensues is prompted by his taunts that, no matter what legal recourse she chooses, 'Nothing can keep me away'. In a way reminiscent of the early modern tragic heroes' insistence on possession of female sexuality, even beyond the grave – Flamineo's promise to Bracciano to kill Vittoria, Giovanni's murder of Annabella, De Flores' suicide pact with Beatrice-Joanna – Martin declares 'I can't live without you; and I won't let you live without me.'

Phyllis Frus finds *Sleeping with the Enemy* typical of this kind of thriller in 'demonizing the abuser, objectifying the woman, eroticizing the victim, and sensationalizing violence'.[13] Lynda Hart is similarly dismissive, writing that 'battered women who kill their spouses can sell tickets at the box office, as long as the heroine is sufficiently pretty and the husband monstrous'.[14] *Sleeping with the Enemy* may be an attempt to address some serious issues about gender and power in general, and spousal abuse in particular. However, its critique is blunted by an odd silence that hovers around the abuse itself. Jacinda Read points out how the opportunities Laura has to share her experiences, once with her mother and once with Ben, are dismissed by Laura herself. In the end, while Laura rebuilds her life largely around her developing relationship with Ben, she has to slay the monstrous husband herself, in a way that is reminiscent of the Final Girl of the slasher movie.[15] Martin even rises up one last time, in classic slasher-killer fashion, and, determined to take her with him, attempts to shoot Laura, only to find the pistol empty. Oddly, the final sequence is not of Laura and Ben in an embrace, but of Laura's wedding ring, just beyond the reach of Martin's frozen, outstretched fingers. A digital effect adds a glint to the metal of the ring, and a corresponding 'pinging' noise to the soundtrack, as the music swells to a climax. It may be that the director intended it as a final, ironic reflection on a dysfunctional relationship, but it also serves to raise the spectre of the idea of marriage as blissful ideal.

Getting even – *Enough* (2002)

Enough was a popular film, though generally poorly reviewed. Both the director Michael Apted and star Jennifer Lopez were keen to emphasise in interviews their intention to root the film in reality.[16] Producer Irwin Winkler states clearly that 'we wanted to get the social issue involved in where women are today'.[17] However, reviewers of the movie, many of whom found its plot laughable, have dismissed out of hand its claims to authenticity, routinely referring to it as a 'revenge fantasy'. It is probably fair to say that the film does sacrifice its claim to realism, and consequently its ability to engage with social issues, on the altar of the sensationalised and unlikely twists and turns of its plot. At the same time, it is important to recognise that Hollywood film works continually within a web of divergent lines of fantasy and reality, and that audience pleasure depends on the successful negotiation of those dimensions.

Jacinda Read has written about *Sleeping with the Enemy* as a continuation of the Cinderella trope begun by Julia Roberts' breakthrough movie *Pretty Woman* (1990).[18] The Cinderella theme is even more explicit in *Enough*, with Lopez herself making the connection in relation to the opening sequence: her character, Slim, is a waitress in a diner, apparently rescued by the gallant Mitch (Bill Campbell) from Robbie (Noah Wyle) who seems to be romancing her, but (as Mitch reveals), is actually working on a bet with a friend that he could 'get inside her pants' within a day. The scene is a startlingly straightforward example of commodification of the female: the bet is either for 200 or 500 dollars, and Slim insists on knowing 'how much I'm worth'. 'The bet was for two hundred,' he tells her; 'but now that I know you ... way too high.' The fairy-tale trope continues in the scene that immediately follows: Slim and Mitch's wedding day, a happy, society family celebration reminiscent of the party scene in *Sleeping with the Enemy* and performing a similar function. The wedding day and Slim and Mitch's early married life are covered in around five minutes of screen-time, creating the image of a perfect marriage, with Slim's every need and desire fulfilled, including Mitch's ostentatious gesture of knocking at the door of the house Slim has fallen in love with, and making the occupier a financial offer he cannot refuse. But, as in *Sleeping with the Enemy*, hairline cracks in the perfect marriage can be traced: Mitch's question at the wedding – 'Are you gonna give me babies... How soon?' hints that his evaluation of Slim stands on functional, patriarchal foundations, reinforced by his later absorption in their newborn child and his failure to respond to Slim's request that he bring the baby to her as she lies in the hospital bed; furthermore, Mitch's emotional distance and vacant stare as they lie on the beach and their daughter Gracie plays in the surf, and his declining Slim's invitation that she join him in the shower, add to the growing unease.

In a short space of screen-time, Slim discovers that Mitch is having an affair. Now, finally, the film begins to work on its central agenda: Slim confronts Mitch, who rehearses familiar, patriarchal attitudes, stating that 'men and women have different needs', and 'I make the money so I set the rules'. The scene is very close in tone and set-up to the corresponding violent scene between Laura and Martin in *Sleeping with the Enemy*, only instead of the male's (groundless) jealousy and half-crazed determination to possess his wife, the male assumes that sexual autonomy is his right, and that his wife should remain his exclusive property. Bracciano in *The White Devil* might be equally combative in his assertion of his right to sexual freedom, but while he demands a divorce from the wife he has grown weary of, Mitch insists on enjoying his other woman, or women, while keeping his family intact. Several times in the course of the movie Mitch insists, 'I refuse to live without you' (echoing Martin in *Enemy*) and, amid his threats, he reminds Slim that 'I am a man who gets what he wants', whether that be a business deal, a house, a wife or a child.

Mitch, like Martin in *Sleeping with the Enemy*, is a monstrous figure, and the grotesque aspect that characterises him again weakens the movie as a whole. After a fleeting glimpse of him as Slim's gallant Prince Charming in the opening scene, he settles into a vaguely discomfiting, menacing mode as early as the wedding scene. In their first violent confrontation, his first slap cuts Slim off in the full flow of righteous anger, and the second blow is a punch, delivered calmly and precisely, that knocks her to the floor. 'You wanna fight?' he challenges, as he looms over her, his voice still calm and level, adding, for an obvious pay-off in the film's final sequence, 'I'm a man, Slim, it's no contest'. Having beaten and intimidated her into silence, he takes her money, driving licence and keys, to make sure she does nothing she might 'regret' later. While *Enemy* relied on the pathological obsessive-compulsive aspect of its male antagonist, the impression of Mitch in *Enough* as a larger than life villain has much to do with the contrast between his violence and his outward calm and level vocal tone. His vicious beating and kicking of Slim when she tries to escape, and his injuring of Gracie at the house in Michigan, further stack audience antipathy towards him.

While *Enemy* relies on a standard romantic figure, with Ben as Laura's white knight, *Enough* is symptomatic of its time: the old romantic myths are either ironised (via the Cinderella trope) or shattered: Slim has no single 'aide', but instead relies on a community of different people, men and women, to survive. Slim's surrogate father, Phil, and ex-boyfriend, Joe, are 'safe' figures in a variety of ways: when Slim comes to Joe first, on the run from Mitch, she explains her decision by saying that she tried to think of the last time she felt safe ('and I saw your face'). In addition, Joe goes out of his way to establish an ironic self-image as an inadequate lover. Although he is in love with Slim, he proves himself to be a faithful, and, crucially, *chaste* friend who can control his desire and love for her.[19] Slim's estranged father, Jupiter (Fred Ward), is at first set up as another faithless and self-centred man. Slim mockingly glosses his unusual name for the benefit of the audience – 'All-powerful mighty king of the gods'. Jupiter rejects Slim the first time she visits him, kicking off her self-styled independent rehabilitation in Northern Michigan. However, soon afterwards, following a visit from Mitch's goons, he changes his mind and sends her enough money to lift her out of the soup kitchen and into a stable and comfortable home. He also helps her to put her plans into operation when she engineers the final confrontation with Mitch. The signals are confused elsewhere, too. Slim finds herself surrounded by other women who have internalised patriarchy, leaving her isolated: on the one hand, Mitch's mother's comment lays the implicit blame on her when she sees Slim's bruised and cut face ('What did you do? What did you say to him?'); on the other, Ginny offers little solace with her cynical conclusion that this is what real men are like ('landmines' waiting to be set off), and makes a disturbing connection between testosterone, sexual potency and violence. At the end of the film, confusingly, it is Ginny who helps to strengthen Slim's resolve to carry out her plan to engineer Mitch's death: 'you have a divine animal right to protect your life and the life of your offspring'.

Just as in *Sleeping with the Enemy*, where lack of faith in the law provides Laura with justification for shooting Martin, there is an emphasis in *Enough* on the impotency of the justice system. Soon after Mitch beats her, Slim tries to get advice at the police station, but the cop's replies to her questions only serve to portray the law as being powerless to protect her. And while Slim recognises that the law favours the mother in custody cases, she is pessimistic, referring to the fact that Mitch has 'a lot of money... and a lot of lawyers'. The lawyer, Toller, whom she visits after Mitch tracks her down in Michigan, is used to press the point home: he (rather implausibly) advises her that Mitch is probably setting up the custody hearing in order to get her where he wants her – and to kill her. The upshot is that Slim decides she can run no longer, and the film prepares its audience for the final reel. There is a strong sense of Slim's motivation being rooted in the abuse she has suffered at Mitch's hands, and despite the attempt to draw Gracie towards the centre, in an 'I will protect you' speech she delivers as Gracie sleeps in the back of the car, the overriding sense is that what Slim wants is not just safety, but revenge. It is at this stage that she plans for a showdown with Mitch, and a sub-*Rocky* sequence follows as she begins a crash-course in Krav Maga self-defence training.

Where *Enough* departs quite radically from its sub-genre is in the final reel. From the beginning, Slim is in control, and the stark difference that a decade makes is very obvious: whereas Martin invaded Laura's new home in *Sleeping with the Enemy* (and, in *The Duchess of Malfi*, Ferdinand invaded and made his own the private space of his sister's bedchamber), here it is Slim who breaks into Mitch's house (which is a new property, Mitch's own personal space, not their old family home). There is a powerful PoV shot as the audience watches with Slim as she hides in the rafters above Mitch's bed (which he is sharing with a blonde woman): Mitch, hearing a noise, wakes up from light sleep, and rises, naked, crossing the room to find a dressing-gown, his pale and wiry body seeming vulnerable in the high angle shot's perspective. Slim prepares Mitch's apartment for their fight, disarming him by removing his hidden pistols, moving the kitchen knives to a place only she can find, and jamming his mobile phone. She dons heavy boots, chunky, bejewelled rings and tapes up her fingers. The final slow tracking shot from a low angle finds Slim standing ready, casting her eye over the battleground in commanding fashion. This time, then, it is Mitch who is in a dangerous space, hunted, stalked, with Slim hidden, her voice echoing around his apartment as she challenges him. The showdown is expertly filmed, managing to maintain tension (notably when Slim is unable to lay the final blow and finish Mitch off), and allowing for a primitive, if effective, catharsis as Slim slaps, punches and kicks Mitch around the house, her final blows intercut with reminders of his brutality towards her.

However, *Enough* is specious in its reasoning and in its attempt to convince the audience (via Ginny's 'divine animal right' line and a despairing attitude to the efficacy of the justice system), that Slim's chosen course of action is a plausible or justifiable one. Nevertheless, in cultural terms, the film is interesting for the way it introduces a number of variations and inversions of the formula. The presence of an oppressive, abusive patriarchy is keenly felt (indeed, far too keenly, some would say, for the film to retain its credibility). However, while Julia Roberts' early-1990s heroine is forced into spur-of-the-moment retaliation, the Jennifer Lopez character of 2002 plans and prepares herself for what amounts to revenge, turning traditionally male tactics (violence, invasion of private space) to her own use, and asserting her right to freedom from a monstrous husband, and the right of her daughter to grow up free of his ownership and influence.

Both *Sleeping with the Enemy* and *Enough* explore conflict and struggles for domination and autonomy between husband and wife. In the earlier film, Laura remains to a large extent objectified as a target of male desire, and the site of struggle between men: Ben, pinned by Martin, spits out a 'Fuck you' before being knocked unconscious and Martin demands that Laura admit that Ben is 'nothing' to her, and to them, as he attempts to claim her back. The audience is acutely aware of Laura's victimhood, and her fight back is retaliatory. Even with Martin dead, her wedding ring, which she purposely discarded and Martin retrieved and offered her again, remains the focal object as the movie closes. There is clear distance between Laura and Slim. The objectified, victimised woman has been exchanged for a woman who makes strong, autonomous assertions of identity: Slim rebuilds her life with only her daughter for company. In the early modern drama, the revenger Bosola triumphs in the slaughter he has perpetrated of the oppressors Ferdinand and the Cardinal, celebrating his 'revenge for the Duchess of Malfi' (5.5.80); De Flores and Beatrice-Joanna die together, with Beatrice begging forgiveness for her transgressions; Giovanni kills Annabella before enacting revenge on her physically abusive husband. The modern equivalents of these women shift from object to subject, from victimhood to retaliation, and in both films the women are represented as justified avengers of the wrongs committed against them.

8
Sex and Violence: *The Changeling* (1622) and *Straw Dogs* (1971)

Sam Peckinpah, whose controversial, patchy and fitfully brilliant body of work includes the violent drama *Straw Dogs* (1971), was not above teasing his public with his roguish reputation, and there is no way of knowing for sure what his motives were when, in an interview for *Playboy* magazine at around this time, he declared, 'There are women, and then there's pussy.'[1] It is tempting but probably unfair to take such a quotable phrase as the last word on the representation of women in Peckinpah's films. Nevertheless, it is a useful starting point for a consideration of the character of Amy in *Straw Dogs*, and is also a binary directly comparable to the virgin/whore formula that is key to understanding representations of women in early modern tragedy. Both *The Changeling* and *Straw Dogs* raise provocative questions about female sexuality. Via the figure of Beatrice-Joanna, *The Changeling* investigates ideas of sin and virtue, and challenges early modern ideas about female sexual desire and sexual autonomy. Roughly 350 years later, *Straw Dogs* presents its audience with another ambivalently sexualised female in the form of Amy (Susan George), a woman prized, appraised and fought over by men in a battle to control her and, indirectly, one another. *Straw Dogs* is a striking example of the ways in which the dynamics of gender, power and violence central to early modern revenge tragedy are echoed in mainstream Western cinema of the late twentieth century. The film's representation of sexualised violence, female sexuality, and patriarchal competition and control, provide fertile ground for the investigation of a set of parallels with *The Changeling*.

At the heart of both *The Changeling* and *Straw Dogs* is an act of rape, the starkest, most brutal expression of the male urge for domination and control of the female. Today, it is not uncommon to understand rape as primarily an act of violence, rather than sex: Susan Brownmiller's

Against Our Will: Men, Women and Rape (1975) was groundbreaking in this respect, forcing a reconsideration of traditional attitudes. During the 1980s and 1990s, further studies uncovered the ways in which rape underpins patriarchal cultures and male-dominated environments. *The Changeling* and *Straw Dogs* are predicated on very different understandings of rape, depict different responses by the men and women involved, and have different sets of implications when re-staged or re-viewed today. There are also surprising, disturbing parallels that endorse feminist concerns about the ways in which cultural representations of rape inscribe and reinscribe male power, and represent its manifestations as natural and inevitable. Jean E. Howard and Phyllis Rackin, in their analysis of the representation of rape, both literal and figurative, in Shakespeare's history plays, note how 'the supposedly instinctive desire of men to rape and the assumed physical vulnerability of women to be raped have provided a remarkably durable rationale for male heterosexual privilege.'[2] When *The Changeling* is revived for a twenty-first-century audience, or when *Straw Dogs* is screened for a group of young adults in 2004, the sometimes fiery, always fascinating, debates about sexual violence that ensue indicate that both texts retain their power to disturb.

There has been a good deal of scholarship in recent years investigating the relationship between representations of rape in early modern literature, and cultural and legal issues in the society of the time. Deborah Burks argues that English rape statutes '[were] designed to redress a wrong committed against a woman's male relatives' and that the men, 'rather than the woman herself, are considered to be the victims of a rape'.[3] Amy Louise Erickson agrees that women were still treated as property around this time, rather than as potential victims of crime.[4] Marion Wynn-Davies focuses on a 1597 Act of Parliament that seems to alter the legal status of rape from being primarily a property crime against the victim's husband or father, and understanding it instead as a crime against the woman herself.[5] Although the evidence suggests that 'this legal gesture towards female self-determination was hardly adhered to in practice,' she continues, 'its very existence suggests that by the 1590s the idea of women as independent subjects was sufficiently substantial to be encoded within a legal text'.[6] In practice, and in spite of the fact that rape recurs frequently in the literature of the period, it seems that instances of actual prosecutions for the crime of rape were scarce, and this may have been because of the difficulty of proving that the crime had been committed, the reluctance of women to expose their shame in public, or a combination of the two.

To cite just one example, Anne Laurence reports that, 'Of twenty-six cases brought in late-sixteenth-century Essex, sixteen resulted in acquittals.'[7]

The Changeling makes room on-stage for an extended, eroticised preparation for the sexual act, but the rape itself is committed off-stage. Sam Peckinpah's film, by contrast, depicts the build-up to Amy's rape, and its execution, in excruciating detail, and controversy has dogged the film ever since. Thirty years later, when Gaspar Noé shot his film *Irréversible* (2002), *Straw Dogs* was a key reference point, and in the years between it has acted as an ambivalent touchstone for films representing, with wildly varying degrees of sensitivity, acts of rape. Karen Bamford claims that, 'Within the "homosocial imaginary" [the phrase is Rebecca Ann Bach's] the raped woman presents a problem to her community: in part because she signifies a potentially explosive grievance between men, in part because she herself is dangerous.'[8] In both *The Changeling* and *Straw Dogs* the rape can be seen primarily as part of a conflict between men, rather than as an act of sexual possession of, or violence against, a woman. Amid these homosocial dynamics, where bonds are forged, challenged, questioned and broken, women's suffering is too often marginalised, elided or erased. The study that follows seeks ways to redress the balance.

'In a labyrinth' – Beatrice-Joanna and *The Changeling*

Middleton and Rowley offer us one of the most provocative (anti-)heroines in all Jacobean drama in the form of Beatrice-Joanna. The most famous Beatrice in literature is Dante's, and because of this the name is most often associated with the tradition of courtly love. For Dante, Beatrice always remains beyond his reach, the epitome of the idealised, perfect woman. Middleton and Rowley's Beatrice-Joanna stands in ironic contrast to Dante's figure. Sara Eaton suggests that the odd, double-barrelled name may be intended to connote heaven and hell, salvation and damnation, with Beatrice read as 'blessed' and Joanna being linked to 'Gehenna' (the New Testament term for Hell).[9] Unlike the pure object of Dante's adoration, Beatrice-Joanna is a noblewoman who is betrothed to one man (Alonzo Piracquo), falls in love with and marries another (Alsemero), and has sex with a servant (De Flores), whom she apparently despises but who blackmails her into a sexual relationship after he has killed Alonzo at her request. When the plots and infidelities finally come to light, De Flores murders Beatrice-Joanna and then kills himself, in full view of Joanna's father and husband, and the brother of the murdered Alonzo.

From the opening scene, *The Changeling* toys with the image of Beatrice, and the gap between a pure and virtuous appearance and inner corruption. As the play begins, Alsemero reflects on the vision of beauty he has seen. The fact that he has seen her twice, and both times 'in the temple' (1.1.1), he interprets as a sign, and there is an air of self-deluding sanctimony as he describes his feelings:

> The place is holy, so is my intent:
> I love her beauties to the holy purpose,
> And that, methinks, admits comparison
> With man's first creation, the place blest,
> And is his right home back, if he achieve it. (1.1.5–9)

For Alsemero, Beatrice-Joanna is his route back to Eden ('his right home back'). His faith in her purity is sustained until the very end of the play, when he realises the full extent of his misconception. The early modern conviction that a beautiful exterior should mirror a morally beautiful interior is evident in the dynamics of their relationship, and Beatrice-Joanna finally inspires so much horror among the male characters in the play because of the striking disjunction between her physical beauty and apparent moral and spiritual degeneracy. De Flores' near-pantomimic ugliness is set in grotesque counterpoint to Beatrice's beauty: in Act 2, Scene 2, Beatrice's insistence that De Flores has improved his appearance, her promises to minister to him, and her apparent obliviousness to the way she is arousing him, work together to comically grotesque effect. (The relationship is also echoed in the sub-plot, with the more traditional mismatch of a beautiful young wife, Isabella, and her foolish, decrepit husband, Alibius.) Beatrice's fall is seen in these specific terms, within the context of physical beauty and its polar opposite. When he discovers her affair with De Flores, Alse-mero exclaims to Beatrice, 'O, thou art all deformed!' (5.3.77). Moments later, confronting the servant, he cries 'oh cunning devils!/How should blind men know you from fair-faced saints?' (5.3.108–9).

The cause of Beatrice-Joanna's tragedy is, in essence, the same as Vittoria's in *The White Devil*, and the same as the Duchess of Malfi's, although the fates of these three women play out very differently. Each woman makes an attempt to assert sexual autonomy, rejecting the choices made on her behalf by the representatives of patriarchy, and instead choosing her own sexual partner. Beatrice-Joanna's early admission to the audience that 'I find/A giddy turning in me' is particularly revealing (1.1.157–8), and would presumably have been even more resonant for a Jacobean audience more accustomed to the notion that women lack the self-control to master their emotions. Nevertheless, there are inherent difficulties in interpreting Beatrice-Joanna as a consistent character in the modern sense. Critics have made sense of her journey through the play in a variety of different ways. Lisa Hopkins believes that 'Beatrice-Joanna's nature seems to be fundamentally altered by the sexual act', and that her behaviour changes from the point she gives in to De Flores' desires.[10] Others choose to interpret her as a woman whose affections are, from the beginning of the play, unnatural, out of control, or both, and this has become the dominant trend in late-twentieth-century critical thinking.

It is not surprising that Freudian readings of the play have influenced stage interpretations in recent years. Roberta Barker and David Nicol have documented many of these readings,[11] connecting them to post-Stanislavskian interpretations of the role on stage, arguing that the two strategies have conspired to create a new sub-textual orthodoxy about the play that casts Beatrice-Joanna as a confused figure, simultaneously repulsed by and sexually drawn to De Flores. Certainly, it is possible, in contemporary productions, to interpret a line such as Joanna's confession to the audience that 'This ominous ill-faced fellow more disturbs me/Than all my other passions' (2.1.53–4) as evidence of unwitting attraction. Joanna continues:

> I never see this fellow but I think
> Of some harm towards me. Danger's in my mind still;
> I scarce leave trembling of an hour after. (2.1.89–91)

The cause of her trembling is not specified, and could be interpreted in a number of ways, but it is most likely that a contemporary actor would choose to pick up an erotic *frisson* from the line. Barker and Nicol show how theatre critics reading twentieth-century stage interpretations of her character have tended to judge performances as being either too brazen, or too innocent. The most highly favoured interpretations seem to be those that have succeeded in balancing these two contradictory elements. The implication is that Beatrice-Joanna's hidden passions are roused unconsciously by De Flores' sexual attention, and, in the wake of his sexual assault, she discovers what she 'really' wants. Barker and Nicol describe this in terms that raise the spectre of debates about rape, and the '"no" means "yes"' myth; they also draw a provocative modern parallel:

> Although the victim may seem unwilling, in fact it's all a bit of saucy fun: no means yes, and one need not feel pity for a heroine whose corruption is also her awakening to her true nature. In a world where rape victims are still subjected to humiliating cross-examination about their sexual pasts on the witness stand, this is hardly a productive way of interpreting ourselves to ourselves.[12]

Barker and Nicol concede that 'a return to [early modern texts'] "authentic" meanings is probably neither possible nor desirable',[13] but argue that the dominant reading of Joanna discovering her repressed sexual desire for De Flores reinforces an interpretation that is true neither to the text's cultural origins, nor to contemporary understandings of femininity. Once again, the gap between the early modern and the postmodern closes, and the spectres of regressive cultural myths and stereotypes return to haunt us.

'Man trap': Amy and *Straw Dogs*

The frequency with which *Straw Dogs* is described as a rape revenge film – most recently by Mark Kermode in his TV documentary *Man Trap*[14] – is alarming, especially when one considers that the film's depiction of a double rape is its most infamous scene, and the source of most of the controversy that has surrounded it. For *Straw Dogs* is in fact not a rape revenge film at all, despite Carol Clover's attempt to file it alongside the likes of *I Spit on Your Grave* (1977), *Lipstick* (1976), *Sudden Impact* (1983), *Extremities* (1986) and even *Deliverance* (1972).[15] Of course, a gruelling double rape does lie at the heart of the film, and revenge drives the plot towards its violent denouement, but the two elements of rape and revenge are connected only indirectly. A brief review of the film's narrative will illustrate the point.

David Sumner, an American professor, takes a sabbatical in Cornwall, accompanying his young wife Amy to the village where she grew up. As he toils away at his mathematical research in the old family farmhouse, Amy becomes idle and bored, while outside a group of local men, including Amy's former boyfriend, Charlie Venner, work on repairing the garage roof. Unspoken hostilities and sexual tensions rise, and in the midst of this, Amy's cat is strangled and hanged in the wardrobe; Amy tells David that one of the other workmen – either the surly, dangerous

Scutt or the rat-catcher Cawsey – killed the animal 'to prove to you they could get into your bedroom'. Venner, Scutt and Cawsey hatch a plot, luring David out on a snipe-hunting trip with them; while he is out, Venner returns to the house to find Amy alone. They have sex; Venner forces himself upon her, with Amy apparently relenting, in what seems to start as a rape but then turns into consensual sex. However, Scutt has followed Venner to the house: he threatens Venner with a shotgun, and brutally rapes Amy while Venner holds her down. David, long since abandoned by the others, returns from the hunting trip humiliated, but Amy tells him nothing of what has happened to her. The next morning, David finally fires the workmen. That evening, the Sumners attend a church social. Meanwhile, the mentally retarded Henry Niles is lured away by a young villager, Janice Hedden (daughter of the village's drunken patriarch figure, Tom Hedden). In the awkward, tentative lover's tryst that follows, Niles accidentally kills her. When she is noted as missing, and an initial search proves fruitless, a posse that includes Venner, Scutt, Cawsey and Tom Hedden is organised to find Niles. In the meantime, driving home through the fog, David and Amy have knocked Niles down with their car, and taken him back to the farm. When the members of the posse learn where he is, they head out to the farm, fired up on whiskey, and demand that David hand Niles over to them. David, sensing the situation is deteriorating into a potential lynching, refuses to comply. Major Scott, a local magistrate, attempts to intervene, and is shot dead by Tom Hedden. The men proceed to lay siege to the house, finally prompting Sumner into violent defensive and retaliatory action. The violence that follows leaves all the members of the posse dead, with only David, Amy and Niles left standing. In the closing scene, David is driving Niles back to the village. When Niles says, 'I don't know my way home,' David replies, 'That's OK. I don't either.'

Over the past thirty years, discussion of the film has gradually shifted from the issue of violence and Peckinpah's attitudes towards male heroism, and focused instead almost exclusively on the representation of Amy. Molly Haskell lambasts her as 'The provocative, sex-obsessed bitch... constantly fantasizing rape.'[16] Bernard F. Dukore points out that there is no evidence in the film that Amy ever fantasises any such thing,[17] but Pauline Kael's reading of Amy is not unlike Haskell's, describing Amy as 'a little beast who wants to be made submissive'.[18] Carol Clover sees the rape in the film as 'a classic in the "asking for it" tradition'.[19] Linda Ruth Williams suggests that, 'In *Straw Dogs*... femininity *is* perversity, and women can *only* misbehave.'[20] And

Gordon Williams, author of the source novel for *Straw Dogs*, claims that the rape scene appeared in the movie because 'Peckinpah "liked to abuse women in his films"'.[21] Just as, in Barker and Nicol's words, the modern reinterpretation of Beatrice-Joanna can be seen to 'embod[y] a fantasy of woman as both virgin and whore, unconscious yet culpable, lacking in agency yet still sinful',[22] Amy can be seen fulfilling a similar function in *Straw Dogs*. Beatrice-Joanna conceals monstrous immorality within a physically beautiful form. Amy is an analogous, though subtly distinct, self-contradiction. The opening shot of Amy, only a minute or so into the film, has been noted by many commentators: the lens frames only her torso, and through her tight white sweater the audience can see she is braless – something that becomes a point of some discord between her and David later in the film, when his anxiety about his ownership of her begins to surface. The camera, having taken its time in establishing this fetishising shot (as Williams notes, it seems 'almost parodic' in its evocation of 'fragmented femininity'),[23] tilts up to focus on her apparently guileless face. In doing so, it establishes the mystery at the heart of her character – her varying levels of awareness about her sexual magnetism, how far she is willing to use it for her own ends, and how much or little control she can exert over the men that are drawn in by it. In the same way that the character of Beatrice-Joanna confuses both her audiences and the fictional men around her with regard to the levels of self-awareness about her sexuality, Amy is constructed as a confusing amalgam of guile and innocence. The scene in which Joanna persuades De Flores to kill Alonzo for her has been played with varying degrees of naïvety or cunning by different performers. She marvels at De Flores, claiming that he has miraculously improved his appearance, and promises to make further improvements with a water she will make with her own fair hands. From here, she indulges in a bout of suggestive sighs and hints expertly pitched to arouse De Flores's interest. 'O my De Flores! . . . No, was I? I forgot, – Oh!' (2.2.98, 101). He jumps at the chance to do her will, despite her warning that 'There's horror in my service, blood and danger' (2.2.119). Joanna is able to detect his hunger ('Belike his wants are greedy' [2.2.125]), but, ironically, is unable to gauge it accurately, interpreting it as greed for gold rather than for her body.

In the opening sequence of *Straw Dogs*, the female protagonist sends out similarly confusing and conflicting signals. Although the aforementioned shot of Amy's body has become something of a critical commonplace, the fascinating sequence that follows has been overlooked: Amy walks towards us, bags in hand, closely followed by the young village girl, Janice, who mimics her walk, highlighting the provocative sway of her hips. Amy smiles and the camera cuts from her face to Charlie Venner emerging from a telephone box with a look of amazement and recognition, and to David approaching from the other direction, carrying a box full of groceries: it is (presumably deliberately) unclear whether Amy is smiling at her husband or her former boyfriend. The framing in this sequence is very provocative: Amy and Charlie exchange a greeting, and the camera gives us a shot of David, looking slightly taken aback. As conversation strikes up, Amy stands shoulder to shoulder with Charlie while David signifies his outsider status, physically set apart from Venner and the other villagers milling around, and even from his wife, who already seems to have been reclaimed by the people she used to live among. Of course, this astute framing of the characters in the opening moments anticipates Amy's shift of loyalties at the climax of the farmhouse siege. Meanwhile, the edginess of the David/Charlie relationship is already being established. Amy suggests Charlie could help with the work on the garage roof, and while David seems a little reluctant, Charlie verbally barges his way into the job. Shortly afterwards, David is clearly preoccupied with Venner, asking Amy whether they went out together when she was younger (her reply is not entirely truthful – 'Oh, by the way, Venner did try to get fresh once – nothing happened'), and soon afterwards asking her why she hired him to help with the garage ('I didn't,' she replies, 'You did'). Amy is at once open and apparently guileless in her smile (acknowledging David or greeting Charlie?), and deceitful (by the time she denies having had a relationship with Charlie, the audience is aware that they *do* have a history); both inviting sexual attention by her mode of dress and at the same time refusing it in her ensuing conversation with Charlie Venner; sending conflicting signals about her loyalties in relation to her new husband, and her old acquaintances of the village.

'I would wear my ring on my own finger' – woman as property

A number of critics, following the work of Gayle Rubin and, later, Luce Irigaray, have considered the place of the female in early modern economies, locating her in relation to the mutually incompatible categories of maid, wife, widow or whore. Pier Paolo Frassinelli, discussing *A Chaste Maid in Cheapside* (1613), argues:

> 'woman' is constituted as a passive object that materialises homosocial relations between men. She is an article for exchange, that is a commodity, an objectified inscription of value whose worth lies

outside herself, in men's desires and investments objectified in the Woman-as-a-commodity.[24]

This attitude is evident in the treatment of the Duchess of Malfi, Annabella in *'Tis Pity She's a Whore*, as well as many women in other plays by Middleton: *Women Beware Women*, *The Revenger's Tragedy* and *A Game at Chess*. In *The Changeling*, Joanna's virginity is highly prized, not only for its 'market value', but also for its own sake – for the specific erotic thrill it entails. In the key scene between Joanna and De Flores in which he shows that he has killed Alonzo de Piracquo and claims his reward, he refuses payment in gold for the murder, declaring:

> I place wealth after the heels of pleasure,
> And were I not resolved in my belief
> That thy virginity were perfect in thee,
> I should take my recompense with grudging,
> As if I had but half my hopes I agreed for. (3.4.115–19)

Beatrice-Joanna is acutely aware of the formula that equates sexual possession with monetary wealth: 'Let me go poor unto my bed with honour,' she begs, 'And I am rich in all things' (3.4.158–9); but De Flores is unmoved, replying in kind: 'The wealth of all Valencia shall not buy/My pleasure from me' (160–1).

Beatrice-Joanna occupies a place familiar to early modern audiences of both comic and tragic drama: her father's possession while a maid, her identity, with dowry and virginity intact, are offered up to an appropriate suitor. Vermandero is evidently well pleased with Alonzo Piracquo, a 'complete' gentleman, 'A courtier and a gallant, enriched/ With many fair and noble ornaments' (1.1.214–16). Later, when Alonzo disappears, he has little hesitation in agreeing to Alsemero as a replacement, so anxious is he to smother any scandal. As a date is negotiated for the marriage to Alonzo, Beatrice-Joanna's virginity is even anthropomorphised: pleading for a delay, she objects:

> with speed
> I cannot render satisfaction
> Unto the dear companion of my soul,
> Virginity, whom I thus long have lived with,
> And part with it so rude and suddenly. (1.1.194–7)

In *The Changeling*, the conflict between males vying for Beatrice-Joanna's attention plays out in a variety of ways. Alonzo's brother,

Tomazo, is deeply suspicious of her affections, and warns Tomazo, 'Think what a torment 'tis to marry one/Whose heart is leapt into another's bosom' (2.1.131–2). Alonzo, however, suffering what Tomazo identifies as 'love's tame madness' (2.1.154), cannot believe 'She knew the meaning of inconstancy', and swears violence against anyone who would doubt her (2.1.145–9).

Amy is not only objectified throughout *Straw Dogs* in visual terms, but also in the way the men commodify her. The precise terms of this sexual economy differ from the system in which characters such as the Duchess of Malfi and Beatrice-Joanna find themselves trapped. However, female sexuality is highly prized by the patriarchy in analogous ways, and Amy becomes contested property, watched over and fought over by men. She is the cause of male competition and explosive, violent conflict. In her first private conversation with Charlie Venner, when she asks why Henry Niles is not in care (or prison), Charlie replies, 'Oh, we can take care of our own here. Usually do.' It is an accurate description of the way things are run in the village, but it can also be interpreted as a veiled hint to Amy that Charlie sees her as being back where she belongs, and that he and the other villagers still exert a degree of ownership over her. Charlie also reminds Amy of their relationship: 'Remember when I took care of you, Amy?' She responds with a barbed reply: 'But you didn't – remember?' As she drives out of the village with David, in a kind of retaliation, she swerves the car towards Charlie and the other men as they stumble home from the pub, prompting outraged curses.

After David and Amy have returned to the farmhouse at the beginning of the film, Cawsey reveals what he has stolen from the house: a pair of Amy's knickers. 'You like my trophy?' he asks. 'Bugger your trophy,' replies Scutt; 'I want what was in 'em'. Amy is quite literally objectified: 'You gonna have a crack at her, Norman?' asks Cawsey; Scutt's reply is an early warning of the violence skulking beneath the surface: 'No, ten months inside is enough for me.' Cawsey muses, 'I could do with some of *that*, too, Normie. Charlie Venner – he had some of *it*. Years ago. When she was here with her father' [my emphasis]. The male competitiveness, often aggression, that erupts repeatedly, makes an early appearance when Scutt comes back with a snarling rejoinder, 'Venner's a bloody liar. And so are you.' Soon afterwards, the knickers make a second appearance in the pub, offering Amy (or at least, the prospect of her) up to wider public consumption. The film cuts from David and Amy having sex to Cawsey throwing the panties to Scutt, who proceeds to taunt Charlie with them, before stuffing them down his own shirt (and from here the film cut straights to Amy and David arguing the following morning).

Amy at first (despite that odd framing in the opening scene discussed above) insists on positioning herself as David's property: much to David's shy discomfort, she kisses him passionately as they draw up outside the farmhouse, in full view of Norman Scutt. Peckinpah's sharp, witty editing underlines the growing tensions and rivalry between the menfolk. From Cawsey brandishing Amy's knickers in the pub, the film cuts to a frustrated, bored, attention-seeking Amy arguing with David, and before long Amy is beginning to position herself more ambiguously: checking her laddered tights and displaying her legs to the workmen as she gets out of the car and, in a move that some claim shows her 'asking for' the sexual attention she will soon receive from Venner and Scutt, removing her sweater and standing topless on the landing, staring angrily back at the men as they watch her through the open window (that motif again, enhanced by the comment David makes as she goes up the stairs – 'Don't forget to draw the curtains').[25]

To David, then, Amy is a trophy wife to be displayed and, in a sharp irony, simultaneously watched over anxiously. However, while he is happy to parade her through the village, he shies away from meeting any challenge to his ownership. As far as the audience is aware, David never asks Amy what she and Charlie spoke about when he observed them from the pub window; neither does he challenge Amy or Scutt and Cawsey when he observes her flirting with them outside the farmhouse. Later, when she comes into the house complaining that Venner and Scutt were 'practically licking my body' as she walked by, David remarks ironically that he congratulates them on their taste, before noting that she 'shouldn't go around without one [a bra] and not expect that type to stare'. Meanwhile, he is irritable and dismissive of her when he is trying to work ('I love you, Amy, but I want you to leave me alone'); and in the company of Major Scott, the vicar and his wife, he patronises her.

As the tension and hostility grow between David and the local men he has employed to fix the garage roof, Amy becomes contested territory. The rape of Amy is, in some sense, only one of a series of flashpoints in the ongoing conflict between David and the others. They needle him (as does Amy) about the violence he has left behind in America ('See anyone get knifed?' asks Cawsey; 'Only between commercials,' David replies), and use their truck to engage him in a game of chicken, initiated by Scutt, nearly forcing him off the road (compare this with Amy's use of the car in the first scene). The car, a familiar phallic signifier, is a rich metaphor: the workmen have just watched David embarrass himself as he tries to find his way around the controls of the unfamiliar vehicle (Amy usually drives). It is also worth noting how Amy emerges from the house, forlorn and perplexed, with no idea where David is going, as he sets out after the truck, further establishing that sense of masculine competitiveness, with no space for the female on the battleground. Most audaciously in the early stages of the conflict, one of the men strangles Amy's cat and hangs it in the wardrobe. This is clearly another attack on David's masculinity and his adequacy as Amy's partner, proving that they can move with ease in these most private spaces.

As in the early modern drama, the invasion of private space, particularly when that space is gendered female, is highly suggestive of sexual violence and possession. In *The Duchess of Malfi*, Duke Ferdinand frets obsessively over his wife's privacy; a number of writers have noticed how *The Changeling* makes use of some complex metaphors in terms of the imagery of private space, property, castles and houses, Mohammad Kowsar reading the image of the castle as one of patriarchy undermined by the alliance between Beatrice and De Flores.[26] Cristina Malcolmson discusses the play's 'recurring image of an invasion that threatens both the city's castle and the female body', and notes how the 'imagery of penetration and invasion' also permeates the sub-plot. Most importantly, however, 'Vermandero's citadel is not only his castle, it is Beatrice-Joanna herself, and the threat of invasion figures the father's loss of control over the female body'.[27] There are similar images of concealment and violation of secrecy in *The Duchess of Malfi*, *The White Devil* and other plays.

In *Straw Dogs*, the invasion of private female space begins when Cawsey steals Amy's knickers from her bedroom, and continues with the invasion of the farmhouse bedroom to hang the casually slaughtered cat in the wardrobe. On the day of the hunting trip, when Venner crosses the threshold at Amy's wary invitation, the assault and rape follow with a terrifying inevitability. The final battle for the farmhouse echoes the rape scene (Venner, Scutt and Amy) when Scutt once again orders Venner to kill David, and to leave him to have his way with Amy. This time, however, codes of masculine loyalty break down, and Venner retaliates by shooting Scutt. However, it is not only the brutish villagers who are guilty of eyeing up what does not belong to them; early on in the film, David ogles Janice and flashes her a flirtatious smile: when she tries to attract his attention at the church social, he ignores her, prompting her flouncing exit and, ironically, leading to her death. There are echoes here of the idea expressed in *The*

Changeling – 'The needle's point will to the fixed north;/Such drawing arctics women's beauties are' (3.3.218–19). If no man can resist the allure of a sexually provocative woman, where does the blame lie – with the subject or the object of that desire? Amy may not be the 'provocative, sex-obsessed bitch' that Molly Haskell describes, but there are clear indications of sexual appetite, another reflection of one side of the virgin/whore binary used to characterise Beatrice-Joanna, Vittoria and even the Duchess of Malfi. Venner remarks, in his first private conversation with Amy, that 'There was once a time, Mrs Sumner, when you were ready to beg me for it.' David twice calls her 'an animal' in this respect, and it is always she, not David, who initiates sex. What is more, Amy's urgency in bed is contrasted with David's comical preoccupations with his glasses, his watch, and winding up the alarm clock. However, the way in which Amy is treated throughout the film reveals the limits on her options: perceived primarily or exclusively as a sexual being, the only means by which she can assert herself, it seems to her, is via her sexuality. Early in the film, she manages to use this to her advantage – when she embarrasses David by kissing him in public, or draws the eyes of the workmen when she feels neglected by her husband. But her power is also her vulnerability, and when primitive instinct overcomes law and custom, the consequences are deeply wounding.[28]

Amy's status has been seen in terms of alliance: Williams' essay ends with the assertion that Amy '[a]t best . . . sees both sides, the native who lives with David but gives voice to his enemies' and '[a]t worst she fucks, disobeys, and betrays them all'.[29] This seems to me to credit Amy with more autonomy and agency than the film itself allows her. Like the early modern women, Annabella and Beatrice-Joanna, Amy is allowed precious little autonomy, or even subjectivity; she is primarily a desired object rather than a desiring subject. Apparently, the backstory developed for the film had Amy as an impressionable student infatuated with David, who, flattered by the attention of a beautiful young woman, married her in what is painfully obviously a dreadful mismatch. The couple bond only in their flirting and lovemaking, and even this has a disturbing sub-text, from Amy's riposte to David that every chair in the farmhouse is 'her Daddy's chair', to David's invitation to her in this playful conversation to take on a Lolita role:

David: You act like you're fourteen.
Amy: I am.
David: Wanna try for twelve?
Amy gazes back at him, silent, chewing gum.
David: How about eight? – I freak out for eight-year-olds.

In a way that relates to early modern patriarchy, and the centrality of the father in the offering up of the maid and her virginity, Amy is linked a number of times with her dead father: Cawsey recalls the time Venner was in a relationship with Amy, when she was living at the farmhouse 'with her father'. Furthermore, David seems to suffer an uneasy sense of trespass in the exchange about her 'Daddy's chair'. Meanwhile, when Amy becomes the centre of local male attention, David can only stand and watch. *Straw Dogs* makes frequent use of PoV shots, and there are several significant sequences where David is depicted peering between the curtains, and through half-open windows, as Amy talks with Charlie (in the opening scene, David is watching from the pub window), and flirts with the workmen at the farmhouse.

Alsemero's anxiety about Beatrice-Joanna's fidelity finds semi-comic expression in *The Changeling*'s virginity test scene. Both Alsemero and Ferdinand in *The Duchess of Malfi* not only have to confront attempts by other males to take possession of their 'property', but also to countenance the threat to social (class) hierarchy that the threat entails. David is a stranger, one set apart from and above most of the other men, notably the workmen spending their time eyeing up Amy. His profession positions him in a class that attracts the curiosity and animosity of almost all the men he encounters, from Venner to the local priest, Barney Hood (Colin Welland), who provokes him into some verbal sparring about the roles and responsibilities of science and the church in the history of human conflict. Part of their competitiveness involves public assertion of the male over the female partner: just as David belittles Amy ('Oh, by the way, did you find your kitty, Amy? Kitty, kitty?'), so the vicar humiliates his own wife with a withering glance when she attempts to intervene in the male, intellectual locking of horns with an innocent question about Montesquieu. For David, his superior education and his lifestyle set him above all the other men in the village: there are frequent juxtapositions of David, the industrious professional, scribbling furiously at his blackboard, and the idle manual labourers, sitting, watching from walls and roofs, with Venner at the centre – the very image of the 'strong-thighed bargeman' Ferdinand imagines his sister mating with in *The Duchess of Malfi* (2.5.42).

In *Straw Dogs*, the male jockeying for position, and competing for property and territory, is explored in ways that, while evident in Peckinpah's earlier work, had never been so rich, complex or perplexing. For most of the film, the likes of Scutt and Cawsey are overly deferential to Sumner (there are lots of 'sirs' and metaphorical tugging of forelocks), but they clearly see him as an unintentionally comic figure, and their deference mocks his blind sense of superiority and patronising attitude. However, while they mock him for his inadequacies and his quirks ('They think you're strange,' Amy tells him), David is still a man in possession of a woman they all desire. Male on male aggression is at the heart of the contest over Amy, but it also manifests itself in other ways. There are signs that Amy is contemptuous of David for his decision to escape from America; she repeatedly berates him for his failure to fix the toaster, and says that if he could only 'hammer a nail', the trouble-some workmen would not be bothering them at all. Although, in the final part of the film, David masters and dominates her entirely, their status is more uncertain in the early scenes: when David notes that their cat 'doesn't answer my call', Amy responds, 'Do *I* ?', and David answers, uncertainly, 'You'd better.' Later, after the cat has been killed, Amy mocks him and his cowardice when he refuses to confront the workmen about it: 'Perhaps you'd like to write them a note on your blackboard,' she sneers.

'Undone...endlessly': *The Changeling* and representations of rape

Jocelyn Catty argues in *Writing Rape, Writing Women in Early Modern England* (1999) that representations of rape in Elizabethan drama function primarily as occasions for staging the spectacle of female suffering, but notes that performance conventions of the time enforced a strange irony: since laws dictated that young men played the roles of female characters in the early modern theatre, acts of rape take place in the off-stage world, making this a peculiar kind of unseen spectacle.[30] However, the implicit eroticism of these encounters is often sublimated via the prologue to the off-stage act itself, and nowhere is this more clearly played out than in Act 3, Scene 4 of *The Changeling*. The moment when De Flores comes to claim his reward for service, and Joanna innocently offers him the gold she believes he craves, sets the stage for a cleverly constructed see-saw action of tension and release. Beatrice-Joanna's offers to increase the amount she will pay him are all rejected, and his rejections are punctuated by her frantic asides to the audience ('I'm in a labyrinth;/What will content him?...Bless me!...I know not what will please him' [3.4.71–2, 75–6]). The audience is very well aware of what De Flores requires as payment, and the erotic tension builds via the oscillation between his shortening patience and growing excitement, and Joanna's apparent bewilderment. The dramatist ratchets up the tension further when De Flores attempts to kiss her: the stage direction '[*He tries to kiss her*]' may be an editor's interpolation, but it seems a sensible one, considering Beatrice's shocked response, 'How now, sir?/This shows not well' and De Flores' cross challenge and second attempt: 'What makes your lip so strange?...Come, kiss me with a zeal now' (89–90, 92).

When Beatrice-Joanna can find no other way to dissuade him from his advances, she makes one last desperate attempt to cling to her high birth. However, according to De Flores, her complicity in the murder has broken down the barrier of social class that would have kept them apart – 'the distance that creation/Set 'twixt thy blood and mine' in Beatrice-Joanna's words (3.4.130–1). Having commissioned the murder, De Flores tells her, 'You're the deed's creature' (3.4.137). For De Flores, the principle of Beatrice's sexual availability is a clinching argument:

> Thou writ'st maid, thou whore in thy affection!
> 'Twas changed from thy first love, and that's a kind
> Of whoredom in thy heart; (3.4.142–4)

The language of the encounter is highly erotically charged: De Flores demands that Joanna must 'ease' him of his (presumably erectile) 'pain', and there is a sexual sub-text in his demand that 'Justice invites your blood to understand me', where blood and sexuality are (as so often in early modern literature) metonymic. Further reinforcing the sense of titillation, there is a heavy emphasis on male physical force overpowering female resistance: 'Can you weep fate from its deter-mined purpose?' De Flores asks rhetorically; 'So soon may you weep me' (162–3). Beatrice-Joanna succumbs in silence, and De Flores' remark, ''Las, how the turtle pants!' also carries an erotic subtext (170). In many productions, De Flores carries Joanna bodily from the stage, further complicating the issue of consent and resistance.

Some of Beatrice's lines in soliloquies and exchanges that follow can certainly be read as confirmation of the myth about female sexual voracity. As Deborah Burks notes, the archetype of the violated but virtuous woman in early modern culture was the figure of Lucrece who, having been raped by Tarquin, took the honourable route of suicide.[31] Jocelyn Catty notes how Jacobean drama repeatedly uses the dramatic spectacle of the threat of rape as 'a means of identifying women as either possessing or lacking the cardinal female virtue: chastity'.[32] The struggle becomes a competition between 'the "male" art of persuasion and the "female" art of *dis*suasion'.[33] In the light of this, Bianca's consenting to becoming the Duke's mistress in *Women Beware Women*, for example, becomes problematic: with the sexual act taken off-stage, as usual, the extent of protest and struggle is impossible to determine. Beatrice-Joanna is more straightforward, however, and is represented as departing quite radically from the supposed ideal of 'chastity by any means necessary' – including suicide. Immediately after the dumb show that follows her exit with De Flores, Beatrice reveals that 'This fellow has undone me endlessly' (4.1.1). The surface meaning is clear – N. W. Bawcutt, fastidiously perhaps, glosses the line as meaning 'caused me infinite trouble (but also implying, probably unconsciously, "damned me eternally")'.[34] However, the word 'undone' can also be interpreted in sexual terms, and it is not difficult to imagine an actor milking the line for these connotations, especially in the light of what Baker and Nicol have established about contemporary renderings of her character.

Later in the same scene, Joanna remarks how 'I'm forced to love thee now,/'Cause thou provid'st so carefully for my honour' (5.1.47–8). De Flores' reply ('Slid, it concerns the safety of us both,/Our pleasure and continuance' [5.1.49–50]) is not challenged by Joanna, and all the signs in this exchange are that she is now enthralled by him: 'But look upon his care, who would not love him?' she marvels. 'The east is not more beauteous than his service' (5.1.72). The lines carry an uncomfortable connotation that relates to the male fantasy about women covertly, or unconsciously, desiring intercourse, even in circumstances where they seem to be refusing it – the 'saying no but meaning yes' idea that has underpinned heated critical debate about the rape scene in *Straw Dogs*, and which perhaps found its earliest expression in literature in Ovid's hateful aphorism, *'Vim licet appellant, vis est ea grata puellis'*, which translates as, 'One may call it force, (but) it is a force which pleases girls.'[35] Karen Bamford has shown how in Jacobean drama, 'the *truly* chaste woman is inviolable; her body may be "defouled" by symbolic rape or erotic torture but not sexually violated'; if a woman values her life above her chastity, 'her deviation is a sign of moral and spiritual corruption'.[36] By portraying Beatrice-Joanna as a young woman in some kind of erotic thrall to De Flores, who in the first half of the play was the object of her spite and disdain, the play clearly marks her out as a unchaste woman, and one embodying a corrupt and unnatural sexuality. The temptation that seems to ensnare many contemporary critics and interpreters for the stage is to encode those desires as latent in Beatrice-Joanna from the beginning of the play. In this way, the idea, flattering to many men, that women often subconsciously desire what they seem to hate and attempt to resist, is starkly reinforced.

'They also serve' – *Straw Dogs* and representations of rape

The precise motivation behind Charlie Venner's visit to the Sumner house remains uncertain. However, the advances he makes towards Amy once she has invited him in and offered him a drink pick up the threads from the first scene together ('Remember when I used to take care of you?' – 'But you didn't take care of me, did you, Charlie?'). The rape itself begins as an unambiguous assault: Amy asks him to 'please leave', and slaps him when he tries to kiss her. His retaliatory slap knocks her down (filmed in agonising slow motion) and he proceeds to drag her by the hair, caveman style, to the sofa. The insistence on display – having already torn her dressing gown, he rips open her t-shirt and forces her arms apart when she crosses them over her breasts – is in keeping with the scopophilic tendency that has characterised Charlie's attitude towards her throughout, but also serves to contradict Susan George's claim that she persuaded Peckinpah to allow her to play the scene with her eyes rather than by the explicit display of her body. At the same time, the heated critical debate over Charlie Venner's rape of Amy is in part attributable to the toning down of the scene that may have come about after the confrontation and discussion between director and female star. At the heart of the controversy has been the eroticisation of the rape scene. Initially the rape is uncomplicated – an aggressive, demanding, sexual assault. However, as it proceeds, Amy's protests turn gradually into groans and cries of pleasure, and it is at this point that it becomes less aggressive, but simultaneously more unnerving for an audience, as the initial stimulus, yielding shock and disgust, is exchanged for one more usually associated with (hetereosexual male) visual pleasure: the display of the female body within the narrative context of consensual sex.

Linda Ruth Williams claims that the juxtaposition of the two rapes – what turns into consensual sex with Venner, followed by the brutal, enforced, non-consensual intercourse (or, it would seem, buggery), by Scutt – implies that one is good and the other is bad: 'In the *Straw Dogs* discourse, rape is not necessarily negative,' she concludes; 'it all depends on who's doing it to you.'[37] While one might argue that the binary does not necessarily hold – it is quite possible that both rapes are being represented as evil acts – it is undeniable that the two rapes (regardless of Peckinpah's intentions) provoke very different responses. Certain critics claim that the director should be exonerated of charges of misogyny by virtue of the fact that he presents the rape from Amy's point of view – this is the claim of the writers who provide a commentary for the UK DVD release of the film in 2002, David Weddle, Paul Seydor and Garner Simmons, as well as Stephen Prince's position in his commentary for the Criterion Edition release in the USA. It is true to say that the breathtakingly swift editing of the scene includes a number of low-angle PoV shots that put the audience in Amy's position, looking up as Venner looms towards her, his hands cradling her face, and even give us an insight into her mental processes as an image of Charlie removing his shirt is intercut with the memory of David doing the same as he made love to her earlier in the film. However, even taking into account these shots and the subsequent scene which depicts, via flash-cuts, Amy reliving the rape in her mind as she and David attend a recital and fete at the local church hall, it is hard to see how this can be argued convincingly as a film shot from the female perspective (see Figure 8.1). Is the voyeuristic tone of the first rape, a depiction of Charlie Venner's scopophilia, a symptom of Peckinpah's own, or an attempt to 'give the audience what they want', whether or not we (or Peckinpah) would be willing to admit it? The uncertainty reflects, perhaps, the kind of ambivalence Karen Bamford notes in terms of male spectatorship of the play *The Maiden's Tragedy*, who 'probably enjoyed identification with Govianus, the heroic revenger, and perhaps – on another level – with the desiring and transgressive Tyrant'; that is, the

Figure 8.1 Eroticizing rape: Del Henney as Charlie Venner and Susan George as Amy in *Straw Dogs* (dir. Sam Peckinpah, 1971)
Source: Screen capture.

man who indulges his necrophiliac urges when he digs up the body of the Lady who has killed herself to avoid the shame of rape at his hands.

The story of the censorship of *Straw Dogs* is complex. The cuts required by the censor in the first place all but excised the second rape, during which Amy is sodomised by Norman Scutt while Venner holds her down. The Motion Picture Association of America (MPAA) demanded the cuts be made, threatening to slap an X certificate on the movie (a rating, now defunct, that at the time was associated almost entirely with hardcore sex films), which would have left it unmarketable. A number of critics have noted that the film, with almost all of Scutt's assault excised, was left (in narrative terms) almost incoherent, while apparently rehearsing the argument that a woman who says no to sexual assault really means yes. According to this argument, Peckinpah's original version was meant to set one rape against the other, the first erotic and second revolting – which takes us back to the troubling ambivalence of Venner's rape. The audience is also left to wonder why Venner complies with Scutt's assault on Amy. Admittedly, Scutt initially uses a shotgun to threaten him (its muzzle shown in alarming close up in a Venner PoV shot), but soon lays it aside to undo his trousers. Venner is obviously horrified at what Scutt does, and the guilt at his betrayal of Amy is etched on his face as the scene ends, but there is no apparent antagonism between the two men after the rape.[38] Later, at the end of the siege of the farmhouse, their long-simmering, but controlled rivalry ends when Scutt, armed and momentarily in control of the bedroom occupied by Amy, Niles, Sumner, Venner and himself, tells Charlie to take Sumner downstairs so he can rape Amy again – 'I'll call you when I'm ready'. This time, Venner chooses the female partner over the male partner, and kills Scutt instead, but up until that point, male homosocial bonds appear to be stronger than heterosexual ones.

The sense of overpowering male subjectivity and control, and female objectivity and compliance, is something that seems to underpin both the film's representations and the context for its actual production. The accounts that we read today of Susan George's experiences on the set of *Straw Dogs* are revealing and disturbing. In terms of ongoing controversies about use of the term 'actress' for a female actor (why should they be distinguished from male actors in this way?), George was very clearly perceived and employed as an *actress* on the *Straw Dogs* set. The air of machismo that seems to have been an inevitable part of Peckinpah's productions seems to have been very prevalent during the filming of *Straw Dogs*. Ken Hutchison tells the story of a late-night expedition to a rocky shore while on location in Cornwall in the company of the director and a supply of Courvoisier (Peckinpah subsequently contracted pneumonia, and the production was temporarily shut down while he recovered).[39] There are also stories of violent, drunken evenings at the local pub, purportedly Actor's-Studio-style exercises in establishing characters and relationships: one of the evenings left the actor T. P. McKenna's arm in a sling for the length of the shoot, lending an appropriate sub-text to the representation of his character (Major Scott), the crippled arm of the law in a volatile society.

All this confirms the idea that the atmosphere on set was markedly male-orientated. George's accounts of the process also report that, while she and Hoffman built up a good rapport in early filming, his commitment to Method acting techniques meant that his attitude towards her (as an actor, not simply as a character) after the rape had been filmed was cold and dismissive. 'From a very kind and humorous and loving friendship, he had become extremely aloof,' she told Weddle. 'Mind games,' she explained, '... incredible mind games, coming from both Dustin and Sam.'[40] As the time to film the crucial double rape scene approached, Peckinpah repeatedly refused to discuss it with Susan George, and when he finally relented and described in detail what he intended to shoot, she threatened to walk off the set. After a long stand-off, George seems to have won the argument: she convinced Peckinpah that she would be able to express Amy's emotional journey 'through her eyes', and that the explicit scene he had envisaged would not be necessary. George told Weddle that she asked Sam to focus on 'my eyes and my body movements'.[41] However, as I have shown, there is a significant mismatch between Susan George's account of her apparent triumph, and what made it on to the screen. Peckinpah apparently declared his intention to film the 'best' rape scene ever committed to celluloid,[42] and no more proof than this is required of the abominable sexism that poisons what is, in many ways, a fascinating and masterfully crafted film. It may be that Susan George was able to tame his vision, through confrontation and the prospect of having his lead actress walk off the set. Nevertheless, the scene led to significant problems with the process of certification, and it is hard to imagine that anything more explicit would have made it past the censor, even if Peckinpah *had* filmed it. According to Kathy Haber, the more graphic scenes were also shot with two body doubles, but, watching the film again for the purposes of the DVD commentary, she had to concede that none of that footage was used in the final cut, with the whole sequence being played by George herself. As the scene was shot, Susan George found herself further undermined by Peckinpah's refusal to engage with her: 'He never moved and he never said a word to me for five days.'[43] Meanwhile, Del Henney was on the receiving end of a different kind of abuse. Reports suggest that Henney hated the scene, and had great difficulty playing it. 'Harrowing' is how he described it to Weddle.[44] Peckinpah reputedly mocked him for his reluctance ('He started saying things like what a dreadful lover he was,' claimed George),[45] adding new, even more disturbing contours to the history of the scene. Having endured the week-long shoot of the scene, Susan George was subsequently barred from the screenings of the rushes, and plunged into a new kind of emotional turmoil (once again, rooted in fear, wondering 'whether I'd managed to pull it off or not, and just how angry he was going to be if I hadn't').[46]

Sarah Projansky sees the 'sheer number of representations of rape that have appeared on screen since the 1970s' as 'a sustained definition of women as sexually victimized and a sustained cultural assault on women'.[47] The graphic depiction of rape, she argues, even in an avowedly progressive film such as *The Accused* (1988) aggravates the problem: 'all representations of rape necessarily contribute to the discursive existence of rape, and...graphic representations do in particularly powerful ways'.[48] The rape scene in *Straw Dogs* exists within a tightly controlled male environment: written by men, enforced on a reluctant young actress isolated and in fear of Peckinpah's capacity for humiliating and intimidating his actors, and filmed in a way that eroticises the sexual assault in a way that is clumsily, not deliberately, discomfiting. Weddle's description of the scene as 'one of the most perversely erotic sequences in cinema history' inadvertently perhaps, cuts to the heart of the matter:[49] in a way that the exploitation movies *I Spit on Your Grave* and *Ms.45: Angel of Vengeance* never do, *Straw Dogs* allows its audience to enjoy their view of a beautiful, naked woman, masking the first physical assault with the sights and sounds of her in sexual ecstasy, before cutting to an even more brutal assault in a way that does nothing to mitigate the preceding, arousing scene. The Gordian knot that binds sexual violence and eroticism in Hollywood film is the 'to-be-looked-at-ness' Mulvey identifies. In an industry that (still) demands that its stars meet certain standards of conventional beauty, the rape of Amy is, almost inevitably, filmed in such a way that her body is the made the object of visual pleasure.

There is a disturbing and rarely mentioned vacuum at the centre of *Straw Dogs*. Having suffered a brutal double rape, hours later Amy is depicted lying in bed, smoking, awaiting David's return. She makes no attempt to talk to David about what has happened to her, restricting herself to a sarcastic reply when her humiliated husband says how 'they stuck it to me out on the moor today'. ('They also serve who only stand and wait,' she mutters). Although some critics claim that the way in which Amy relives the rape in flash-cuts throughout the subsequent scene in the village hall expresses her inner turmoil and anguish, there is in fact very little space allowed for Amy's mental suffering following her ordeal. In the same way that female suffering in Jacobean drama is so often appropriated by the male tragic figure (transferred from Gloriana to Vindice in *The Revenger's Tragedy*, Lavinia to Marcus and then to Titus in *Titus Andronicus*, the Lady to Govianus in *The Maiden's Tragedy*), the fall-out of Amy's rape is eclipsed by the male territorial aggression of the siege of Trencher Farm in *Straw Dogs*. Tellingly, Beatrice-Joanna internalises patriarchal ideology at the point of death, locating the pollution in blood that she acknowledges as belonging to her father:

> Oh, come not near me, sir; I shall defile you.
> I am that of your blood was taken from you
> For your better health; look no more upon't,
> But cast it to the ground regardlessly.
> Let the common sewer take it from distinction. (5.3.149–53)

The image she uses simultaneously denies her self-ownership, and accepts full culpability. In death she becomes 'that blood "taken" from the patriarchal body in order to purge it, to relieve it from a plethoric disease ... [a disease caused by having too much blood in the body] ... this blood has been poured into a common "sewer", a drain, where it will mix with all forms of filth and waste'.[50]

Whatever its merits, Peckinpah's *Straw Dogs* remains bound by patriarchal attitudes that position the woman as disputed property; that makes tentative connections between a woman's supposed 'flaunting' of her sexuality and containment and punishment; and that (*pace* its mostly male apologists) presents sexual assault from an almost exclusively male perspective. From the beginning, Amy is objectified, and comparisons can be drawn between the presentation of Amy and the introduction of the female protagonists in the drama, especially in relation to the virgin/whore binary. Conflicting images of the Duchess of Malfi are set up in the first scene: is she Antonio's beautiful icon whose beauty inspires awe while she simultaneously 'cuts off all lascivious and vain hope' [1.1.200]; or is she the whore that Ferdinand imagines; or merely a woman of flesh and blood, with accompanying needs and desires, as she herself pleads (1.1.453)? Is Beatrice-Joanna the holy vision Alsemero imagines in the opening scene of *The Changeling*, or is she the 'deformed' creature of his nightmares (5.3.77)? The extent to which Amy is aware of the power of her sexuality is debatable, and just as Beatrice-Joanna's naïvety leads her into a doomed, forbidden relationship, Amy finds herself triangulated between David and Charlie.

Amy is given little sexual autonomy, policed in different ways by David's guarded jealousy, and by the aggressive, invasive gaze of Charlie, Scutt, Cawsey and the others. Amy, like the early modern women, is object rather than subject and she (and in particular her sexuality) functions as disputed property. David, Charlie and Scutt all lay claim to her, in a way analogous to the status of Beatrice-Joanna (Piracquo, Alsemero, De Flores), the Duchess (Ferdinand, her dead husband, Antonio) and Annabella (Giovanni, Soranzo). The representation of Amy's expression of her sexuality, its containment and violation, mirrors age-old attitudes that inform the punishment of the Duchess, Beatrice, Vittoria and Annabella. There are more similarities in the ways in which male homosocial bonds are forged, threatened and broken around the possession of female sexuality. Sarah Projansky notes a strand of rape narratives in film that are structured around transgressions of economic and social class, remarking that such films 'express an underlying ambivalence about a classed society'.[51] Amy transgresses gender and class hierarchies in the relationship that is (re)forged between her and Venner: even if it is with reluctance and resistance on her part, it is impossible to ignore either the modulating of her response to his sexual assault, or the fact that she cries out to him, not David, for help at the climax of the farmhouse siege. The lure of female sexuality, and the male anxieties so tightly wound around that lure, finally leads to explosions of bloody violence that envelop men and women alike.

9
White Devils and Basic Instincts

'The devil in crystal': Vittoria in *The White Devil*

John Webster's *The White Devil* recounts the story of Vittoria, a woman who, having fallen in love with Bracciano, a married man, persuades him to arrange the deaths of her husband (Camillo) and his wife (Isabella), freeing Bracciano and Vittoria to marry one another. This Bracciano does, with the help of Vittoria's brother – his secretary, Flamineo. In the aftermath, Vittoria is arrested and put on trial, ostensibly for conspiracy in the murder plot. When the case collapses, the Cardinal steps down from his position as judge and accuses Vittoria of being a prostitute, ordering that she be punished with imprisonment in a house of penitent whores. Bracciano springs her from her prison, and they marry. However, the murder plots have aroused the suspicions of Isabella's brother, the Duke Francisco, and he infiltrates Bracciano and Vittoria's wedding celebrations. There, his assassins murder Bracciano, and, finally, Vittoria herself, her maid, and Flamineo.

Vittoria, despite being *The White Devil*'s titular heroine, has only four key scenes that are crucial in her portrayal: the love scene between her and Bracciano (1.2), the arraignment (3.2), the house of penitent whores (4.2), and her death scene (5.6). In each instance, her behaviour can be construed as being radically different from her preceding appearance. David Gunby, writing in 1995, suggests that Webster's presentation of her is 'quite consciously disjunctive'.[1] John Russell Brown, in his edition of the play published over thirty years earlier, had already noted the way in which Vittoria's 'mood, or tone, is very different' in each of her four major scenes. '[E]ach of Vittoria's scenes starts on a new note, with little or no preparation in earlier scenes', he believes; and he

147

suggests, rather vaguely, 'Such was Webster's style, the instrument he forged out of many elements.'[2] Roma Gill works hard to establish a greater consistency for Vittoria, but has to admit that what she has to offer is a 'modern' interpretation 'owing more to post-Freudian psychology than to Jacobean writings on the passions'.[3] In the same way that modern critics and stage interpreters tend to read Beatrice-Joanna as a model of Freudian sexual repression, so Vittoria has been more readily decipherable in a similar conceptual framework.

Whether such disjunctions should be interpreted as evidence of complex characterisation is debatable. It may be more feasible to interpret such contradictions and inconsistencies as evidence that the construction of 'realistic' characters was not a dramatist's first priority during this period, and that our attempts to read them in this fashion betrays a lack of understanding of cultural specificity. Vittoria, like other women in Jacobean tragedy, works better if understood as a site of ideological struggle, a tablet on which different ideas of woman, and the relations between men and women in early modern society, are inscribed (or scrawled). Catherine Belsey argues that, in *The White Devil*, Vittoria's 'discursive discontinuity' has an ideological root cause: 'in a society where the circulation of discourses is controlled by men the definition of women is inevitably patriarchal and reductive'.[4] She quotes the line of Bracciano's that I have already noted – 'Woman to man/Is either a god or a wolf' (4.2.91–2) – and describes how females in early modern plays tend to include contrasted female stereotypes, reducible to the 'devilish Vittoria and the patient Isabella [in *Measure for Measure*]'. She continues, 'Stereotypes define what the social body endorses and what it wants to exclude.'[5] The conflicted representation of Vittoria embodies the stereotypes, but in forms that may make an audience think again, and consider more closely, the attitudes that lie behind them.

Vittoria is, from her first appearance, a much more obviously morally compromised figure than Beatrice-Joanna. She is presented as being at the centre of a sexual intrigue that brings about the murder of both her husband and Bracciano's wife. Her first scene depicts a lovers' tryst between herself and Bracciano, during which she recounts a dream that, as Flamineo informs the audience, hints to her lover that he should 'make away with his duchess and her husband' (1.2.247). Her cunning provokes Flamineo's admiration ('Excellent devil', he marvels [1.2.245]). Christina Luckyj, studying the famous arraignment scene in which Vittoria stands trial for her part in the murder of her husband, points out that Vittoria does not fit the mould of the wrongly accused woman, in the tradition of Desdemona (*Othello*) and Hermione (*The*

Winter's Tale [1609]). The audience is aware in both these cases that the woman is innocent, accused by a husband driven half-insane with jealous suspicion (and one should not forget how the drama often exposes masculine folly in extreme, usually groundless, responses to suspected infidelity). Vittoria, by contrast, is deeply implicated in the crimes of which she stands accused.[6]

Several critics have interpreted Vittoria's striving for sexual autonomy in gendered terms. Gayle Greene describes Vittoria as 'the very antithesis of the Renaissance ideal of woman: disobedient, defiant of convention, sexual, subversive, she displays the assertion rather than the subordination of self'.[7] If Greene reads Vittoria as the Renaissance 'anti-woman', Laura L. Behling ventures to suggest that Vittoria has 'in effect, played the masculine role in sexual relations',[8] and it is easy to see how such an interpretation could be enacted on stage, especially during her exchange with Bracciano described above. In the light of this, Webster's audience may have interpreted Vittoria's attempt to defend herself against Monticelso's accusations as inappropriate simply by virtue of the fact that she was speaking out in public. As usual, the prohibition on women's discourse had a biblical basis, taking a cue from the Apostle Paul's edict in his first epistle to the Corinthians:

> Let your women keep silence in the churches: for it is not permitted unto them to speak; but they are commanded to be under obedience, as also saith the law. And if they will learn anything, let them ask their husbands at home: for it is a shame for women to speak in the church. (1 Corinthians 14, 34–5)

The biblical restrictions were often extrapolated into all kinds of secular contexts in order to prohibit women's public speaking, with some writers and preachers seeking to extend their relevance into the private sphere. One educational treatise of the period, which 'emphasises the ideal godly woman as one who refrains from speaking',[9] usefully throws into relief the transgressive nature of Vittoria's behaviour.

Nevertheless, it is possible to interpret *The White Devil* as something more than a reiteration of familiar myths about women in general, and female sexuality and temerity in particular. Jonathan Dollimore, in a chapter of *Radical Tragedy* indebted to Foucault, discusses the misogyny that inhabits Webster's *The White Devil*, mostly via Flamineo's conventional malcontent denigration of women, and in Cardinal Monticelso's 'character of a whore' speech. 'To be male,' Dollimore writes, '*is* to have power – in particular, power over women.' Moreover, '[n]ot only does the language of the dominant actually confer identity on the subordinate, but the latter can only resist this process in terms of the same language'.[10] The patriarchy asserts its power stridently and overtly, most obviously in the famed arraignment scene. Vittoria, labelled a 'whore' by the Cardinal is, as Dollimore points out, forced to defend herself by 'personat[ing] masculine virtue' (3.2.136). Since male (misogynistic) discourse is predominant, women are forced to participate in these debates on male terms: the fact that women were actively discouraged or, in some contexts, forbidden to speak in public, is symptomatic, and part of a vicious cycle.

It is clear that the arraignment scene operates not to *establish* Vittoria's guilt, but to *parade* her guilt and shame (as Monticelso hopes), on stage, for all to see. 'She scandals our proceedings,' Monticelso protests, as she attempts to speak in her own defence (3.2.129). Even critics who endorse a more sympathetic reading of Vittoria find her duplicity in this scene inexcusable, while still admiring the courage she displays as she challenges the Cardinal's authority and accusations. Gunby writes that 'the gap between Vittoria's claims to womanly modesty and her vituperative and indecorous outburst points up the danger of taking what she says at face value'.[11] It is here that charges of hypocrisy are most common, and certainly her protestations of innocence are at best disingenuous, at worst brazen, bearing in mind her part in persuading Bracciano to kill Camillo and Isabella. Monticelso repeatedly reminds his audience that what may appear beautiful on the outside may hide an inner corruption – again, a familiar trope of early modernist ideology. Vittoria's willingness to challenge and confront the figure of patriarchal (and religious) authority may have made her actions even more shocking, although it is also possible to read anti-Italian, anti-Catholic satire in the depiction of the Cardinal. Would a Jacobean audience have seen Vittoria's behaviour as indefensible, and interpreted her shameless protestation of innocence as evil hypocrisy, typical of the deceitful woman? Would Vittoria arouse hostility and distrust simply by virtue (or fault) of being a confident woman ready to challenge male authority? Or is there room for a more complex and ambivalent response to Webster's (anti-)heroine?

Cardinal Monticelso describes in great detail his understanding of the character of a 'whore'. For his purposes, 'whore' means any woman who steps outside the legitimate bounds of sexual abstinence (for an unmarried woman or widow), or fidelity (to a husband). His speech is a catalogue of misogynistic metaphors, concluding, 'You know what whore is: next the devil, adultery,/Enters the devil, Murder' (3.2.109–10).

According to Monticelso, whores operate as a kind of index to man's sinful nature:

> They are worse,
> Worse then dead bodies, which are begged at gallows
> And wrought upon by surgeons, to teach man
> Wherein he is imperfect. (3.2.96–9)

Vittoria offends by her refusal to remain silent, and is punished accordingly. Her death, repeatedly delayed and then prolonged when it finally happens, is in part an act of revenge orchestrated by the brother of Bracciano's wife (another casualty in the plot that has rid Vittoria of her tedious and inconvenient husband). Before this, however, she is seen to commit one more act of duplicity as she attempts to turn her brother Flamineo's proposed three-way suicide pact into an escape route for herself and her servant, Zanche. As they line up in a triangle, each with a pistol trained on the other,[12] the two women both turn their pistols on Flamineo. Flamineo delivers a ludicrously elaborate death speech before standing up and announcing that the pistols had no bullets in them:

> Trust a woman? Never, never. Bracciano be my precedent: we lay our souls to pawn to the devil for a little pleasure and a woman makes the bill of sale. (5.6.158–61)

Flamineo and Lodovico are both desperate to be the one who has the pleasure of killing Vittoria: 'You shall not take justice from forth my hands – O let me kill her!' pleads Flamineo (5.6.173–4). Lodovico himself expresses his contempt and disgust at Vittoria in an unusual, vehement turn of phrase:

> O thou glorious strumpet,
> Could I divide thy breath from this pure air
> When 't leaves thy body, I would suck it up
> And breathe't upon some dunghill. (5.6.204–7)

The text is open once more to provocative interpretations in the staging of her death. Christina Luckyj cites a review of the 1991 London National Theatre production which noted how Vittoria met Lodovico's dagger thrusts 'as though they represented a tempestuously flattering act of copulation'.[13] To have Vittoria stabbed repeatedly in the groin has become a familiar directorial choice, and it emphasises in the most brutal fashion that connection between sexuality and punishment.

In *The White Devil*, Vittoria's *hic mulier* tendencies are emphasised throughout, most especially in the dominant role she plays in the early stages of her relationship with Bracciano, and in her insistence on speaking up in her own defence during the arraignment scene. In the final scene, as she defies her killer, Flamineo marvels at her courage: 'If woman do breed man,/She ought to teach him manhood' (5.6.241–2). She taunts Lodovico as her blood drips from his dagger:

> 'Twas a manly blow.
> The next thou giv'st, murder some sucking infant,
> And then thou wilt be famous. (5.6.231–3)

But, for all her defiance, she too internalises the patriarchal line in her final moments: 'O my greatest sin lay in my blood; now my blood pays for't' (5.6.239–40). The parallels between this and Beatrice-Joanna's dying speech in *The Changeling* are striking. However, Vittoria remains a provocative and potentially subversive figure, and the analysis that follows attempts to map her on to the template of the *femme fatale*, thereby tapping into that subversive potential, and discovering how the same archetype has, perhaps unconsciously, dominated interpretations of her in the past.

'A vagina and an attitude': white devils, femme fatales, *Basic Instinct*

The figure of the objectified, victimised woman is ubiquitous in Hollywood; the contextual discussion at the beginning of Part II considered how the role of the female in contemporary violent cinema has traditionally been a limited one, and how the evolution of more active women in horror, science fiction and thriller genres has been contained. However, there are instances of more radical, 'dangerous' women emerging, especially since the late 1980s. The Hollywood star, Sharon Stone, who enjoyed major celebrity status in the 1990s primarily because of her barnstorming performance as the murderous, bisexual writer-with-a-degree-in-psychology, Catherine Tramell, in Paul Verhoeven's *Basic Instinct*, has made her way into on-line quotation reference sites with her remark that, 'If you have a vagina *and* an attitude in this town, then that's a *lethal* combination.'[14] The remark has entered the annals of film history in part because it represents one of those moments where star and role merge: it was the kind of quip her *Basic Instinct* character might have made during her interrogation scene (discussed in detail below). Furthermore, it came at a moment of significant change in Hollywood, as female stars began to command higher salaries and demand greater attention from the Hollywood fantasy industry. The gap between Susan George in 1971 and Sharon Stone in 1992 seems in some respects very wide, though such distances can prove deceptive on closer inspection.

The *femme fatale* figure was a staple of *film noir* in particular, reaching her peak in the 1940s in films such as *Double Indemnity* (1944), *The Big Sleep*, *The Postman Always Rings Twice* and *Gilda* (all 1946), but the genre withered and all but died out between the 1960s and 1980s, as E. Ann Kaplan notes in her introduction to the new (1998) edition of the seminal collection of essays *Women in Film Noir*, first published in 1978.[15] The kind of dangerous woman that emerged as more explicit sex and violence began to seep into the Hollywood mainstream in the late 1980s was something bold and new. The new *femme fatale* was a version of Amy with an attitude and no guilt, a woman unafraid of expressing and exploring her sexuality, and setting up very different power dynamics in the arena where men and women battle for sexual autonomy and control. At the same time, in an era that had seen traditional models of masculinity fragment or shatter, it is probably not surprising that the threat of the powerful, sexual woman should return to haunt the Hollywood hero. So Ellen Barkin took apart Al Pacino's cynical cop in *Sea of Love* (1989); female cop Debra Winger pursued husband-killing Theresa Russell in the overly-literal *Black Widow* (1987); Madonna played a hyper-version of the black widow type, killing off her husbands via overly-energetic sex in the unintentionally comic *Body of Evidence* (1993); Linda Fiorentino forged a unique brand of male-bashing amorality for *The Last Seduction* (1994); and Matt Dillon found himself caught between poor little rich girl Denise Richards and trailer trash Neve Campbell in *Wild Things* (1998).

Alongside these dangerously seductive women runs another line of transgressive women whose danger lies primarily in their obsessive pursuit of the male protagonist – they are what Kate Stables refers to as the 'psycho-femmes',[16] usually engaged in wilful destruction of the family unit. Glenn Close terrorised her married lover Michael Douglas in *Fatal Attraction* (1987); Rebecca De Mornay threatened to steal husband and child from the woman who employed her as a nanny in *The Hand That Rocks the Cradle* (1992); Drew Barrymore provided a disturbingly Lolita-esque twist on the genre as *Poison Ivy* (1992), seducing her best friend's father; and *Disclosure* (1994) transposed the template into a corporate business context, with Demi Moore preying on (once again) poor old Michael Douglas. It is also notable that many of these women simultaneously pandered to and subverted male fantasy via their ambiguous sexuality (*Basic Instinct, Wild Things* and, most blatantly, *Bound* [1996], with its fashionable, butch/femme lesbianism): any debate about the ways in which lesbianism and bisexuality may operate as threats to male sexual potency would do well to bear in mind the widely documented appeal to the typical heterosexual male viewer of 'girl on girl action', and the way it has traditionally been filmed for a mainstream audience.[17]

Although Mary Ann Doane argues that the *femme fatale*, that classic 'symptom of male fears about feminism'[18] emerges as a central figure in the nineteenth century, and that '[h]er appearance marks the confluence of modernity, urbanization, Freudian psychoanalysis and new technologies of production and reproduction (photography, the cinema)',[19] it is possible to see earlier incarnations of this figure stretching back into classical and even biblical literature. Janey Place writes that '[t]he dark lady, the spider woman, the evil seductress who tempts man and brings about his destruction is among the oldest themes of art, literature, mythology and religion in Western culture'.[20] According to Yvonne Tasker, the *femme fatale* draws on a tradition in which 'women are mysteriously seductive but evil, in which "woman" is not only defined by her sexuality but also by the power that this generates',[21] and she lists four significant aspects of the *femme fatale*:

> First, her seductive sexuality. Second, the power and strength (over men) that this sexuality generates for the *femme fatale*. Third, the deceptions, disguises and confusion that surrounds her, producing her as an ambiguous figure for both the audience and the hero. Fourth, as a consequence the sense of woman as 'enigma', typically located within an investigative narrative structure which seeks to find 'truth' amidst the deception.[22]

As Kate Stables argues, the *femme fatale* is 'a timeless fantasy, a cross-cultural myth, but also a historical construct, whose ingredients vary according to the time and climate of her creation'.[23]

It is possible to discern at least the first three of the elements Tasker identifies in Webster's Vittoria (*The White Devil*), as critics and theatre practitioners have interpreted her over the years. Furthermore, Mary Anne Doane's contention that the *femme fatale*'s power is peculiar in that 'it is not usually subject to her conscious will, hence appearing to blur the distinction between passivity and activity' is commensurable with dominant readings of Vittoria in literary and theatrical criticism.[24] She has always inspired conflicting and conflicted responses among audiences, theatre critics, literary critics and theatre practitioners; the tension is neatly encapsulated by the writer for *Blackwood's Magazine* (1818), who described Vittoria as 'startling by her beauty and wickedness'.[25] D. C. Gunby, editing the first volume of Webster's *Complete Works*, suggests that while there is little to admire in Bracciano, there is 'in Vittoria much, with wit, intelligence, and courage allied to beauty in a combination which Webster renders both seductive and mysterious'.[26] In contrast to Vittoria stands the faithful, unfortunate Isabella. As in conventional *film noir*, the evil woman is 'contrasted... with a marginal female figure representing the good woman, who is worthy of being a wife, and often the victim'.[27] These attitudes lurk in literary and theatrical critical responses to the figure of Vittoria as far back as the nineteenth century. Alexander Dyce, discussing the arraignment scene, writes of 'that forced and practised presence of mind which the hardened criminal may bring to the place of accusation', noting Vittoria's reliance on 'the quickness of her wit' and 'the influence of her beauty'.[28] Dyce's view is perhaps representative of nineteenth-century attitudes to sexual morality. Charles Kingsley similarly regards her conduct in the arraignment scene as 'not an insight into Vittoria's especial heart and brain, but a general acquaintance with the conduct of all bold bad women when brought to bay'.[29] The reviewer for *Blackwood's Magazine*, quoted earlier, found her 'startling by her beauty and wickedness' but also noted that Webster's portrait was 'true enough to nature',[30] implying an analogous attitude towards Kingsley's 'bold bad women'.

The role of Vittoria, then, is predicated on her sexuality, and there are ways in which she works as an early modern example of the *femme fatale* mythotype. In pure narrative terms, she operates as the mainspring of the revenge plot in so far as Bracciano's desire to marry her leads him to plot the murder of his wife and her husband. In contemporary cultural forms, the figure of Catherine Tramell in *Basic Instinct* is one of the finest examples of the *femme fatale* in her own period. The film's director, Paul Verhoeven, describes how, unusually for a movie in the thriller genre, 'the woman has the power just because of the strength, openness and outrageousness of her sexuality'.[31] The description could as easily be applied to Vittoria, and its attitude contrasts markedly with some of the nineteenth-century reviewers of *The White Devil* cited above. Camille Paglia celebrates the movie and delights in Stone's portrayal of the powerful and beautiful 'bad girl' who, unlike the standard *femme fatale* of films fifty years earlier, literally gets away with murder.[32] In early modern tragedy, women are punished for sexual transgression: in *The Duchess of Malfi* we eavesdrop on Ferdinand's hellish, sexually inflected, sadistic plans of punishment for his wayward sister, and watch the Duchess slowly prepare for death, before being garrotted by two executioners, her relatively restrained death swiftly followed by the panicky, confused murder of her waiting-woman. We hear the orgasmic death cries of Beatrice-Joanna in *The Changeling*, and watch with her as her blood streams from her body. Punishment for transgressive sexuality is most evident in contemporary Hollywood in the slasher genre (to be considered in Part IV), although it can also be traced in certain kinds of thriller, in particular serial killer movies.

What marks *Basic Instinct* out as particularly interesting for our present purposes is the way it reverses the polarities of the standard gender/power circuit. The opening sequence sets the subversive tone. The camera's odd angle and the direction of the panning is disorientating, and it takes a moment for the audience to get its bearings, as the camera settles and focuses on a man lying on a bed, straddled by a woman, with the two of them in the throes of passion. The scene plays knowingly and expertly on audience expectations. The movie had been sold largely on its promise of graphic sex, and, within minutes, it seems to be delivering on that promise, as the woman ties the man by his wrists to the wrought iron bedhead, and their lovemaking becomes more frenzied. The shots capitalise on the woman's naked body, with medium close-ups sometimes working as point of view shots of her partner on the bed. Suddenly, as the woman seems to be climaxing, 'the woman steals the man's penis and uses it against him', as Camille Paglia puts it:[33] she slides an ice-pick from beneath the bedspread behind her, and stabs him repeatedly in the face and the body. In gruesomely witty fashion, male ejaculation is supplanted by spurts of blood from his wounds, in close-up and medium long-shot. In this way, the film's key elements – graphic sex and brutal violence – are established in decisive fashion. The film's key sequence, however, is the interrogation scene, described by Camille Paglia as 'probably one of the great scenes in the whole history of film-making demonstrating woman's power over men'.[34] Catherine has been brought in for questioning after the murder of her lover Johnny Boz (the man the audience has seen stabbed to death in the opening scene). From her first meeting with detective Nick Curran (Michael Douglas) and his partner Gus (George Dzundza), she is uncompromising about her language and her sexuality, making a distinction between 'dating' and 'fucking' (what she did with Johnny Boz was emphatically the latter); asked if she is sad Boz is dead, she replies, 'Yeah, I liked fucking him.' Catherine's direct style will serve her well in the interrogation that follows.

For our purposes, the trial of Vittoria in *The White Devil* provides an instructive contrast. Catherine's white suit in the interrogation scene is an evocative signifier. Not only does it make reference to Hitchcock's thrillers and *femmes fatales*, it also makes an ironic comment on the question of Catherine's innocence or guilt. Furthermore, the fact that she is wearing no underwear (the shot in which she uncrosses and recrosses her legs has become one of the most fabled moments in modern cinema history) brings into even sharper focus the virgin/whore binary central to early modern drama, and especially *The White Devil* itself, when Monticelso draws attention to the gap between the beautiful exterior and morally corrupt soul of Vittoria. As we saw in the last chapter, in an ideal order, where it was assumed that inner and outer should mirror one another, the radical disjunction between physical beauty and moral impurity provoked deep unease, and both Catherine and Vittoria upset the beliefs that are fundamental to the patriarchy's assessment of what is safe and what is threatening. Although it is impossible to know what costumes may have been used when *The White Devil* premiered, recent productions have often paid careful attention to Vittoria's appearance. The National Theatre production of the play (1969) featured a piece of stage business that sought to emblematise her moral status with a bold, theatrical stroke. Rowland Wymer reports that, in the middle of the arraignment scene, 'Vittoria's white cloak fell away to reveal a dress of flaming red, confirming her accusers' picture of her as a "scarlet woman".'[35] Christina Luckyj notes how, in the text, the Cardinal 'insistently foregrounds the visual in a protracted display of misogynistic scopophilia'.[36] The Royal Shakespeare Company (RSC) production emphasised this by some stage business used during the arraignment scene that was noted by almost every critic who reviewed the show: Jane Edwardes remarked how 'Philip Voss's cardinal can't take his eyes off her [Vittoria's] bosom as he condemns her to a home for repentant whores', and Benedict Nightingale noted that '[t]he fact that [Monticelso] is staring bug-eyed down her cleavage adds to the prurient disdain this actor expresses so effectively'.[37]

It is not difficult to imagine a Jacobean audience responding appreciatively to this kind of ironic touch in the depiction of the Cardinal, as modern audiences, for different reasons, do today. In *The Duchess of*

Malfi, the unnamed Cardinal has a lover, and this kind of hypocrisy was probably standard anti-Catholic satire at the time. Martin Orkin believes that the fact that the misogyny of the 'character of a whore' speech is voiced by the morally equivocal Cardinal 'seems strongly to argue Webster's own disparagement of dominant patriarchy'.[38] The RSC's production was not the only one to portray the Cardinal as a sexual hypocrite; Benedict Nightingale, reviewing the 1969 National production, wrote:

> John Moffatt's Cardinal exceeds the demands of text and sub-text alike; during the trial, 'he lingers over words like "whore" and "Gomorrah" and, fascinated, frustrated, can scarcely control his wandering hands... he jerks abruptly and repeatedly towards Vittoria's breasts, galvanized by their electricity.[39]

Each of these examples shows how stage interpreters have found imaginative ways of revealing the hypocrisy that fatally compromises the Cardinal's self-righteous attack on Vittoria's moral character. While her guilt is well-known to the audience, the play clearly encourages the spectators to give careful thought to the way in which the trial is conducted. The frequent direct appeals to the audience, by both Vittoria and the Cardinal, as if it were the jury at the trial, are deliberate. Equally significant is the commentary by the French and English Ambassadors ('She hath lived ill'; 'True, but the Cardinal's too bitter' [3.2.106–7]; and, a little later, 'She hath a brave spirit' [140]).

I have already shown how a number of critics have interpreted Vittoria's striving for autonomy in gendered terms. There are also very clear parallels between Vittoria and Catherine in *Basic Instinct* in this respect. Webster's audience may have interpreted Vittoria's attempt to defend herself against Monticelso's accusations as inappropriate behaviour ('She scandals our proceedings' [3.2.129]), simply by virtue of the fact that she was speaking out in public. She is denied the benefit of legal defence, and Bracciano's intervention only makes matters worse. Her only recourse is flat denial of her crimes, and an insistence on her honour. Although the audience is very well aware of Vittoria's guilt, it watches as she flatly denies the charges laid against her, insisting on an honour the audience knows to be tarnished. Alexander Dyce writes of 'that forced and practised presence of mind which the hardened criminal may bring to the place of accusation', noting Vittoria's reliance on 'the quickness of her wit' and 'the influence of her beauty',[40] weapons also used by Catherine in *Basic Instinct*'s parallel scene.

In *Basic Instinct*, Catherine waives her right to an attorney, claiming she has nothing to hide. Her defence is reliant on wit and beauty, and she wastes no time in turning the tables on her male inquisitors. Invited to extinguish her cigarette, she responds coolly, 'What are you gonna do? Charge me with smoking?', and when the direct questions begin, she turns accusation into innuendo-soaked invitation: asked whether she ever engaged in any sado-masochistic activity, she leans forward and coos, 'Just exactly what did you have in mind, Mr Correlli?' Her effect on the men is unmistakable, literally raising the temperature in the room: as the camera switches from her to the cops, Correlli is spied mopping his sweating brow, and Walker fetches himself a drink from the water cooler. If 'To be male *is* to have power', as Dollimore claims, and the subordinate (that is, women) 'can only resist this process in terms of the same language',[41] then Catherine gains and retains control in the scene, as Verhoeven notes,[42] via her willingness to be much more daring in her use of sexual innuendo than are the men, as the analysis below will show.

Intriguingly, the men begin the interrogation scene (see Figure 9.1) with working assumptions and value systems not unlike Cardinal Monticelso's. However, Catherine makes a shameless claim for the traditionally masculine privilege of sex without commitment: asked about her relationship with Johnny Boz, she replies, 'I had sex with him for about a year and a half. I liked having sex with him. I like men like that. Men who give me pleasure. He gave me a lot of pleasure.' Quizzed about drug use, she confounds expectations of denial: not only does she freely admit to cocaine abuse, without skipping a beat, she strikes

Figure 9.1 A white devil on trial: Catherine Tramell (Sharon Stone) under interrogation in *Basic Instinct* (dir. Paul Verhoeven, 1992)
Source: Screen capture.

back: 'Have you ever fucked on cocaine, Nick? It's nice.' A key accusation (since cocaine was found at the crime scene) is defused by Catherine's retaliation, enhanced by the infamous 'crotch shot' that throws the concentration of every man in the room. What is going on at this moment has been hotly debated, and there are obvious reasons why these few frames may be considered objectionable. It is possible to interpret the fetishising focus of the camera in the context of the *femme fatale* tradition, where the woman is 'overwhelmingly the compositional focus, generally centre frame and/or in the foreground, with the focus often on particular body parts, usually the legs'.[43] Catherine is, in theory, the object of the male gaze – the view of the audience is intensified and focused through the stares of Nick and the other police officers, most acutely at the moment she opens her legs. However, the voyeuristic moment can also be read as an act of subversion on Catherine/Sharon Stone's part. Verhoeven insists that the shot is 'the complete expression of her dominance'.[44] Janey Place suggests that the traditional *femmes fatales* 'control camera movement, seeming to direct the camera (and the hero's gaze, with our own) irresistibly with them as they move'.[45] Midway through the act of crossing her legs, we cut from Catherine to the stunned faces of the cops, chiefly that of her main interrogator Correlli. Catherine meets the male gaze as if with a mirror, and dazzles the men with a reflection of their own, prying eyes. Nick tries to regain the offensive, asking how she felt when her former boyfriend Manny died ('I loved him; it hurt'), and establishing that she did not feel the same about Johnny Boz's death 'because you didn't love him ... Even though you were fucking him'. Again, Catherine turns his attack against him: 'You still get the pleasure. Didn't you ever fuck anybody else while you were married, Nick?' When Walker pursues a similar moral line ('You didn't feel anything for him, you just had sex with him for your book?'), and Nick's partner Gus expresses similar distaste ('That's pretty cold, ain't it, lady?'), her response is no more apologetic.

In terms of the pleasure of the audience, the effect of Catherine's easy use of obscenities is a matter for some debate. Kate Stables, in her consideration of Bridget's frequent deployment of such language in *The Last Seduction*, suggests that they may be subversive in one respect, while at the same time pandering to the fantasies of the male auditor:

As she offers up obscenities like sweets, the terms gain an additional friction and pornographic quality from their context (since these are lower-class words enunciated be elegant upper-class females) ... these are words which rub up against and unbalance the law of the father, and disturb and titillate the male auditor.[46]

Nevertheless, Catherine's appropriation of traditionally male discourse and, crucially, the assumptions that underline that discourse, is perhaps what unsettles her interrogators most deeply. Her mimicking, or mirroring, acts may even go beyond appropriation, bringing to mind Luce Irigaray's conceptualisation of a feminine discourse that refuses the linearity and binary of dominant, masculine thought in the Western tradition. The curved mirror of the *speculum* serves not only to reflect the male gaze back at Catherine's inquisitors, but also to subvert and distort their perceptions. And if Catherine's appropriations of traditional male discourse and male assumptions about sexuality can be interpreted as bold challenges to the patriarchy, then, in its own context, Vittoria's contempt for her male accusers can be seen as equally radical:

> For your names
> Of whore and murd'ress, they proceed from you,
> As if a man should spit against the wind,
> The filth returns in 's face. (3.2.148–51)

However, Vittoria, in spite of her subversive potential, and in spite of the challenges the play as a whole offers to the hypocrisies and failings of the patriarchy, must finally be contained. Janey Place, commenting on the overall impression of the *femme fatale* in Hollywood movies of the 1940s, notes how '[I]t is not their inevitable demise we remember but rather their strong, dangerous, and above all, exciting sexuality.'[47] Just as the classic Hollywood narrative works to neutralize the *femme fatale* (either by killing her or marrying her off), the destabilising force of Vittoria must be controlled too. Having seen Vittoria established as an intensely sexual and dangerous figure, the audience also has to witness her destruction: as Janey Place writes, 'the myth of the sexually aggressive woman ... first allows sensuous expression of that idea and then destroys it.'[48] Vittoria becomes an object lesson in the dangers of unfettered female sexuality. Nearly 400 years later, the new *femme fatale*, Catherine Tramell, impersonates the masculine 'virtue' of power and control, and, notoriously, gets away with it, both in the film's narrative and, undoubtedly, in the eyes of the majority of the audience. Time and again Catherine defeats her male antagonists (which usually means Nick), in verbal combat, in sexual encounters, and elsewhere: the centrepiece sex scene between Catherine and Nick reaches its first (literal) climax with Nick dominant, but it is swiftly followed by Catherine reversing the dynamic, and tying Nick to the bed before they climax again. Her defeat of Nick in the car chase sequence is another triumph over his masculinity, and throughout the film her preternatural ability to remain at least one step ahead of Nick is a frequent source of humiliation. Indeed, Michael Douglas insisted on certain script changes to lessen the impression that he is completely under her control.

This is not to say that all the representations of power and gender relations in *Basic Instinct* are unproblematic; the scene between Nick and his former lover Beth is particularly poorly judged. It begins as a passionate and apparently consensual sex scene, and ends with Nick throwing Beth over the back of a couch and entering her from behind (Verhoeven claims whether or not it is an act of anal sex is left deliberately ambiguous). The remarks made by Verhoeven during his commentary for the DVD bring to mind the controversies surrounding *Straw Dogs*, especially his admission that the scene does indeed '[go] up and down between she wanting it and basically…perhaps…being brutalised…She's not sure if she likes it, but at least she is adventurous enough to find out if she does.'[49] What Verhoeven signally fails to comment on is the way in which Nick's act of forced anal sex reveals his own insecurities, unsettled by Catherine and in need of finding some way of reassuring himself about his own phallic power. In fact, although Nick Curran is purportedly the movie's chief protagonist, he comes across as a dislikeable character in general. Just as in *The White Devil* Bracciano betrays selfishness, cowardice lurking behind bluster, and a carnal self-centredness, so Curran is represented repeatedly as being weak, vain and sex-obsessed (shown via the scene with Beth, his voyeuristic peek at Catherine as she changes in her bedroom, and so on).

The men in *Basic Instinct* are, in general, unsympathetic, and from their first appearance at the scene of Johnny Boz's death onwards, tend to exhibit a casual misogyny that Catherine coolly challenges in the interrogation scene. The scenes with Catherine's lover, Roxy, are also controversial and tend to show Curran in a poor light: there is a facile sub-plot in which Roxy challenges Nick's attempt to claim Catherine, is 'defeated' when she apparently watches Nick's self-proclaimed 'fuck of the century' with Catherine, and attempts to kill him in an act of revenge. Catherine Tramell is a triumphant *femme fatale* who defeats all attempts to contain her. Probing the production history of *Straw Dogs*, and in particular the treatment of Susan George during filming, uncovered processes of subjugation and marginalisation analogous to the treatment of her character in the fictive world of the movie. The (occasionally revisionist) histories of the making of *Basic Instinct* are more ambivalent in these terms, and Sharon Stone has accused her director of manipulating and deceiving her in the filming of the interrogation scene, for example. On the other hand, even Michael Douglas's revisions to the film's script, in vain attempts to redress the balance of power between his character and Sharon Stone's, could not wrest control back again. Just as Catherine determines the narrative of the film, scripting it for the novel she says she is writing, so Stone eclipses Douglas and maintains a firm grip on audience expectations and fantasies, both male and female.

There are significant areas of crossover between early modern revenge tragedy and contemporary thrillers in relation to gender, power and violence. While some contemporary representations rehearse old paradigms and patterns of patriarchal control and female objectivity, drawing such parallels can also highlight provocative areas of difference, as the comparison between two 'white devils', Vittoria and Catherine Tramell, does. However, it is in the horror genre, and in particular the slasher movie, that some of the most startling examples of the intersection of gender and violence can be traced. The subject of the human body – damaged, decayed, mutilated, opened up or obliterated – is a preoccupation of revenge tragedy. It is also the *raison d'être* of much contemporary horror. As I shall argue in the next section, the body in pieces, and the body in various states of physical distress, can signify many things, but more often than not such representations are bound up tightly in the politics of gender and sexuality.

Part III
Death and the Damaged Body

10
Introduction: Vile Bodies

'And though continually we bear about us
A rotten and dead body, we delight
To hide it in rich tissue: all our fear,
Nay, all our terror, is lest our physician
Should put us in the ground, to be made sweet.'
(John Webster, *The Duchess of Malfi*, 2.1.52–6)

Specificity, transhistoricism and cultural value

Part III investigates an important common feature of both the early modern and contemporary genres, a feature that provokes more controversy, perhaps, than any other: the depiction of extreme episodes of physical violence, often presented in the most graphic terms that the different performance media allow, focusing on the exposure of the fragility and mortality of the human body via representations of the damage and destruction that can be wrought upon it. What pleasure do horror audiences derive from those things that are generally accepted as being discomfiting, unpleasant or repulsive? What was it about early modern tragedy's dedication to increasingly inventive forms of torture, bodily mutilation and murder that attracted its audiences, and seemed to inspire its writers to ever more ingenious variations on the theme? Andrew Tudor, writing about the critical reception of the horror film, identifies two contrasting strands of thought in attempts to theorise the appeal of horror that usefully cross over with the tension I have nominated as being crucial to the current study. He compares what he terms 'beast within' theories on the one hand – the idea that there is something universal in all of us, something repressed and bestial, which takes pleasure in transgressive representations – with particularising

167

approaches on the other, views positing that the appeal of horror is understood 'to be a product of the interaction between specific textual features and distinct social circumstances'.[1] To take just one illustrative example of cultural specificity, an overview of the history of the horror film reveals certain trends that reflect the changing preoccupations of Western society: advances in science, especially in terms of nuclear technology, lie behind the sudden rise of the monster movies of the 1950s such as *The Beast from 20,000 Fathoms* (1953), *Them* (1954), *Godzilla* (1956), *Attack of the Crab Monsters* (1957) and *The Fly* (1958), all of which feature monsters created via accidents with atomic weapons, tests or inventions. The alien/UFO films of the same era are frequently read as sublimations of Cold War paranoia: listing *The Thing* (1951), *Red Planet Mars* (1952), *It Came from Outer Space* (1953), and *Invasion of the Body Snatchers* (1956) only scratches the surface of this particular trend. In the 1980s, the revival of the vampire genre, and the way in which conventions were retooled by screenwriters and directors, has been linked to the emergence of AIDS/HIV, first discovered in 1981, but only becoming common knowledge in the West in the second half of the decade: *The Lost Boys* (1987), *Near Dark* (1987), *Bram Stoker's Dracula* (1992) and *Interview with the Vampire* (1994).

The historical specificity of these, and many other, trends, is relatively easily identified. At the same time, there is a good deal of evidence to suggest that there is something trans-historical about the fascination with body horror, which has reanimated itself periodically across the centuries. The early modern theatre was determined to stage the violence that had, in the Greek and Roman models provided by Sophocles, Seneca and others, been committed off-stage and only reported to the audience (admittedly, in Seneca's case especially, with bloody, detailed descriptions of the acts and their consequences). A few centuries after the Elizabethans, the Grand Guignol theatre in Paris scandalised audiences for over sixty years with its depictions of poisonings, stabbings, mutilation, necrophilia, child-killing and worse. For a long time, it seemed to be a peculiarly Parisian phenomenon: on tour, the shows would often fall foul of censors in other countries. However, the influence of this melodramatic, violent and grotesque genre on both early expressionist film and the longer history of the horror film is unquestionable. The Grand Guignol's last director, Charles Nonon, believed that the decline of the theatre was connected with the Western worldwide culture shift following the revelation of the Nazi Holocaust: 'We could never compete with Buchenwald,' he claimed. 'Before the war, everyone believed that what happened on stage was purely imaginary;

now we know that these things – and worse – are possible.'[2] However, the fact that cinema very quickly took up the challenge, working with increasingly extreme, graphic violence in a medium more conducive to realistic representation, suggests that audiences never really lost their appetite for such spectacles, and that, even after staring into the hollow eyes of concentration camp survivors, there has always been space for ever more extravagant imaginary terrors.

There are two specific areas that this chapter does *not* seek to address: first, what I would term, loosely, 'extreme' cinema; and, second, debates about the effects of violence in the media. The focus of the whole study has been mainstream film, and plays that we know formed part of the common repertoire of the public playhouses and private theatres of the Elizabethan and Jacobean periods. When one begins to consider representations of graphic violence in contemporary media, the varied, shadowy forms of extreme cinema inevitably loom large: so-called 'mondo cinema', including films purportedly including actual footage of rail and air disasters, suicides and autopsies, such as *Faces of Death* (1978) and *Autopsy* (1973) comes into this category, as do most of the Italian horror-thrillers made by writer-directors such as Dario Argento, Lucio Fulci and Mario Bava. Also included here are the zombie movies of the 1970s, epitomised by George A. Romero's *Dead* trilogy[3] and the more extreme *Zombie Flesh Eaters* (1979, aka *Zombie* or *Zombi 2*) and *Return of the Living Dead* (1985), alongside cannibal movies, including Ruggero Deodato's *Cannibal* (1976) and *Cannibal Holocaust* (1979), and Umberto Lenzi's *Cannibal Ferox* (1980). Even the more mainstream efforts among them, such as George A. Romero's zombie trilogy, remain largely in the domain of cult viewing, inspiring small, fanatical followings (with low-circulation fanzines gradually being superceded by websites). While the remake of *Dawn of the Dead* (2004) was a surprise box office hit (making almost US$60 million in its first month in the USA alone), the bloodier original has earned its keep over a longer period, largely via home video release. More highbrow films that deal in explicit violence, what we might designate 'art-house' films, are given a little more detailed attention (in the UK, two notable examples are the controversial French films *Baise Moi* [2000] and *Irreversible* [2002], neither of which, I would contest, are as clever as they think they are). However, the discussion remains centred on mainstream popular culture, and in particular on popular entries into the horror genre since the 1970s. In terms of debates about media violence affecting the understanding, attitudes and even the behaviour of its viewers, it is relevant to the extent that I am concerned with the ways popular texts interact with their social and political contexts; however, any discussion in this study is, of necessity, tangential and speculative, since such a vast, deeply researched and interdisciplinary field cannot be addressed in any comprehensive way here.

Carol Clover notes that 'all that lies between the visible, knowable outside of the body and its secret insides is one thin membrane, protected only by a collective taboo against its violation'.[4] The painfully sensitive awareness of the fragility of the body emerges in the poetry of the early modern period (it is very close to the surface in the works of John Donne), and, repeatedly, within the genre of revenge tragedy. 'What's this flesh?' asks Bosola in *The Duchess of Malfi*; 'A little curded milk, fantastical puff-paste; our bodies are weaker than those paper prisons boys use to keep flies in' (4.2.120–22). Time and again in these plays, the body is violated: mutilated, punctured, caused to bleed. Characters have limbs and other body parts (often the tongue) removed at the drop of a hat – Hieronimo bites his own tongue out to ensure that torture will yield no secrets in *The Spanish Tragedy* (4.4.191); in Shakespeare's *Titus Andronicus*, Lavinia, Titus's daughter, is raped, has her tongue cut out and her hands cut off (2.3). Later, Titus's enemy, Tamora, is served her own sons baked in a pie (5.3.59–61). Probably drawing on the same Greek legend as Shakespeare did for *Titus*, Marston depicts in *Antonio's Revenge* (1600) the revenger murdering Julio, the young son of the villain, Piero, and serving up the boy's limbs at a banquet. Piero is bound, his tongue is plucked out, and he is presented with a dish *'containing Julio's limbs'*, according to Keith Sturgess's interpolated stage direction.[5] Piero's response is contained in one of the eeriest and most moving of all original early modern stage directions: *'Piero seems to condole his son'* (5.3.81 s.d.). Ever more ingenious deaths are designed, varied and imaginative in their planning and execution: the Duchess of Malfi is garroted (4.2.229); in the same play, another character kisses a poisoned bible (5.2.284). In *The White Devil*, Isabella kisses a portrait of her husband that has been coated with poison (2.2.23), while Bracciano has a corrosive poison spread on the inside of his helmet which, eating away at his skull, sends him mad (5.3); he dies at the hands of his enemies, who have disguised themselves as monks come to offer him comfort in his final hours (V.iii.173). In *The Tragedy of Hoffman* (1602), Hoffman dies when a white-hot iron crown is placed on his head. Vindice and Hippolito's acts of violence against the Duke are brutal and graphically represented in both word and deed (see pp. 193–4). Close family ties, as we might expect, provide the most profound, wounding shocks. In *'Tis Pity She's a Whore*, Annabella, the central female character, has her heart cut out by her incestuous brother and it is presented to her husband at a banquet celebrating his birthday (5.6.31–34). 'Considering the way narrative poems about rape and popular stage plays featuring dismemberment and gory death proliferated in the early modern period,' writes Cynthia Marshall, 'it seems obvious that early modern codes of textual pleasure depended upon a significant charge of violence.'[6]

Contemporary horror's fascination with bodily destruction and death is a field too immense to explore in any depth, and an overview, followed by a brief specific, recent example must suffice. There is, of course, a danger of homogenising horror, when in fact the genre is broad enough to encompass a very wide range of different films, with its conventions permeating genres as diverse as the thriller (*Silence of the Lambs* [1991]), science-fiction (the *Alien* series [1979–97], *Event Horizon* [1997]), and comedy (mainly via parodies such as the *Scary Movie* franchise [2000–3]). However, it is possible to narrow the focus by restricting our attention to those films where graphically violent horror, in a real-life (as opposed to a supernatural) context, is central. Herschell Gordon Lewis is often credited with launching this breed of cinematic horror with the low budget shocker *Blood Feast* (1963). Although the production values were low, the screenplay and acting laughable, Lewis's eagerness to show, and to linger over, the (preferably female) bloodied and mutilated body, tapped into a nerve that had been left almost completely untouched since the beginning of motion pictures. As Lewis himself said, a 'combination of pretty girls and crazy violence makes for good box office',[7] and it is certainly true to say that that precise combination has served many film-makers well since Lewis's time: *Halloween*, for example, was made on a budget of US$325,000 and went on to gross US$47 million in the USA alone. The hyper-violent horror film launched offshoot sub-genres such as the zombie and cannibal movies and other extreme forms mentioned above, but in the Hollywood mainstream it was the teen slasher that carried the torch, and the genre exploded, creatively and commercially, in the early 1980s. John Carpenter created the serial killer Michael Myers for *Halloween* (1978), which spawned seven sequels between 1981 and 2002. Sean Cunningham's *Friday the 13th* followed soon afterwards (1980), with its psychotic killer, Jason Voorhees, clocking up ten sequels between 1981 and 2003. In 1985, Wes Craven introduced child-killer Freddy Kruger to the movie-going public in *A Nightmare on Elm Street*, and while Craven quickly dissociated himself from the franchise, it too had spawned four sequels by 1989, before moving to television for the

Freddy's Nightmares show. It resurfaced as an interesting precursor of the postmodern horror of *Scream* when Craven reappropriated Kruger for *Wes Craven's New Nightmare* (1994).

After a fallow, formulaic period that saw the slasher movie playing to shrinking audiences, retaining a hold only in the home video market, the genre experienced a mainstream revival in the 1990s and 2000s that owed a great debt to the success of Wes Craven's *Scream* series (1996, 1997, 2000). However, the post-*Scream* slashers picked up their own momentum as the movement re-gathered pace. Ingenious deaths had been a feature of the first generation of the sub-genre, the most frequently cited being the death of Kevin Bacon's character, Jack, in *Friday the 13th*: as he lies on a bed, post coital, smoking a joint, an arrow passes from beneath through the mattress and into the back of his neck, emerging through his throat with a shockingly profuse spurt of blood. Nevertheless, none of the earlier films can match the very brutal, graphic, bloody and imaginative deaths that characterise more recent entries in the genre. The saga of slasher franchises perhaps reached its logical endpoint, and low point, in the all-star death match *Freddy vs. Jason* (2003), in which the two kings of mass murder finally sacrificed all credibility upon the box office counter. The movie was marketed on the showdown between Freddy and Jason, as everything from the poster to the Las Vegas wrestling-bout-style press conference indicated. The teen slayings in reality act only as a prelude to the battle between the two super-villains, which resembles more closely the kind of super-hero movies that had been box-office hits at around the same time,[8] and other spectacular combat films such as the three *Matrix* instalments (1999, 2003), than it does a horror film.

Scream is superior to most of the films that followed in its wake, chiefly because of its witty script, its effortless self-referentiality, and Wes Craven's well-honed skill in setting up and editing suspense and shock sequences. The focus on what Paul Wells neatly encapsulates as 'the fear of death, the multiple ways in which it can occur, and the untimely nature of its occurrence'[9] has given these films a new lease of life. Wells suggests that this theme 'makes the horror genre continually relevant', since 'societies are constantly having to address the things which threaten the maintenance of life and its defining practices'.[10] In this respect, they work in a way analogous to the *memento mori* tradition that many critics have noted as an integral part of the revenge tragedy genre, with a crucial distinction: in the early modern period, the reminder of death had always been intended as a warning to mortals that life was short, death might come at any moment and, unless one's soul was in a state of readiness, hell was a terrifyingly real inevitability. In a post-Christian age (even while acknowledging that, in the USA at least, Christianity remains central to the culture), as the discussion of *Se7en* and *Doctor Faustus* suggested in the Introduction to this book, such certainties are absent, triggering a different set of fears about death.

The 2000 film *Final Destination* is a good example of the contemporary horror film,[11] since it is a movie that installs this precise notion (fear of death, and its untimely and unpredictable nature) as its very *raison d'être*, and unashamedly plays repeated riffs on it: in *Final Destination*, the traditional serial killer is replaced by the unseen figure of Death itself 'stalking' its victims. The movie begins with a horrific plane crash that kills a group of high school students and their teacher – except that the crash turns out to have been a premonition experienced by one of the teenagers, Alex (Devon Sawa), as he daydreams while awaiting take-off. Panicking, he, a few friends caught in the fracas, and one of the teachers, are bundled off the flight. While they stand in the airport lounge arguing, they see the plane carrying the rest of the party explode in mid-air. As the survivors struggle to come to terms with the deaths of their friends and the freak nature of their own survival, one by one, they begin to die in unlikely circumstances. Gradually, Alex, haunted by barely intelligible premonitions of each of the deaths that follow, figures out that Death has come to reclaim the survivors, and is killing each of them in the order in which they would have died if his first vision of the plane crash had come true, and all of them had died that night. The depiction of these deaths follows a particular pattern, establishing each of the victims in turn as Death's quarry, hunted down often with PoV shots of the imaginary stalker (a standard feature of the slasher movie, and a good example of the way in which the most recent generation of teen horror takes advantage of the knowledge of conventions it shares with its audience). In one sequence, the teacher who survived the plane crash (Valerie Lewton, played by Kristen Cloke) pours a hot drink, then throws it away and fills the mug with vodka from the icebox. The mug cracks, and we see the liquid drop into the monitor of her computer as she leans over to switch it on. She turns away and when she turns back, smoke is rising from the machine. As she steps in to investigate, it explodes, and a flying shard of glass from the screen embeds itself in her throat. The rest of the scene plays out in similar fashion, as she tracks back to the kitchen where she has already laid the seeds for her own destruction, like a booby-trapped stage set, including a gas stove, the open vodka bottle, and a tea-towel discarded over a block of large, sharp kitchen knives. Each item falls into place in a series of close-up insert shots, like tiny gears locking into motion. By contrast, the death of Terry (Amanda Detmer) is shocking because it is so sudden, and because it is so physically devastating. Stepping out into the street without looking, she is hit at speed by a bus, her body disintegrating in a smash and splatter of red that sprays her horrified friends left on the sidewalk.

The purpose of the discussion that follows is to consider the preoccupation with the damaged and destroyed human body that seems to be shared between early modern tragedy and mainstream horror films of the past thirty years, with an emphasis on the body horror cinema of the past decade. It is my contention that the fascination with body horror in the early modern and contemporary contexts is rooted in different aspects of the cultures, but that there are deeper connections that might cause us to reappraise the value of trans-historical approaches. The theme of untimely, unpredictable and inevitable death has universal resonance, but can also be read in specific terms, in view of the fact that in contemporary, affluent Western society we have become 'more aware of risks...less convinced by the systems of expertise that surround us and the institutions that seek to regulate our lives', in a world where 'anxiety and fear have become ubiquitous'.[12] Nevertheless, Terry Eagleton suggests:

> It is because of the body...that we can speak of morality as universal. The material body is what we share most significantly with the whole of the rest of our species, extended both in time and space. Of course it is true that our needs, desires and sufferings are always culturally specific. But our material bodies are such that they are, indeed must be, in principle capable of feeling compassion for any others of their kind.[13]

If Eagleton is right that our material bodies comprise the fundamental element that we share in common with all cultures, synchronically and diachronically, then there may well be aspects of the appeal of body horror that cannot, or should not be, explicable in specific, cultural terms. Furthermore, there are distinct parallels in the critical fortunes of the genres – revenge tragedy and contemporary horror – which seem to signal a reluctance on the part of the dominant ideology to engage with explorations of the taboo of bodily destruction: both revenge tragedy and contemporary horror have in the past been dismissed in cultural terms via labels such as 'exploitative' and 'formulaic'. What we see is a kind of 'pull–push' effect in the reception of these texts: while they hold an undeniable fascination for their audiences, at the same time, a society built on a principle of self-preservation will inevitably be inclined to reject artworks that threaten those principles. 'Dead bodies are indecent,' writes Terry Eagleton; 'they proclaim with embarrassing candour the secret of all matter, that it has no obvious relation to meaning.'[14] Robert Watson suggests that 'Murder and incest are sensational precisely because they are important; they are primal violations of human bodies and of the social order established to protect them', and he speculates that, if we do find pleasure in watching the deaths, then it has to do with 'the Freudian relief of confronting the forbidden, here safely encased within the frame of artistic ritual and convention'.[15]

Critical consensus will often attempt to reject, and class as being aesthetically worthless, cultural artefacts that confront taboos. Those works that do manage to confront and overcome such prejudice are, almost without exception, valorised by being designated as 'high culture' and, for a number of reasons, considered 'safer' because of such a designation: the logic, not always fully articulated, is that art-house audiences are more capable, intellectually and morally, of dealing with such violations of what is understood to be acceptable in a culture. The revenge tragedy genre's taste for episodes of extreme violence has in the past earned it the casual and dismissive labels 'decadent', 'exploitative' and 'gratuitous'. A number of critics have noted a historical trend in the genre to develop ever more sensational and curious innovations in the representation of such acts of violence, and Fredson Bowers set a kind of precedent when he interpreted it as a sign of the collapse of the tradition, a turn towards decadence:

> The drift towards sensationalism and artificiality in the Jacobean age inevitably led audiences to demand more variety with less high seriousness. The earlier tragedy had had its share of horrible incident but had used it as background material, as a testing ground for the human spirit. The violence of these new plays is portrayed for its own sake...The sound and fury is chiefly on the surface and characterization weakens and grows conventional, since it was sufficient for the dramatist...merely to portray types which would be recognizable.[16]

At a time when the Shakespearean era was identified in theatrical terms as the golden age of English drama, and in literary terms as the distillation of the finest insights into the human condition, revenge tragedies were embarrassing blemishes that were best ignored. John

Webster, for example, was dismissed by George Bernard Shaw as 'Tussaud Laureate', and in the 1940s and 1950s, influential critics such as Ian Jack and L. G. Salingar regularly described his work as 'decadent'. According to Jack, Webster has 'no deeper purpose than to make our flesh creep', and Salingar, while conceding that Webster is 'sophisticated', qualifies his judgement by adding that 'his sophistication belongs to decadence', remarking how in the plays 'every sensation is inflamed, every emotion becomes an orgy'.[17] Muriel Bradbrook named one chapter in her *Themes and Conventions of Elizabethan Tragedy* 'The Decadence', and her analysis is full of references to the 'coarsening of the fibre'[18] of the earlier, supposedly purer, drama. She also remarks how '[i]t is not surprising therefore to find a taste for the more extraordinary sexual themes (rape, impotence, incest) combined with a blurring of the aesthetic difference between tragedy and comedy and the moral distinction between right and wrong'.[19] Such critical consensus, of course, had an impact upon one of Shakespeare's own revenge tragedies: while the relatively restrained *Hamlet* remained central to the canon, his *Titus Andronicus* was seen as an embarrassment by many of its editors. The consensus in the eighteenth century was that it must have been the work of another writer. When *Titus* is rehabilitated, as in Jonathan Bate's Arden edition (third series, 1995), this is achieved by clawing back its high cultural status: Bate argues that the play has been misjudged by dismissive critics, and that it is in fact 'one of the dramatist's most inventive plays, a complex and self-conscious improvisation upon classical sources'.[20]

If we were to read the quotation above from Bowers again, simply removing the words 'earlier tragedy' and 'plays' and substituting 'earlier horror' and 'films', the quotation could be read as a fairly familiar critique of the horror film since the 1970s. Similarly, Bradbrook's objection to an emphasis on sex, and the blurring of the boundaries of comedy and tragedy, and right and wrong, are accusations regularly levelled at the contemporary horror film. It has also been ignored until recently by most academic critics, and more often than not also dismissed by most mainstream cinema critics, because of its allegedly formulaic nature. Such criticism lays the genre open to dismissal on Frankfurt-School-like terms: horror is easy to consume because it conforms to audience expectations and therefore breeds passivity in its audiences. Even a critic like James B. Twitchell, who has offered several in-depth studies of horror film and fiction, complains about what he perceives as a decline in the genre: 'Whatever "art" the myths once had has been replaced by "craft",' he writes, 'and craft has been dominated by gory special effects.'[21] It is what Paul Wells, after George Ritzer, refers to as the 'McDonaldisation of horror',[22] with the fundamental principles of efficiency and predictability. None of these critiques, it seems, is prepared to offer any kind of explanation for the appeal of the genre, beyond the idea of 'giving the audience what it thinks it wants'. The discussion that follows will attempt to draw out the key elements of the culture, both early modern and contemporary, that might help us to understand why spectacles of violent death have an enduring fascination for audiences, at different points in history.

11
Spectacles of Death

The anatomist, the playhouse and the technology of violence

One way to understand the preoccupation with explicit, and often heavily stylised, self-consciously theatrical representations of violence in the early modern period is to see it in the context of a growing interest in the structure of the human body that has, in recent years, been recognised as a significant development in Western culture at that time. The second half of the sixteenth century witnessed the sudden, startling rise to prominence of the anatomist. Developments in dissection practices in the sixteenth and seventeenth centuries, and a widening interest in the anatomists' discoveries, is illustrated by the popularity of texts such as *De Humani Corporis Fabrica* (Vesalius, 1543), *De Dissectione* (Charles Estienne, 1545), *Historia de la Composicion del Cuerpo Humano* (Valverde, 1556), *De conceptu et generatione hominis* (Jacob Rüff, 1580) and *De Formato Foeto* (Spigelius, 1627), which both revolutionised the understanding of the human body and began to reach beyond the members of a nascent medical profession, unravelling the secrets of the human body for the literate population. Furthermore, evidence suggests that the study of anatomy also took on the status of entertainment for a paying public, with crowds flocking to see demonstrations in cities such as Bologna, Padua, Paris, Leiden, Amsterdam and London. The engraving of the Leiden Anatomy theatre (see Figure 11.1) shows how religion and science still co-existed in this pre-Enlightenment setting. Installed around the space are animal skeletons provided for comparative anatomy, as well as the mounted figure symbolising the vanity of human glory and the skeletal forms of Adam and Eve at the apple tree in the foreground, raising the provocative issue of knowledge that may be forbidden. However, Jonathan Sawday argues that the

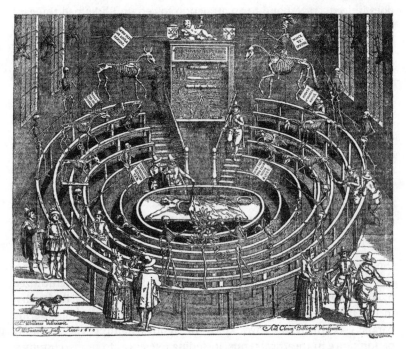

Figure 11.1 The anatomist as performer: anatomy hall of the University in Leiden; copper engraving (1610) by Willem Sdwanenburgh (1581/2–1612) after a drawing by Jan Cornelisz van't Woudt, known as Woudanus (c. 1570–1615)
Source: Photo from akg-images.

developments in the study of anatomy undermined the Western tradition that understood the body to be invested with great spiritual significance. The highly organised structure of the body seemed to endorse the notion of a hierarchical universe ordered by the divine hand, 'the harmony between one part of creation and another…the analogical comparison and reductions of all things', in the words of Nicholas Culpepper, defending the old order of understanding in a work published as late as 1654.[1] In the anatomy theatre, it seems, an ideological shift was taking place, and although it would take fifty years or so for the intellectual climate to change dramatically, the origins of a new rationalism was already emerging from the discoveries of the anatomists. 'The inwardly directed gaze traversed not simply regions of doubt,' writes Sawday, 'but transformed the body into the *locus* of all doubt'.[2] If, as Philipe Ariès suggests, the 'fashionable success of anatomy' does indeed 'correspond to an attraction to certain ill-defined things at the outer limits of life and death, sexuality and pain', then it is possible to see an analogous attraction in our own culture's determination to explore such limits.[3]

Even more striking is the way in which the anatomy theatre resembles the public playhouses of the time (Inigo Jones, a notable architect and designer of more than one London playhouse, designed a theatre for the London Company of Barber Surgeons in 1636). A second engraving of the Leiden anatomy theatre (included in Jonathan Sawday's *The Body Emblazoned*) shows the stalls packed with eager spectators, while the anatomist delivers his lecture, one hand gesturing towards his lectern and the other on his anatomical subject. This engraving emphasises the *memento mori* aspects of the theatre's layout, with the skeletal figures and their banners looming large and impassive over the citizens in the audience, wrapped in cloaks and hats, listening and watching intently. Kate Cregan presses the connection between playhouse and anatomy theatre even further, referring to 'a raised central area upon which a formalized scene was enacted on the bodies of the subjects scrutinized by an audience prepared to be confronted by a gory spectacle, familiar in the Jacobean playhouses'.[4] She goes on to draw other fascinating parallels between the two kinds of venue, framing the anatomy performance in theatrical terms, including references to props, costumes, scripts and stage areas.[5] Certainly, in some places, the public dissections became major events, accompanied by carnival-like processions, music and feasting.

The link between the practice of the early modern anatomists and the punishment and execution of criminals is well known: various universities and societies were granted the corpses of executed criminals for medical purposes. When the Barber Surgeons of London formed in 1540, for example, Henry VIII granted them the use of the bodies of four executed criminals each year for the purposes of anatomical study.[6] Both Kate Cregan and Jonathan Sawday invest a good deal of significance in these facts, and close examination of these paintings and other representations of anatomy practices at the time, and in the decades following, reveals that the connections have intriguing ramifications. Rembrandt's famous *The Anatomy Lesson of Dr. Nicolaas Tulp* depicts the dissection of the body of a petty thief, Aris Kindt. The body is on display, and Dr Tulp performs his public lecture over this exposed body. Francis Barker suggests the fact that the anatomy lesson begins with a dissection of the arm and hand – the criminal's tools – is instructive.[7] The punishment of the criminal does not end with a hanging, but continues with this public stripping away and breaking down of the body. The punishment devised is seen as an apt one (the dissection of the instrument of the crime); furthermore, by refusing to allow the criminal the dignity of immediate burial, the public shaming continues even beyond death. Webster's *The White Devil* makes a direct reference to the anatomists. In his attack on Vittoria during the arraignment scene, Cardinal Monticelso talks of bodies removed from the gallows and worked on by surgeons – 'to teach man wherein he is imperfect' (3.2.98). The nakedness of death is dramatised by the gradual stripping away of the layers of skin to expose the signs of death and corruption beneath. The associations are obvious: the body fails and dies, and the signs of corruption are discovered by the anatomist; similarly, the soul is corrupted, and the signs of sin can be revealed by a similar process of spiritual anatomy.

A number of plays from this period feature bodies put on display for other characters, as well as for the audience, and while some literary critics have related these moments to the execution scaffold (with interesting, Foucauldian implications in terms of displays of power),[8] connections with the anatomy theatres in the cultural consciousness is equally likely and enlightening. In Henry Chettle's little-read *The Tragedy of Hoffman*, the play opens with the hero drawing back a curtain to reveal a body, rescued from the gallows and hung up for display – the body of his father. In seeking his revenge, in true eye for eye (or skin for skin) fashion, Hoffman kills Otho and strips his bones to hang this second 'anatomy' next to that of his father.[9] In Kyd's *The Spanish Tragedy*, Hieronimo's son, Horatio, is murdered and his body hung in the arbor – graphically illustrated in a famous woodcut which may reveal something about early modern staging practices in terms of audience expectations of realism. In *The Duchess of Malfi*, Ferdinand first gives his sister a dead hand, supposedly her husband's, and proceeds to present her with the bodies of her family: '*Here is discovered, behind a traverse, the figures of Antonio and his children, appearing as if they were dead*' (4.1.55 s.d.).[10]

The technology involved in the representation of stage violence is an area that has been relatively neglected, partly, no doubt, because of the paucity and ambiguity of evidence about early modern stage practices. It should not surprise us, however, if members of an early modern London audience, many of whom would have been familiar with the spectacle of executions at Tyburn, had demanded a level of realism in the theatre, in the depiction of woundings and death in its myriad forms. Among the more monied sections of the audience, there may well have been an increasing interest in, and knowledge of, the dissected, opened human body. Furthermore, it is a commonplace that early modern citizens would have had much more of an everyday familiarity with death, disease and mutilation than most of us have today in the West. It is believed that, as far back as medieval times, drama included graphic depictions of violence: J. D. Martinez cites the example of *The Death of Herod* in the fifteenth-century collection *Ludus Coventriae*, which apparently included 'a detailed portrayal of the Massacre of the Innocents, complete with blood effects and dismembered bodies'.[11] Jean MacIntyre and Garrett P. J. Epp cite a stage direction in the roughly contemporaneous *Chester Last Judgement* which instructs that blood should flow visibly from the wound in Christ's side.[12] In the Elizabethan period, we know that Philip Henslowe had a severed head listed amongst his props, and it is generally agreed that concealed animal bladders were often used as blood-packs for sword-fights and stabbings. Andrew Gurr refers to the book-holder's instructions for *Battle of Alcazar* (c.1592), which included ' "3 violls of blood & a sheeps gather", that is, a bladder holding liver, heart and lungs'.[13] Colleen Kelly refers to the practice of swordplay in tournaments, masques, and the fact that '[i]t was a fashionable pastime to watch expert swordsmen test and prove their sword skill'. She concludes that 'exposure to such a variety of functional and theatrical sword events created an audience capable of brutally judging a "staged" fight'.[14]

Andrew Gurr also includes in his book *The Shakespearean Stage 1574–1642* a woodcut depicting a device for displaying decapitated bodies, and speculates that it 'may resemble the kind of device used to display decapitated bodies on stage'.[15] It is reproduced here as Figure 11.2. Alan Dessen cites examples of beheadings in *Apius and Virginia*, *The Virgin Martyr* and *Sir John van Olden Barnavelt*.[16] While stage props were often used figuratively (again, Henslowe's diaries tell us that they included a hell's mouth and numerous animal heads and skins, presumably for actors to depict wild beasts), it is also safe to assume that at least some of the death scenes were staged with a careful eye on realism and, possibly, with ambitions to outdo rival companies and previous productions. Other stage directions that startle in this respect include the flaying of the judge Sisamnes' skin in *Cambyses* (c.1560) (the stage direction in the fifth scene calls for 'a false skin' to achieve the effect),[17] the corrosive poison on Bracciano's helmet in *The White Devil* (5.3), as well as the various amputations already mentioned. It is likely that scenes such as the garrotting of the Duchess of Malfi would have been performed with a similar commitment to realism; it would seem to be the natural climax to a scene that is excruciatingly protracted in terms of the Duchess's

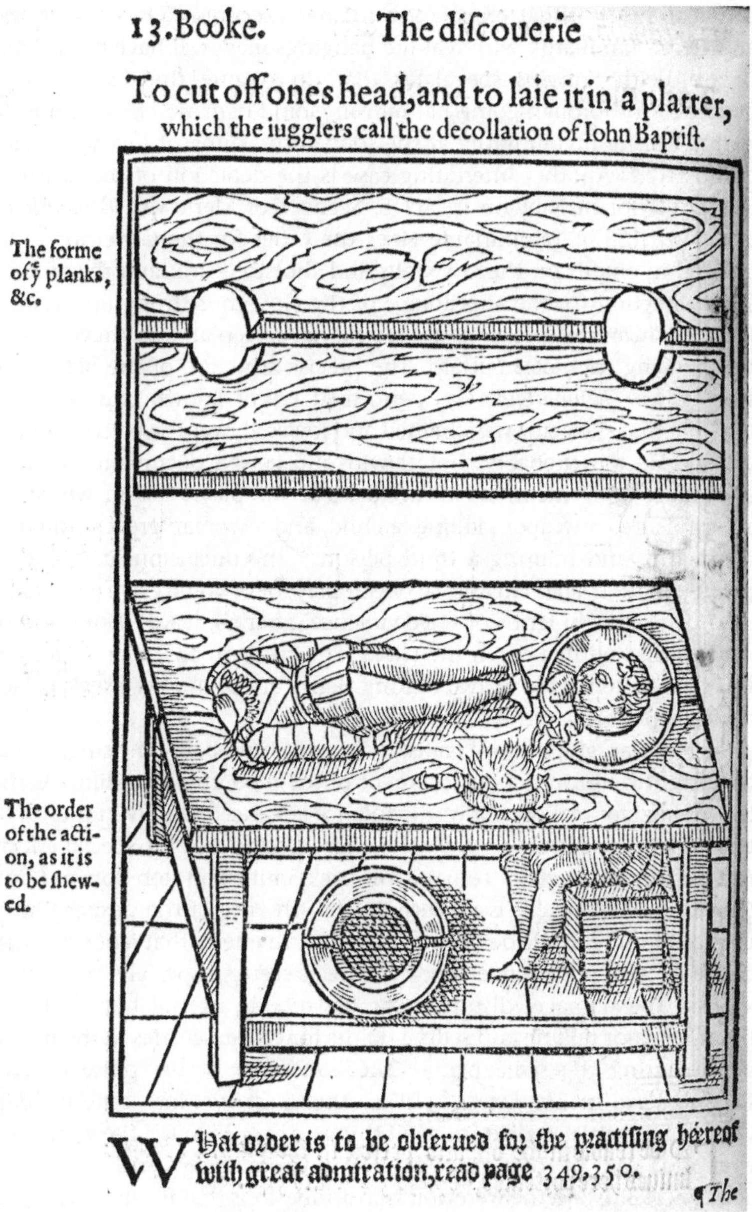

13.Booke. The diſcouerie

To cut off ones head, and to laie it in a platter, which the iugglers call the decollation of Iohn Baptiſt.

The forme of ye planks, &c.

The order of the acti-on, as it is to be ſhew-ed.

What order is to be obſerued for the practiſing hereof with great admiration, read page 349, 350.

¶The

Figure 11.2 The technology of stage violence: late-sixteenth-century woodcut of device for displaying the illusion of the decapitated body. From Reginald Scot, *Discoverie of Witchcraft* (1584); and described by Scot as 'a juggler's trick for deceiving the ignorant'

Source: By permission of the British Library.

physical and spiritual preparation for her execution. Once again, the audience's familiarity with real-life hangings may well have been significant: Keith Sturgess speculates that, in staging the death of the Duchess, 'a thorough-going naturalism would demand choking noises, hands tearing involuntarily at the rope, a thrashing of limbs, the face contorted'.[18] Another interesting case is the depiction of the death of the Governor of Babylon in Act 5, Scene 1 of Marlowe's *Tamburlaine Part Two* (1587): Tamburlaine gives the order for the Governor to be hanged in chains on the city walls and shot to death, and the editor's stage direction for the appearance of the Governor strung up uses the term '*is discovered*', presuming it would have been an effect revealed by the drawing back of a curtain. The precise structure of the playhouse stage where *Tamburlaine* was performed is not known, but it is also possible that the actor was chained and lowered over the balcony of the gallery. He was probably shot at with muskets; a document dated 16 November 1587 mentions an accident at the playhouse in which an actor misfired a weapon, killing 'a child, and a woman great with child forthwith', and injuring a third person.[19] In conclusion, it is safe to assume that Elizabethan and Jacobean playgoers would have expected a level of realism in terms of stage violence: after all, it was dedication to realism that burned down the Globe Theatre in 1613, when a cannon was fired to signal the arrival of King Henry at Cardinal Wolsey's palace during a performance of *Henry VIII*.

Spectacular, graphic and realistic violence is probably the single most important factor in the development of the modern horror film. As the technology for realistic shows of violence advanced rapidly in the 1970s and 1980s, personality cults sprang up around certain special-effects make-up artists such as Tom Savini, Dick Smith and Rob Bottin. Carol Clover notes that, '[i]t is no surprise that the rise of the slasher film is concomitant with the development of special effects that let us see with our own eyes the "opened" body'.[20] Effects scenes, especially those built around the damage, distortion or destruction of the human body, became major talking and selling points for certain entries in the horror genre during the same period: the 360° turn of the possessed girl Regan's head in *The Exorcist* (1973); the chest-bursting scene in *Alien* (1979), recently parodied in, of all things, *Shrek 2* (2004); the exploding eyes and heads of *Scanners* (1981); David Cronenberg's grisly remake of *The Fly* (1986); and the werewolf transformations that formed their own sub-genre at this time – *The Howling* and *An American Werewolf in London* (both 1981) and *The Company of Wolves* (1984) being good early examples. The horror–political satire *Society* (1989), which climaxes in a bizarre orgy during which bodies merge and turn inside out is another startling instance, and in *The Thing* (1982), which won an Oscar for its special effects, there is a nicely judged meta-cinematic moment when a severed human head sprouts spider's legs and skitters away while one character looks on incredulously, voicing the sentiments of the audience with a flabbergasted, 'You've got to be fucking kidding me.' Meanwhile, the aforementioned zombie sub-genre put explosive special effects at the centre of its creative process.

The popularity of the slasher movie encouraged further innovation in the graphic depiction of grisly deaths. *Friday the 13th* serves as a useful example of the increasing concentration on inventiveness in this respect: the original (1980) begins fairly mundanely (knives, axes, arrows), but the first sequel (1982) is more adventurous (ice pick, hammer, machete, spear), and after that, the writers and directors begin to stretch the capabilities of the special-effects departments much further: Part 3 (1982) featured death by knitting needle, pitchfork (in the neck and stomach on two different victims), meat cleaver, a spear through the eye, and electrocution, while one of the final victims has his head squeezed until an eye pops out and another, the pregnant Debbie, is knifed from beneath a hammock, in a clear case of self-reflexivity, recalling Jack's death in the first part. By the time the series reaches *Jason X* (2002), which pitches the anti-hero, via cryogenic freezing, into the future and into outer space, a whole new world of destruction is opened up to the filmmakers, their ingenuity epitomised by the death of Adrienne, whose face is frozen in liquid nitrogen until it is solid and brittle before being smashed to splinters on a counter.

In the *Nightmare on Elm Street* series, transposing the slasher into a semi-fantastic context (Freddy Kruger visits the teenagers while they sleep and kills them in their dreams) allowed the filmmakers to combine the realism of slasher violence with the kind of monstrous effects usually reserved for supernatural or science fiction horror. In *Dream Warriors*, for example, the third instalment in the franchise (1987), one of Freddy's victims has his veins pulled from beneath his skin and used as marionette strings to guide him out of the window of an abandoned building, while another, a recovering drug addict, is repeatedly punctured by multiple syringes and has her body drained of its blood. Spectacular on-screen deaths have become centrepieces of the genre in recent years. *Freddy vs. Jason* features the conventional set-up of the four teenagers alone in a house, with a familiar atmosphere of booze, drugs and sex. The mean-spirited, selfish, sexist Trey and his girlfriend Gibb retire upstairs to make love. When Gibb goes into the bathroom for a shower, Trey falls victim to Jason: stabbed through the back as he lies in bed (presumably another echo of Jack's death in the first *Friday the 13th* film), he is then virtually folded in half, the wrong way, as Jason snaps the bed-frame together. The slayings at the rave, one of the film's key scenes, include a crushed skull and a head turned through 180°, as well as many brutal cuts with the machete (cueing spectacular sprays and gushes of blood) and a double impalement: as Gibb lies unconscious at the party, she is mounted by an intoxicated party-goer, before they are simultaneously skewered by Jason. In the hospital, Freeburg (possessed by Freddy Krueger) is sliced in two at the waist by Jason, his torso sliding and toppling away off his hips. This particular effect – the literal 'slicing' of the body – was very much in vogue in the early years of the new millennium. *Resident Evil* (2002) featured a group of soldiers trapped in a corridor and being picked off one by one as a laser cuts through them from different angles. As the last man left standing prepares to jump, duck or dodge the laser as it makes another pass, it suddenly becomes a deadly, criss-crossed mesh that passes right through him, cutting him into a jigsaw-puzzle of pieces that the audience hears rather than sees fall apart, while his companions watch helplessly from the other side of a security door they cannot break open. The opening scene of *Ghost Ship* (also released in 2002) depicts the supernaturally inspired 'accident' of a high-tension cable being released from the rigging as the ship's crew and passengers dance on deck. The cable passes through each one of them, cutting through necks,

Figure 11.3   The technology of screen violence: Rory (Jonathan Cherry) goes to pieces; screen capture from *Final Destination 2* (dir. David R. Ellis, 2002).

chests and heads, and presenting an extraordinary spectacle as they all stand frozen for a second, before neatly falling apart, leaving only one young girl alive (the cable has passed harmlessly over her head), amidst a mass of neatly sliced bodies. And in *Final Destination 2* (2003), one of the characters is sliced into three pieces by a flying razor-wire fence, launched by a car exploding in the field behind him (see Figure 11.3, and compare with Figure 11.2 on page 183).

The significance of graphic, creative violence such as this (and I have chosen just a few examples out of an immense range of possibilities) is highlighted by the rapid take-up in recent years of DVD as a home entertainment format: in the bonus features that populate DVD releases of horror movies, viewers are given access to behind-the-scenes footage that explains the way in which the film's special effects are achieved. The DVD menu for *Jeepers Creepers 2* (2003), for example, includes a navigation point entitled 'Body Parts', and the release of the remake of *Dawn of the Dead* (2004) reserves space for an 'Exploding Heads' documentary. *Wrong Turn* (2003), meanwhile, includes a featurette entitled 'Fresh Meat: The Wounds of Wrong Turn' which focuses on the depiction of a victim, hiding high in a tree, whose head is split horizontally across by an axe, just below the upper jaw. The lower part of the face falls away, and the body with it, tumbling out of the tree, leaving the upper part of the face sitting on the flat of the axe against the tree-trunk. Concomitant with the rise of increasingly violent and, more importantly, *realistic* video games, the centrality of the imaginative, and graphically and realistically staged, death in the contemporary horror film is an indicator of a preoccupation with the fragility of the body, in a culture where the vast majority of the population is shielded from direct encounters with the reality of death, and it is this paradox that forms the basis of the section that follows.

Opening up: bodily destruction and corruption

As well as a preoccupation with violent death, early modern tragedy shares with contemporary horror a puzzled fascination with the corruptibility and fragility of the human body. In *The Revenger's Tragedy*, Vindice's first soliloquy frets over Gloriana's skull, stripped of its 'three-piled flesh', and later, preparing her remains for her fatal meeting with the Duke, he muses ironically on her skeletal beauty; in *The Duchess of Malfi*, Bosola has a number of meditations on the corruptibility of human flesh, which he perceives to be linked inextricably both with moral decay, and with the ever-hovering proximity of death. He speaks of 'a lady in

France that having had the smallpox, flayed the skin of her face to make it more level; and whereas before she looked like a nutmeg grater, after she resembled an abortive hedgehog' (2.1.24–27). In his reply to the Duchess at her death, in a strongly *memento mori*-inflected speech, he answers her question 'What am I?' in these words:

> Thou art a box of worm-seed, at best but a salvatory of green mummy. What's this flesh? A little crudded milk, fantastical puff paste. Our bodies are weaker than those paper-prisons boys use to keep flies in; more contemptible, since ours is to preserve earth-worms. (4.2.119–24)

I have already noted the likelihood that many members of an early modern theatre audience would have witnessed public executions. Since, often, the bodies of those who had been executed would be left to rot in order to extend their punishment by shaming their corpses, the sight of scavenged and decaying flesh would probably also have been familiar.

In our own time, the acute fascination with the fragility and corruptibility of the human body seems to have spread far beyond the relatively rarified zone of violent horror. The hugely successful and long-running TV show *E.R.* (first aired in September 1994, and in its eleventh season at the time of writing) was in part structured around its graphic presentation of the messy everyday reality of an emergency ward. More recently, the plastic-surgery soap opera *Nip/Tuck* (first aired in July 2003) has taken a similar approach to a growing industry, and there has also been an explosion of interest in documentary-style programming showing surgical procedures in close-up detail. Footage of crime scenes, combat (from so-called 'embedded' news teams), bombings and other atrocities on TV news reports today reveal much more than they did in the early 1990s. In a different context, Jonathan Sawday refers to scandalous stories circulating in the Danish press in 1994 concerning a practice of displaying corpses at the University of Copenhagen where, since the early 1980s, there had been a practice of exhibiting the corpses to interested and paying members of the public. The scandal, when uncovered, sparked intense media attention and a police investigation.[21]

These changes in the representation of the human body (and the treatment of real human bodies) in contemporary culture could be interpreted as a sign that the body no longer enjoys the protection of any kind of taboo. *Robocop* (1987) presents the audience with the notion of the body as a walking auto-repair shop, while, back in the real world, plastic surgery slices and folds, pumps and drains the body in the pursuit of physical perfection, and metal body piercings mould the skin and flesh into new patterns. In *Texas Chainsaw Massacre* (1974), as Paul Wells writes,

'Leatherface treats all human life as "meat"...[The film] shows only contempt for the body and with it the tangible credentials of humanity'.[22] In the teen horror film *Jeepers Creepers 2*, the bodies of the high school basketball team are almost literally served up as fresh meat when their bus blows a tyre, leaving them stranded in the creature's territory: in one early scene, a number of them are depicted sunbathing on the roof of the bus, grilling like barbecue steaks. As in the original *Jeepers Creepers* (2001), the creature picks out from his victims the precise body parts he requires. When one of the plucky cheerleaders manages to put a javelin through the creature's skull, it takes the head of one of the students and ingests it, from where the head travels up through the creature's temporarily head-less frame to replace its damaged one. The body is recycled in whatever form latex and CGI effects will allow. Even in a film as mainstream as *Bad Boys II* (2003), rated 15 in the UK and R in the USA, the cops Mike (Will Smith) and Marcus (Martin Lawrence) are depicted throwing body parts around an autopsy room; during a car chase, the criminals they are pursuing tumble frozen cadavers out of the back of a mortuary van.

The work of the artist Gunther von Hagens has caused debate on an international scale via his touring 'Body Worlds' exhibition. Von Hagens has perfected a technique called plastination, in which human bodies are first preserved in formaldehyde, frozen, thawed, then dissected

Figure 11.4 The opened female body 1: exhibit from Gunther von Hagens' 'Body Worlds' exhibition

Source: Rex Features. Photograph by Nils Jorgensen.

and drained of their fluids. The fluids are replaced with polymers and the result is a preserved, coloured, odourless body. His touring exhibition includes specimens that can be perceived as medically significant (damaged spinal columns, polluted lungs, swollen livers), but is more memorable for its imaginative, 'artistic' examples: a figure playing chess; a woman reclining, her womb occupied by an eight-month-old foetus (see Figure 11.4); a man mounted on a horse, the animal also stripped to its sinews, the rider holding the horse's brain in one hand and his own in the other. Von Hagens sees himself standing in the tradition of the anatomists (he performed a live autopsy on UK TV Channel 4 in November 2002 in a stunt that caused huge controversy). In an interview with Imogen O'Rorke for the *Observer* newspaper, he claimed his mission was to bring anatomy to the people, making an interesting connection between representations of the opened body in science and in entertainment:

> Except for the short period of the Renaissance when anatomy was studied widely and available to artists, intellectuals and medical students, the interior of the body has always been connected with horror and gruesome effects – it is Hitchcock, it is Frankenstein, or the movie industry obsessed with killing. At Korperwelten [Body Worlds] the gap between life and death is narrowed.[23]

Although his work has caused much offence, including condemnation by many religious groups who claim it violates the sanctity of the human body, von Hagens (predictably) begs to differ, citing the fact that his list of voluntary donors includes many young people. In a post-Christian age, it seems, plastination offers some kind of immortality: 'It eliminates anxiety,' von Hagens claims, 'because I am able to extend my physical existence after death.'[24]

In contemporary Western society, many of us have no direct contact with death for much of our lives. Whereas in the past, the death of a loved one was dealt with by the community, the body kept in the home and prepared for burial by family members, today the process of death has been handed over to a small group of professionals, pathologists and undertakers. Vivian Sobchack, in a fascinating 'Personal Memoir of Death in the Movies', reflects back on an essay written twenty-five years earlier, and notes he no longer finds himself drawn to violent film, possibly because of a growing acknowledgement of his own mortality (the main essay was written when he was in his early thirties, the afterword in his late fifties), possibly 'because now, after various and intense experiences of physical pain, it affects me more strongly than it did before, writing itself on my body as it writes itself on the screen'.[25] Such matters are guaranteed to provoke conflicted, ambivalent responses, not only culturally and generationally, but also within each one of us. William Paul considers the ambivalence involved in a reaction of disgust, a 'simultaneous attraction and repulsion' which is at the heart of what he calls the 'gross-out' aesthetic: 'a strategy of working against meaning in favor of spectacle, the ascendancy of the physical over the conceptual';[26] the gross-out reaction depends fundamentally upon the gratuitous nature of the spectacle, recalling the value judgements considered at the beginning of the chapter, and the bandying of terms such as 'gratuitous' and 'exploitative'. Frequently, the judgement has a historical frame: Bernard Kolker believes that, in the wake of Peckinpah's *The Wild Bunch*, 'aesthetics, prosthetics, cinematic ritual, and cultural consent sutured violence into the very structure of cinema'. He continues:

> Once the heroes of eighties action films began surviving the most horrendous acts of violence to their bodies, or showed their bodies to be cyborg instruments, violence turned from convention to display. It has become a kind of joke and spectacle, curiously, perhaps shockingly, a kind of pleasure.[27]

Pete Boss complains that, '[t]he bodily destruction of the modern horror film is... often casual to the point of randomness; devoid of metaphysical import, it is frequently squalid, incidental to the main action, [and] mechanically routine in its execution'.[28]

Certainly, there is an aspect of early modern tragedy's preoccupation with violence, and contemporary horror's compulsion to repeatedly push back the boundaries of taste, which has to do with the desire to shock. However, this does not necessarily and straightforwardly imply mere exploitation. Noel Carroll talks about horror appealing to our hunger for knowledge that may be forbidden – 'horror attracts because anomalies command attention and elicit curiosity'[29] – and Paul Wells agrees, arguing that '[t]he *frisson* of the horror text for the audience is underpinned by the expressed desire to experience feelings which relate to taboo agendas and the limits of gratification'.[30] Horror movies repeatedly set up taboos, acknowledging societal norms in order to shatter them. Carol Clover compares the effect of the shower scene in *Psycho* (1960) – showing little but implying much – with the modern slasher films' explicitness. Where violence in *Psycho* was taken seriously by its audiences in 1960, the reaction to a killing in a modern slasher is very different: silence during a stalking scene, a scream at the first gesture of attack, followed by cries of 'Gross!' or something similar, usually mingling laughter and expressions of disgust, as the attacker severs a limb or slits a throat. In this 'cultivation of intentionally outrageous excess', Clover continues, there is an alternation between so-called 'real' horror and the camp of self-parody.[31]

Early modern tragedies, like graphically violent horror movies, often walk a fine line between seriousness and camp, between shock and laughter. Both as a director and as a member of an audience, I have experienced both species of reaction. In one instance, over a run of five performances, the climactic slaughter in a production of *The Duchess of Malfi* I directed (with an emphasis on realism, including the use of blood-packs, and a syringe to pump stage blood from Bosola's neck after he was bitten by the lycanthropic Ferdinand) was received in silence, punctuated by gasps. At one Friday night performance, the sight of the blood provoked a few spectators to laughter, which seemed to set off a wave of similar responses in one area of the auditorium; the result was fascinating (though, for the actors, deeply frustrating): a far more mixed and diverse response to a scene that repeatedly tips either (or both) ways. Of course, it is difficult to make any accurate guesses at early modern audience responses, and even more difficult to decipher the intentions of the plays' authors. The violence depicted in, for example, *'Tis Pity She's a Whore*, climaxing with Giovanni entering, presumably covered in blood, bearing his sister's heart on his dagger, seems to remain resolutely straight-faced, but this is no guarantee, of course, that the audience will oblige, particularly when Annabella's father Florio keels over dead, presumably from a heart attack. Similarly tricky in this respect is the ending of *The Atheist's Tragedy*, a play which, despite some amusing comic scenes, is apparently committed to a po-faced rebuttal of the idea of justifiable revenge. The play reaches a bathetic climax when D'Amville mounts the scaffold and snatches the axe from the hands of the executioner, determined to take his revenge on the (self-)righteous couple, Charlemont and Castabella. But, as he raises his axe, the bizarre stage direction tells us that D'Amville '*strikes out his own brains. [He] staggers off the scaffold*' (5.2.239 s.d.). Just in case the audience is in need of a clear explanation (or, who knows, perhaps to cover any mishaps with rigged props), the executioner tells us, 'In lifting up the axe, I think h'as knocked/His brains out' (240–1). If the notion of poetic justice has not been hammered hard enough already, D'Amville has a couple of lengthy speeches before he dies (given this, one wonders how the actor might have signalled his apparently severe head injury), ending with the excruciating lines, 'O!/The lust of death commits a rape upon me,/As I would ha' done on Castabella' (264–6). Although it is impossible to be certain about a Jacobean audience's response to this, it is hard to imagine it being taken entirely seriously. On the other hand, books such as Thomas Beard's *Theatre of God's Judgements* (1597), with its moral tales of godless lives cut short (including, interestingly enough, the 'atheist' Christopher Marlowe's), were popular at the time, and it is not entirely outside the bounds of credibility that the audiences *did* watch in awe rather than mirth, although it is impossible to imagine a production being mounted today that would be able to carry this off as anything other than comedy – another indicator of historical and cultural differences.

At the other end of the spectrum, the blinding of Gloucester in Act 3, Scene 7 of *King Lear* (1604) provokes nothing but shock and horror, unless performed ineptly, or with parodic intentions. Cynthia Marshall believes that the power of a scene like this arises from the fact that it 'register[s] in more immediate phenomenological ways, with compelling physical and emotional resonance for viewers', reminding them of the vulnerability of their own observing eyes.[32] The author of *The Revenger's Tragedy*, on the other hand, is more adventurous. The death of the Duke strikes sparks by clashing the blackly comic and the horrific, in a fashion analogous to the ironic horror movies of the 1980s and 1990s discussed above. There is a carefully paced preparation for the revenge: Vindice begins the scene barely able to contain his excitement ('O, 'tis able/To make a man spring up, and knock his forehead/Against yon silver ceiling' [3.5.2–4]), and he presents Gloriana (according to the stage direction, he leaves the stage briefly and returns '*with the skull of his love dressed up in tires*' [42 s.d.]) to Hippolito, who is evidently shocked virtually speechless: 'Why, brother! Brother!' (49). Vindice launches into a crazily ironic speech praising the skull's beauty: an eye (socket) 'Able to tempt a man – to serve God'; 'A pretty hanging lip' that would be enough to make a drunkard 'clasp his teeth and not undo 'em/To suffer wet damnation to run through 'em'; and a cheek that keeps its (bone-white) colour, 'let the wind go whistle' (as it should, through the hollows of the skull face) (54–60). The audience's response is complicated by Vindice's double vision: his ironic praise of Gloriana's beauty is both amusing and poignant, reminding us of the beauty of his lost beloved. However, the jokes continue as Vindice, in his Piato guise, introduces the Duke to her ('Sh'as somewhat a grave look with her' [135–6]), and the murder itself works partly via the physical action, and partly by Middleton's deployment of hyper-extended, violent rhetoric: immediately after the Duke kisses the poisoned skull, Vindice orders Hippolito to 'Place the torch here, that his affrighted eyeballs/May start into those hollows' (146–7) – that is, the hollows of Gloriana's eye-sockets that

Vindice praised so lavishly moments earlier. Triumphant, Vindice crows, 'The very ragged bone has been sufficiently revenged', once again pressing home the full horror of his act of vengeance (152), before declaring that he has hardly started: 'Puh, 'tis early yet; now I'll begin/ To stick thy soul with ulcers' (170–1). Soon after, as they prepare to put the finishing touches to their revenge by forcing the Duke to watch himself being cuckolded by his bastard son, he insists that Hippolito 'with thy dagger/Nail down his tongue', and, should he 'but wink . . . Let our two other hands tear up his lids/And make his eyes like comets shine through blood' (197–8).

Set against the horror and startling violence, physical and rhetorical, is the acidic, deep black comedy: as the Duke cries out, the poison corroding his teeth, Vindice remarks, 'Then those that did eat are eaten' (159), and as it burns out his tongue, he adds, 'twill teach you to kiss closer,/Not like a slobbering Dutchman' (161–2). Hippolito joins in the sport. In one startlingly modern moment, the Duke, unaware that Hippolito is a co-conspirator against him, cries out to him to raise the alarm: 'O Hippolito, call treason!' (153). 'Yes, my good lord,' replies Hippolito, '*Stamping on him*' (154 s.d.): 'Treason, treason, treason!', presumably with another kick punctuating each reiteration (154). The final masterstroke is a meta-theatrical touch by Middleton: Vindice's grim, satisfied, 'When the bad bleeds, then is the tragedy good' (199), inviting the audience, as the character observing the spider-head in *The Thing* also does, to recognise the spectacle as consummate performance. In the final scene of *Revenger's*, the mass slaughter reaches a farcical pitch: although the revenge is enacted via a masque – a performance – and this further heightens the sense of ritualised violence, the multiplying of revenge and murder leads to a blackly farcical (anti-)climax: when the second set of revengers arrive, they find their job already done.[33]

A brief example of a parallel moment in contemporary cinema shows how a similar juxtaposition of comedy and extreme violence works to analogous effect: Mr Blonde's torture of a police officer in *Reservoir Dogs* (1992) is a scene that has acquired a canonical status. The movie tells the story of the robbery of a jewellery store that goes badly wrong, and observes the deterioration and self-destruction of the gang in the aftermath. The torture scene in question takes place in the warehouse hideout where the captured policemen, Marvin (Kirk Baltz), has been taken, and tied to a chair. The audience is given some preparation for what might follow, an argument between the gang members over the botched heist during which Mr White (Harvey Keitel), already established for the audience as a trustworthy point of engagement and perspective (he has formed a strong bond with undercover cop Mr Orange [Tim Roth]), reveals that Mr Blonde (Michael Madsen) began shooting indiscriminately when the store's alarm was activated. Mr White is extremely reluctant to leave Mr Blonde alone with the captured policeman and the wounded Mr Orange, being convinced that he is psychotic, having witnessed his 'kill-crazy rampage' in the store. When they are finally ordered to leave by Nice Guy Eddie (Chris Penn), there is a moment of silence as the echoes of the shouted argument die away, and then Mr Blonde jumps down from his perch, removes his jacket (with an implication of "getting down to business"), and utters the menacing words (spoken in a neutral, harmless tone): 'Alone at last.'

Marvin's insistence that he knows nothing about the set-up the gang suspects played havoc with their plans is what provides Mr Blonde with his cue: 'Nobody tells me shit, you can torture me all you want,' Marvin tells him; 'torture, that's a good...that's a good idea, like that one, yeah, sounds fun.' The growing sense of menace is created partly by Mr Blonde's unnerving juxtaposition of humour and mock-friendliness; in a familiar rehearsal of standard 'psychotic gangster' tropes, he switches between ostensibly chummy colloquialisms ('Scuse me' pal') and sudden, random violence ('You hear what I said, you son of a bitch?', punctuating his speech with a hard slap across Marvin's face). He proceeds to tape up Marvin's mouth, while informing him, in very level, clinical tones, that he's going to torture him, not to get information, but simply because 'it's amusing to me to torture a cop'; the only thing Marvin can do is 'pray for a quick death...which you ain't gonna get'. Having pulled his pistol and aimed it at Marvin's head (the cop's writhing provoking Mr Blonde to laughter), his next move is to step over to the radio with another slip into casual friendliness: 'Ever listened to "K-Billy's Supersounds of the Seventies"?' He turns on the radio and, in close-up, removes a straight razor from his boot. As the Stealer's Wheel tune "Stuck in the Middle with You" kicks off, Mr Blonde begins to sing along and starts a soft shoe shuffle dance to the music, while Marvin watches, bloodied and dumbfounded. Suddenly, Mr Blonde stops, makes one slashing lunge at his victim's face and then moves in, heavy and deliberate, grabbing Marvin's face with one hand and attacking his ear with the razor in his other hand (see Figure 11.5). The camera, in a gesture that seems almost a conscious courtesy to the audience, pans up and away and fixes on the warehouse wall; the audience hears Marvin cry out, his voice muffled by the tape over his mouth, and Mr Blonde's brutal, 'hold still, hold still, you fuck...'. The next thing it sees is Mr Blonde holding the bloody, severed ear, and once again the

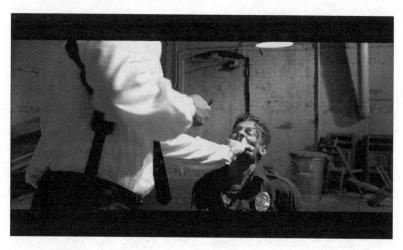

Figure 11.5   Michael Madsen as Mr Blonde and Kirk Baltz as Marvin in *Reservoir Dogs* (dir. Quentin Tarantino, 1992)
Source: Screen capture.

script and performance lurch back into black comedy. 'Was that as good for you as it was for me?' he asks Marvin, in a perverse, ironic eroticisation of the torture; then, putting the ear closer to his mouth, 'Hey, what's going on? You hear that?', followed by more laughter, and another sudden switch into mean irritation as he discards the ear and wipes his bloodied hand on Marvin's shirt.

There are obvious differences between this and the torture and execution of the Duke in *The Revenger's Tragedy*, not least the identity of the Duke as a villain deserving of some kind of punishment, compared to the innocent victim Marvin, whose humanity is brought home as he pleads for his life, telling his torturer that he has a child, while Mr Blonde, oblivious, dowses him in petrol (Mr Orange will shoot Mr Blonde before he can set the prisoner alight). Vindice's sanity may be in question by this point in the play, but the audience has a detailed insight into the reasons for his actions; Mr Blonde, in contrast, is simply sadistic, turned on by the power he can exert, the terror he can inspire, and the damage he can inflict on his victim. However, the scenes also bear strong resemblances in tone, notably in their negotiation of the comic and horrific. In both scenes, the sadism is carefully deliberate, savoured by the one inflicting pain, and offered to the audience in a way that invites them to participate vicariously in it. Both Mr Blonde and Vindice enhance their performances of violence by their manipulation of tone, and by drawing attention to the gap between the vicious nature of their actions and their casual attitude towards it. Both of them make jokes about the specific impact of their violence upon their victims ('those that did eat are eaten' ... 'What's going on; you hear that?'), and invite the audience to respond to their comic, ironic touches.[34] On the other hand, though Mr Blonde may be blessed with a charismatic performance by Michael Madsen (from which, ironically, the actor's career has never really recovered), there is very little one could identify as psychologically real or complex in his characterisation. In this respect, his act of violence takes place in a kind of vacuum, and, more than is so with many such instances in contemporary cinema, it seems vulnerable to charges of gratuitousness, since its purpose is obscure in terms of the narrative progression. For writer–director Quentin Tarantino, commenting on the way his scene works, the comedy is crucial: 'I kinda defy anybody to watch Michael Madsen do that dance and not kind of enjoy it', he remarks on the DVD commentary, claiming that the comic lead into the torture implicates the audience: 'You are a co-conspirator.'[35] However, Tarantino makes no attempt to analyse any further what this might mean in terms of audience response, or the audience's *awareness* of its response. Perhaps this lacuna, conscious or not, is simply a recognition that the scene does not have the power to make the audience do any such thing.

Although Tarantino's stylish brand of screen violence arguably often fails to proceed past an infatuation with its own cleverness, the tendency to dismiss contemporary graphic violence as both exploitative and gratuitous may be challenged in many other cases. It is my contention that a number of contemporary horror films, often denounced as trite and formulaic, can be read as sublimations of fears about the vulnerability of the body and the imminence of death, particularly in a society largely protected from the spectacle of the consequences of actual physical harm and fatality. At the same time, as I intend to demonstrate in the next chapter, graphic representations of violence in particular contexts – notably certain sub-genres of horror – once again alert us to complexities of gender and power that can carry disturbing sub-texts, and resonate with analogous representations 400 years old.

12
Punishment and Redemption

'In a mist': perdition and redemption

The preoccupation with body horror no doubt taps into fundamental fears about the fragility of the human body, and the unpredictability and inevitability of death. The fascination that these mysteries hold for many of us is no doubt one of the reasons why representations of spectacular deaths recur in our culture. In our own time, in our own culture, part of the appeal may well lie in the fact that the sight, smell and feel of a dead body is as mysterious to many of us as the conception of what may lie beyond it. For the Elizabethans and Jacobeans, more familiar with the reality of death (and more sure of its consequences in terms of damnation and salvation), spectacles of death may well have been a way of sublimating their own fears, and answering their curiosity about the body and its obscure relationship with the soul, and the life that they understood to lie beyond the grave. This is not the place for a comprehensive investigation of different understandings of death and the after-life in early modern culture, along the lines of the major studies offered by Michael Neill and Robert N. Watson.[1] However, there is a striking parallel between deaths in revenge tragedy (often protracted to ensure the relevant characters have the opportunity to voice lengthy dying speeches), and many instances of violent death in contemporary violent cinema, where the impact of the key scenes is enhanced by ensuring that the characters concerned are given time and space to register their imminent doom.

The deaths of key characters in early modern tragedy are extended more often than not, the dying character's rhetoric lingering long past the logical endpoint that realism would dictate. At times this will involve characters making peace with others witnessing their death

(Laertes and his offer to 'exchange forgiveness' with Hamlet [5.2.282]), or else preparing their souls for divine judgement. The martyred Duchess of Malfi, for example, is depicted rapt in a vision of heaven's gates opening as she prepares for her execution, and she welcomes her end on her knees: 'Come, violent death,/Serve for mandragora to make me sleep' (4.2.226–7). Doctor Faustus also sees a vision of heaven where 'Christ's blood streams in the firmament' (A-text, 5.2.70), but for him there is no salvation. The dying speeches of many of Webster's other protagonists, on the other hand, are notable for their apparent failure to envisage their characters' imminent fates, or to determine anything of value in their lives and deaths: in *The Duchess of Malfi*, Julia, poisoned by her lover, the Cardinal, dies with the words 'I go,/I know not whither' (5.2.284–5); Bosola declares 'We are only like dead walls, or vaulted graves,/That, ruined, yields no echo' (5.5.96–7); his victim the Cardinal asks, 'let me/Be laid by, and never thought of' (88–9); Ferdinand declares, 'I do account this world but a dog-kennel' (66). In *The White Devil*, Flamineo finds himself 'in a mist' (5.6.259), and Vittoria despairs that 'My soul, like to a ship in a black storm,/Is driven I know not whither' (248). Macbeth can make no sense of the way in which his life has careered off its rails, finding only 'a tale told by an idiot, full of sound and fury, signifying nothing' (5.5.26–8). Religious scepticism is most acute, it seems, when these characters are *in extremis*, caught in the agonising and prolonged death throes that is the inevitable fate of so many of them.

In the slasher movie, deaths may be sudden and unexpected, functioning to elicit shock responses in the audience (the scene in *Final Destination*, mentioned earlier, when Terry is hit at high speed by a bus, has never failed, in my experience, and the DVD release includes fascinating footage of the responses of a test audience filmed with a hidden camera).[2] However, while for obvious reasons they do not leave the bounds of realism as early modern texts often do, they will often adopt a different strategy: characters are frequently confronted with terrifying, painful deaths, and part of the filmmakers' strategy is to allow the audience to witness and participate vicariously in that moment of abject terror. However, if the characters are offered anything at all to verbalise their terror, it rarely passes beyond redundant, inarticulate screams for help. Part of the poignancy of the death of Nora in *Final Destination 2* is the juxtaposition of her avowal that she's ready to 'go to heaven to be with her family' (widowed already, her son is the most recent victim of Death, the Stalker) with the scene, moments later, when she is trapped with her head caught in the elevator doors, screaming, 'Help me, I don't want to die', as her friends struggle in vain to save her from decapitation.

Both early modern revenge tragedy and contemporary violent film can be playful with their representations of violence, seemingly disrupting the tragic grain by approaching death and traumatic, sadistic injury from blackly comic angles. One of the key differences is that, despite the charges of gratuitousness that have in the past been levelled against revenge tragedy, the violence is, in almost all cases, sutured into the thematic and narrative fabric of the text. It rarely seems extraneous to the action in the way that the torture of Marvin in *Reservoir Dogs* does. On the other hand, there are forms of violence in the earlier texts that may still surprise or shock us, notably the depiction of deaths of young children: while the subject remains relatively (though not entirely) taboo in contemporary cinema, early modern tragedy features a number of child killings, frequently bloody, and dwelt on both visually and rhetorically. Often, the child speaks, before or after being struck, thus heightening the pathos. Maurice Charney notes the interesting example of *Cambyses* (c.1560), in which the King of the play's title, offended by his counsellor Praxaspes' warnings about his drunkenness, offers to prove his sobriety by shooting an arrow through the heart of Praxaspes' youngest son. The boy pleads for his life ('Alas, alas, father, will you me kill?/Good Master king, do not shoot at me;/My mother loves me best of all'), but is shot nevertheless, and a few lines later his heart is brought on stage as evidence of the king's skill with a bow.[3] Charney also refers to *A Yorkshire Tragedy*, in which a boy is knocked over the head by his father, before being stabbed to death; and the death of Macduff's son in *Macbeth*.[4] The audience is shown the bodies of the Duchess of Malfi's slaughtered children (accompanied by Bosola's moving line, 'Alas, how have these offended?' [4.2.249]). However, even in the most violent mainstream contemporary horror, the representation of the death of a child is still seen as something to be approached tentatively. The French horror movie *Haute Tension* (aka *Switchblade Romance* [2004]) depicted in detail the slaughter of an entire family, including the spectacle of the killer jamming the father's head between stair rails before decapitating him with a chest of drawers, and the mutilation of the mother, her hands cut off and her throat slit. However, the young boy, after escaping into a cornfield, is tracked down and killed with a shotgun blast off-camera. In the aftermath, his body is only seen in semi-darkness in a high-angle long shot. Both genres are ready to confront their audiences with violent spectacles that shock by unexpected tonal shifts, juxtapositions and double exposures of the comic and the horrific. However, these brief examples suggest that the differences are also, at times, just as striking as the similarities, and act as reminders of the gaps that still need to be negotiated in attempts to make sense of the culture of the past, and the audiences that consumed it.

'A manly blow': the female body, abjection and punishment

In Chapter 6, discussing the context for gender and violence in early modern tragedy, I noted the prevalence of the virgin/whore binary in the representation of female characters. I also discussed the violent responses provoked in the patriarchy by sexually transgressive women, and disjunctions and disruptions of the ideological status quo, as, for example, when physical beauty is mirrored not by spiritual beauty, but by moral debasement and sexual immorality. Ferdinand cannot endure the sight of his sister, the Duchess of Malfi, once he knows she has remarried in secret; Beatrice-Joanna is, in the eyes of Alsemero, 'all deform'd'; Vittoria, a 'white devil'. Disobedient, sexually transgressive women are monstrous in the eyes of the patriarchy (if not the audience). In the wider culture and social structures of the time, assertive women are aberrations associated with witchcraft; shrewish wives were paraded, muzzled, in the streets like animals. In contemporary horror, images of the female monster abound, and it is beyond the scope of the current project to document them fully. However, there are some specific connections to be made: just as the image of the *femme fatale* recurs throughout the history of Western culture, so the image of what Barbara Creed has designated the 'monstrous-feminine' can be traced back to ancient folklore. Mark Jancovich, introducing an extract from Creed's *The Monstrous-Feminine* (1993), cites Freud's theory of castration anxiety ('Probably no male human being is spared the terrifying shock of threatened castration at the sight of the female genitals'), Joseph Campbell's identification of the motif of the *vagina dentata* (the 'toothed vagina'), and the symbol of the Medusa's head as examples.[5] The female vampire has always been an important component of the mythology of vampirism, and Mark Jancovich points out the significance of this depiction of an insatiable need for blood, an analogue for a boundless sexual appetite, and in this sense another threat to male potency.[6]

Nothing has attracted more attention in terms of the representation of the female in the horror genre than blood. In *Violence and the Sacred*, René Girard writes:

> Among primitive taboos the one that has perhaps been most analysed is the taboo surrounding menstrual blood. Menstrual blood is regarded as impure; menstruating women are segregated from the community. They are forbidden to touch any objects of communal usage, sometimes even their own food, for risk of contamination.[7]

He continues: 'in many societies [menstrual blood] is regarded as the most impure of impurities. We can only assume that this extreme reaction has to do with the sexual aspect of menstruation'.[8] Feminist readings indebted to Freud and Lacan and, more directly, Julia Kristeva have focused on the significance of the idea of the 'abject' female.[9] In Kristeva's conceptualisation, the female is associated with all the taboo aspects of the body such as bodily emission and waste, defilement, disease and death. The female is seen by the patriarchy as something 'monstrous', a threat to the male that must be contained or destroyed, since it signals above all the failure of the male to control his environment and, crucially, embodies the threat of annihilation. Barbara Creed applies Kristeva's theory of the abject to the horror genre specifically, and explains the prevalence of the monstrous-feminine by positing the genre's typical audience as male, trapped in an ideology that constructs feminine difference as terrible and threatening. While Kristeva argues that religion functions to purify the abject, Creed builds an analogous argument that the horror film attempts to bring about a confrontation with the abject in order to eject it and 'redraw the boundaries between the human and the non-human'.[10]

One of the most direct expressions of this kind of anxiety in popular film is the opening scene of *Carrie*, depicting the eponymous heroine in the shower and experiencing her first period. Slow-motion, semi-pornographic images of Carrie and her high school classmates showering and soaping themselves dissolve into the sudden, shocking stream of blood running down Carrie's leg, and causing her to panic: her sheltered upbringing, under the wing of her religious fanatic mother, means she has no idea what is happening to her, and her terror is only exacerbated by the other girls' mockery, as they pelt her with tampons. Carrie's classmates act in the shower scene as the representatives of the patriarchy, young women who have accepted and internalised the demand to keep their own bodies under control, to avoid the display of those signs that provoke male fears. At the film's climax, Carrie is once again humiliated by her peers when, while she is being crowned prom queen, a bucket of pig's blood rigged above the stage is poured over her head. In response, Carrie, rendered monstrous, blood-streaked and wild-eyed with fury (see Figure 12.1), goes on the rampage, wiping out indiscriminately all those who cross her path, before eventually killing her mother and herself.

The films of David Cronenberg offer perhaps the most sustained and detailed expression of the idea of the monstrous-feminine. In *Rabid* (1975), Rose (Marilyn Chambers) has a phallic organ implanted in her body, which emerges from a vulva-shaped opening in her armpit to feed on human blood. Those she infects (her attacks often involving seduction and sex – it is no coincidence that Chambers was most famous in the 1970s as a soft-porn actress) contract a rabies-like disease and attack others, driven by a similar blood-thirst. In *The Brood* (1979), Nola (Samantha Eggar), a patient under the care of psychotherapist Dr Raglan (Oliver Reed) as she recovers from a traumatic divorce, manifests her rage through mutant progeny that grow on her body like blisters, emerging to carry out revenge on the targets of her fury. Cronenberg's later film *Dead Ringers* (1988) is even more extreme in its depiction of male

Figure 12.1 The monstrous-feminine: Sissy Spacek as *Carrie* (dir. Brian De Palma, 1976)
Source: Screen capture.

fear of the female body. The relationship between twin gynaecologists Beverly and Eliott Mantel (both played by Jeremy Irons), who are accustomed to sharing women as sexual partners, begins to unravel when Beverly descends into paranoid insanity, developing a set of horrifying gynaecological instruments to use on the object of his obsession, Claire (Genevieve Bujold), a woman with a mysterious 'gynaecological mutation'.

The rise of the slasher horror film in the late 1970s and early 1980s is a phenomenon worthy of close attention, since many have seen in it a perpetual recycling of the enactment of punishment on the female transgressor. Barbara Creed connects the slasher genre with the concept of castration anxiety:

> The horror film's obsession with blood, particularly the bleeding body of woman, where her body is transformed into the 'gaping wound', suggests that castration anxiety is a central concern of the horror film – particularly the slasher sub-genre . . . In the guise of a 'madman' he enacts on her body the one act he most fears for himself, transforming her entire body into a bleeding wound.[11]

Tony Williams sees the genre as revealing 'an unconscious patriarchal hysteria trying to hold back contradictory tensions, especially those involving changing gender roles'.[12] The slasher film's key conventions include extreme, graphic and sadistic acts of violence, usually committed by a serial killer whose identity remains obscure until a strategic moment in the narrative, and most often executed using pre-technological weapons such as spiked and bladed implements. His victims are commonly groups of teenagers and young adults, though the body count will often include older characters (parents, police) caught in whatever the knife's equivalent of crossfire might be. Many films in the genre, including *Friday the 13th* and its sequels, some of the *Halloween* films, and lower-budget efforts such as *Sleepaway Camp* (1980), *Terror Train* (1980), *My Bloody Valentine* (1981) and *The Slumber Party Massacre* (1982), feature teenagers indulging in pre-marital sex before death comes knocking.[13]

Frequently, one standard-issue virginal female will survive for a climactic showdown with the killer. This familiar paradigm has provided fodder both for scholars (notably in Carol Clover's 'Final Girl' formulation)[14] and for postmodern reworkings of the genre. Clover's concept of the Final Girl acknowledges that the survivor and vanquisher of the killer tends to be a girl set apart from her female friends, generally less (or not at all) sexually available, serious, smart and competent; in other words, closer to a male than a female stereotype, and commonly given a non-gender-specific first name such as Laurie or Stevie. Wes Craven's *Scream* plays self-consciously with the idea through the character of Sidney, while the 2000 movie *Cherry Falls* cleverly reverses the premise by presenting a serial killer who kills only virgins, prompting what one character calls a 'hymen holocaust' as all the young women of the town attempt to exempt themselves as targets by losing their virginity: in the orgy that follows, the killer runs rampant.

Within its social context, the original slasher sub-genre is interpretable as one of several traces in popular culture of a response to the breakdown of the nuclear family, increased liberalism and what many saw as a rise in immorality, and in particular sexual immorality. Michael Ryan and Douglas Kellner suggest that they should be seen as part of an attempt to 'restabilize the patriarchal social system as a whole, by reasserting discipline over youth and by repositioning women as the submissive other of a primary, aggressive male subject'.[15] Robin Wood sees the slasher figure as 'essentially a superego figure, avenging itself on liberated female sexuality or the sexual freedom of the young'.[16] Viewed in less psychological, more political terms than the Kristeva/Creed model allows, it is also possible to interpret the phenomenon as an expression of the fears that feminism has engendered in a society where men have been accustomed to power and control. In the first *Friday the 13th*, promiscuous teens are picked off one by one at the camp by Crystal Lake – variously knifed in the stomach, throat slit, or, more inventively, impaled by an arrow through the throat from below the bed, an axe in the face, or pinned to a door with arrows. However, the slasher turns out to be not, as the audience had been led to believe, Jason Vorhees, the child who drowned at the camp more than twenty-two years earlier, but his mother, Pamela, intent on symbolic revenge, since Jason had died while the camp counsellors looking after him were having sex. Tony Williams describes her as 'a phallic avenging mother, speaking with his voice'.[17] The idea of young women being targeted for sexual immorality is a popular assumption in the genre (the impression strengthened by recent parodies of the genre such as *Scream, Cherry Falls* and the *Scary Movie* franchise [2000–3]), even though statistically-based research by Barry S. Sapolsky and Fred Molitor disputes these common perceptions.[18] However, it is certainly true that the eroticised (female) deaths seem to have a much greater impact on an audience than do male deaths: statistical data in this sense can be misleading, since its empirical approach cannot account for the difference between what an audience in fact sees, and what it processes, or what it *thinks* it sees. As Carol Clover points out, male victims are generally dispatched fairly quickly, usually filmed at a distance, or in obscure lighting or weak focus, while female victims' deaths are generally depicted in detail and at some length.[19]

It should be no surprise that, in a genre predicated on spectacle, and structured around very rigid gender binaries, Laura Mulvey's theories about the male gaze have been significant in the proliferation of scholarship on the horror movie. The frequent use of PoV camera in the murder scenes has been singled out for attention, critics claiming that it works to identify the audience with the killer as the female victims are the objects of the slasher's gaze, and the targets of (usually) his violence. Roger Ebert, for instance, claims that 'the visual strategy of these [slasher] films displaced the villain from his traditional place within the film – and moved him into the audience'.[20] Others demur: Paul Wells, for example, argues that there is nothing more sinister in the choice of PoV camera than convenience: 'The audience is merely situated in the best place to observe the extreme effects of violence,' he writes, and often, he claims, the director eschews PoV shots; instead, the audience is 'made to observe the unseen monster in the back of the frame, ready to pounce'.[21] Carol Clover also questions the idea that the slasher film works to identify the audience with the killer, pointing out how the female hero, when she fights back, effectively reverses the gender positions and allows the male spectator a point of masochistic identification.

In Chapter 6 I discussed the significance of sexual jealousy and intrigue, adultery and sexually-motivated revenge in early modern tragedy. I also noted how the combination of sex and violence becomes more common in the drama, with women's sexualities perceived as being male property, strictly policed and fought over. Frequently, the interiority and secrecy of female privacy provokes male anxiety and aggression, directed either at competing males, or, perhaps most often, at the female herself. In Ben Jonson's *Volpone* (1606), Corvino interrogates his wife, whom he suspects of adultery, and his interrogation is an anatomy and a punishment, framed in these words:

> I will make thee an anatomy,
> Dissect thee mine own self, and read a lecture
> Upon thee to the city, and in public. (2.3.70–2)

Hélène Cixous asks the provocative question,

> how, as women, can we go to the theatre without lending our complicity to the sadism directed against women, or being asked

to assume, in the patriarchal family structure that the theatre reproduces *ad infintum*, the position of the victim?[22]

Michael Neill suggests that these obsessions with violating, breaking open female secrecy, betray a preoccupation with the opacity of the human body and its resistance to internal examination.[23] Frustration erupts in episodes of shocking anatomical violence, notably in the death and mutilation of Annabella in *'Tis Pity She's a Whore*.

The anatomy books of the early modern period are revealing about attitudes towards the human body in general, both in terms of the body as a physical object and as a sign of absence – in other words, as a signifier of death. Sawday suggests that the growth of interest in human anatomy reawakened an interest in what he calls the body's *'penetrable'* nature, and he cites a number of poets who seem fascinated by the possibilities of the human body's legibility: 'The body was evoked . . . so that it could be peered into, opened out, "displayed"'.[24] However, Sawday, Cregan and others have noted key differences in the representations of the male and female forms in the anatomy books of the period. In the illustration from Jacob Rüff's *De conceptu et generatione hominis* (1580) reproduced as Figure 12.2, the woman presents her body for display as her eyes look up and away from the observer, inviting a gaze without any sign of resistance or confrontation. Some similar images feature the subject represented as opening up her body for scrutiny, holding the flaps of skin that have been drawn back. In the Rüff image, the hands rest on the arms of an ornate chair, and the woman's legs are open, exposing the genitalia, clearly visible beneath the opened womb with its small but detailed foetus. The images of the female body reveal, as one might expect, a fascination (and legitimate research interest in) the processes of pregnancy and childbirth. However, the sheer volume of illustrations, and the way in which the subjects are presented, signals something more subtle: an attempt to grasp intellectually and own metaphorically the mystery of the uterus, that organ so vital to the survival of the patriarchy, but which was perceived as unruly and potentially treacherous, and is consequently the root of so much emotional and physical violence in the drama.

I have already noted the suspicions that female secrecy arouses in the patriarchy. In *The Changeling*, for example, bedchambers are invaded, cabinets broken open, and Alsemero's final attempt to control his wayward wife and treacherous servant – by locking them both in his closet – leads, in most stage and study interpretations of Joanna's death, only to another, final, fatal sexual assault. In *Malfi*, the Duchess has her

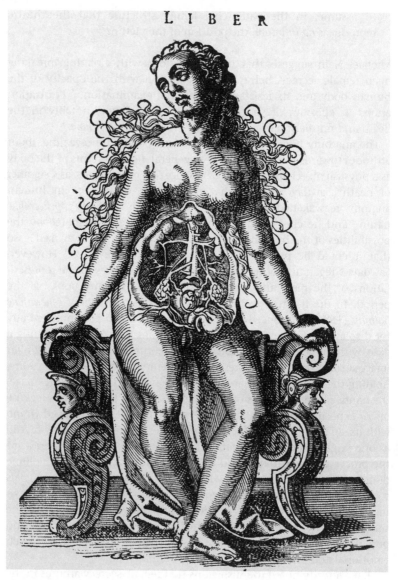

Figure 12.2 The opened female body 2: from Jacob Rüff's *De conceptu et generatione hominis* (1580)
Source: © The Trustees of the British Museum.

bedchamber invaded by her vengeful brother Ferdinand; in *'Tis Pity She's a Whore*, Giovanni slaughters Annabella on her bed in the room in which she has been imprisoned by Soranzo; in *The White Devil*, it would seem that Vittoria is hunted down and killed in her private rooms by Lodovico and his men; the Lady of *The Maiden's Tragedy* suffers the ultimate violation when her body is removed from its tomb by the sexually obsessed Tyrant. Time and again the idea returns of exposing the vulnerabilities, and frequently the hidden transgressions, of the female. In the usual course of events, the revelation is swiftly followed by retribution, which may involve public shaming and drastic punishment, and murder or execution. Bosola plots to discover the Duchess's concealed pregnancy with the apricots:

> A whirlwind strike off these bawd farthingales,
> For, but for that and the loose-bodied gown,
> I should have discovered apparently
> The young springal cutting a caper in her belly. (2.1.152–5)

The spectacular punishment of transgressive women is an effective means of reinforcing patriarchal control. As Sara Eaton makes clear, 'Men's power to punish is made visible by their actions, and is rarely questioned, demonstrating the power of the patriarchy to construct the "realities" of women's lives.'[25] In *The Changeling*, Alsemero locks Beatrice and De Flores away until he can gather an audience of men to stand witness to her wicked duplicity, and Beatrice herself declares her guilt to the assembled company as she lies bleeding to death.

In *The Duchess of Malfi*, *The Changeling* and *The White Devil*, as well as other, less well-known works, such as *The Maid's Tragedy*, the transgressive female is efficiently and often brutally 'neutralised' by murder or execution. Furthermore, the punishment of the women is very often spectacular – a spectacle, something to be observed by the audience. In many instances, the stage is populated by other characters, a second audience assembled to witness the act of punishment, or its aftermath. As Foucault has shown, display is crucial to the operation of power: 'If torture was so strongly embedded in legal practice,' he writes, 'it was because it revealed truth and showed the operation of power.'[26] Very often, the punishments, executions and deaths of transgressive women carry sexual overtones. In *'Tis Pity*, when Annabella's husband, Soranzo, discovers that his new wife is not a virgin and – worse – that she is pregnant, he drags her around the stage by her hair, declaring he will discover the identity of her lover by 'rip[ping] up thy heart and find[ing] it there' (4.3.53–4). Later, the fatal violence inflicted on Annabella is given a sexual accent by Giovanni's declaration that 'this dagger's point ploughed up/Her fruitful womb' (5.6.32–3). Soranzo's metaphorical expression of his desire to rip out her heart is made bleeding flesh by Giovanni himself, who presents his audience with Annabella's heart skewered on his dagger's point. To Giovanni, Annabella's body is a site of devotion, but also of betrayal: 'For her too fruitful womb too soon bewrayed/The happy passage of our stol'n delights' (5.6.48–9). Her heart is a symbol of himself, the secret lover whose identity she refused to reveal, and his possession of it is, after 'the rape of life and beauty/Which I have acted' (5.6.19–20), the one, undeniable sign that she belongs to him and not to her husband (''Tis a heart,/A heart, my lords, in which is mine entombed' [26–7]). Like the anatomists, Giovanni has opened Annabella's body to expose and possess its secrets: as he tells the horrified onlookers, 'I digged for food/ In a much richer mine than gold or stone/Of any value balanced' (24–6).

The punishments Ferdinand plans for his wayward sister in *The Duchess of Malfi* are also sexually charged: he rants of making a sponge...of her bleeding heart' (2.5.15); and threatens to 'toss her palace 'bout her ears,/Root up her goodly forests, blast her meads' (2.5.18–19), and to 'hew...her to pieces' (31). Most explicitly, at the climax of this raging scene, he cries:

> Go to, mistress!
> 'Tis not your whore's milk that shall quench my wildfire,
> But your whore's blood. (2.5.46–8)

His final vision in this scene is of stringing whips with scorpions to chastise her for her betrayal of their royal lineage (2.5.78). Blood is central to the way he perceives her crimes, as well as the necessary punishment and redemption. John Russell Brown traces the connection between witchcraft and sexuality that Ferdinand makes in interpreting his sister's behaviour: 'The witchcraft lies in her rank blood,' he retorts when Bosola suggests someone may have used 'sorcery' on the Duchess to make her fall in love (3.1.78). In Ferdinand's mind, the bloodline has been contaminated by the Duchess's union with someone of lower birth: 'Damn her! That body of hers,/While that my blood ran pure in 't, was more worth/Than that which thou wouldst comfort, called a soul' (4.2.121–3). Although, in general, the Cardinal does not express his feelings with as much violence as his brother, he is also enraged by the contamination: 'Shall our blood,/The royal blood of Aragon and

Castile, be thus attainted?' (2.5.21–3). The execution of the Duchess's children is not merely gratuitous: Ferdinand sees it as the extermination of the offspring of her socially 'impure' alliance with Antonio. The line of succession in *Malfi* has been disrupted by the injection of base, servant-class blood, and Ferdinand and the Cardinal seek to sever that line. The same threat arises in *The Changeling* as a result of the relationship between Beatrice-Joanna and De Flores. Annabella is due to suffer at the hands of Soranzo for having the child of her brother, but Soranzo is pre-empted by Giovanni, who consumes all three of them (and the unborn child) in a murder/suicide pact. Transgressors such as the Duchess of Malfi, Vittoria and Beatrice-Joanna are considered to be polluters of the purity of the blood of the aristocratic body and, according to the logic of this ideology, they purge that body of its pollutants by their deaths. Once again, there are hints that it may be the patriarchy, its paranoid suspicions and hysterical reactions to female autonomy, that is being critiqued, and not the Duchess's own behaviour.

For both societies, however, it seems that the spectacle of woman as victim remains a constant, even if it is interpreted in different ways. One of the characteristics of the women perceived as sexual transgressors, duly punished, is their tendency to internalise the judgements men pass upon them: as Beatrice-Joanna tells her father, as she bleeds to death, 'I am that of your blood was taken from you/For your better health' (5.3.150–1). Once again, it is blood that is central: tainted blood that the patriarchal body must be purged of, blood that must be spilt in an act of purification. The Duchess of Malfi is exceptional in this respect. Judging how Webster's first audiences may have responded to her is not easy: some critics argue that the Duchess's behaviour could not have been condoned by a Jacobean audience, and that the tendency to view her as a heroine is misguided. However, most interpreters of the play, both literary critics and actors and directors, have, particularly in the twentieth and twenty-first centuries, ennobled her, seeing her as a woman who chooses love over the outmoded and distorted priorities set for her by her brothers. Such interpretations view her death as a kind of martyrdom. The Duchess sees her blood not as being polluted (Ferdinand's perception) but as potentially redemptive: 'I have so much obedience in my blood,/I wish it in their veins, to do them good' (4.2.168–9), and for Bosola, the Duchess is his potential saviour: 'Her eye opes,/And heaven in it seems to ope, that late was shut,/To take me up to mercy' (5.2.346–8). The image of the Duchess as martyr offers us no clear way out of this trapped, repetitive loop of representations: Beatrice-Joanna and Vittoria are bleeding wounds being purged of their monstrous impurities; the Duchess, by contrast, is an image of pure, sanctified suffering; but for all of them, death is inevitable.

Each of the three parts of this study has been concerned, in different ways, with woman trouble. Revenge narratives circle obsessively around sexual intrigue and betrayal; dynamics of gender, power and control are played out in violent confrontations between men and women, and between men as they fight over women. And spectacles of death frequently stage in the most graphic form the anxieties and fantasies of a society that clings grimly to patriarchy, whether explicitly or subconsciously. In the conclusion, I shall offer some reflections on a number of modern and early modern texts, in which the three key themes that have formed the book's three sections come together in the shape of the female revenger.

Conclusion: Gendered Revenge

'Sweet is Revenge – especially to women.'

(Lord Byron, *Don Juan*, canto 1, stanza 124)

Revenge and the iconic female

In the king's bedchamber on the island of Rhodes, a beautiful young woman ties his arms to the bed while he sleeps. In a retired rock star's opulent bedroom, viewed in a mirrored ceiling, a beautiful naked woman straddles her lover, reveals a hidden silk scarf, and ties his wrists to the bedrails. In the bedchamber, the king wakes. Discovering the bonds around his wrists and ankles, he turns to the woman hovering at his bedside: 'What pretty new device is this, Evadne?' he asks, his voice heavy with arousal. 'What, do you tie me to you by my love?'[1] In the rock star's bedroom, the naked woman, her face obscured by tumbling blonde hair, rocks back and forth as she approaches her climax. Throwing back her head, her hand reaches behind her, beneath the bedcovers. In the bedchamber, the king invites Evadne to bed: 'There thou shalt know the state of my body better,' he promises her. 'I know you have a surfeited foul body,' Evadne spits back, drawing a dagger, 'And you must bleed.'[2] In the bedroom, the blonde woman propels herself forward, ice-pick in hand, and stabs her lover repeatedly in the face; he screams as blood spurts from his wounds. In the bedchamber, Evadne stabs the king over and over, heedless of his cries for mercy. 'Thus, thus, thou foul man,' she screams, punctuating her words with dagger blows; 'Thus I begin my vengeance.'[3]

The previous sections have explored issues of revenge in a wide range of texts. In *Taxi Driver*, the object of Travis Bickle's affection, Betsy, and the prostitute he tries to save, Iris, are crucial figures. The former is

213

Travis's 'angel' and his potential saviour. When Betsy takes herself out of the picture, and Travis goes into a psychic tailspin, the young prostitute, Iris, becomes a symbol of redemption, someone he can save from the filth that is drowning the city, and threatening to take him with it. Iris is a focus for his obsession with human corruption, his fury crystallised by the idea that her innocence has not only been destroyed but also cynically exploited by her pimp, Sport. In this way, the Betsy/Iris nexus is analogous to Gloriana's skull in *The Revenger's Tragedy*, a signifier of purity amidst the mire of moral and sexual corruption:

> Thee, when thou wert apparelled in thy flesh,
> The old duke poisoned,
> Because thy purer part would not consent
> Unto his palsy-lust (1.1.29–32)

In the movie *Se7en*, Tracy (Gwyneth Paltrow) is the redemptive figure – the one to whom Mills escapes from the squalor of the crime-ridden city, the one whose unborn child represents a fragile chance for something to survive the unremitting bleakness. Her death flatlines any hope of redemption that may have remained. The other women in the film form the flipside of the madonna/whore binary: the prostitute killed as the sin of lust, and the woman who kills herself with an overdose once Doe has cut off her nose and left her with a phone glued in one hand (to call for help) and a bottle of sleeping pills in the other (to kill herself and avoid the horror of permanent disfigurement) – the sin of pride. With a bloody-mindedness characteristic of the movie, Tracy's head is cut off and the gruesome discovery precipitates Mills' act of revenge – or 'wrath', as Doe would have it, in his obsession with finishing his masterpiece of the seven deadly sins. When he shoots Doe dead, Mills seals his own damnation.

The plays and films I have considered are all preoccupied, in different ways, with what contorts Doe's psyche: the disjunction between what is and what should be in a fallen (or degenerate) world. And, frequently, the female becomes the key symbol of that tension. However, while women are repeatedly used as the *motivation* for, or *object* of revenge, the active female revenger is a rare anomaly – certainly in the early modern period, where the notion of the female as the perpetrator of physical violence seems to be almost unimaginable. There are a handful of notable examples. Perhaps the most familiar is the figure of Lady Macbeth, who can prepare herself for murder only after she has renounced her female nature, calling on spirits to 'unsex' her and fill her 'from the crown to the toe, top-full/Of direst cruelty' (1.5.40–2). However, although it would appear that her plan is to murder Duncan herself (1.5.49–53), she finds that she is unable to follow through ('Had he not resembled/My father as he slept, I had done 't' [2.2.13–14]), and soon afterwards she descends into a turmoil of guilt that drives her to insanity and suicide. It is not difficult to read a subtext here of the unnatural, demonic woman denying her true nature and subsequently self-destructing in spectacular fashion. Like the bloody figure of Beatrice-Joanna, the sight of Lady Macbeth sleepwalking, desperately rubbing imaginary blood from her guilty hands, can be decoded as a warning to women in the audience. She finds her contemporary counterpart in the likes of Rebecca De Mornay's psychotic, vengeful nanny in *The Hand That Rocks the Cradle* (1992) and the Glenn Close 'other woman' character who becomes violent when her lover (Michael Douglas) attempts to return to his wife and children (*Fatal Attraction*, 1987).

Evadne, the wronged woman at the centre of *The Maid's Tragedy* (1611) is a female protagonist unlike any other in early modern drama. Not only does she enact bloody revenge, she also moves against a king: her crime is an act of treason. When the king's attendants discover his body, one cries, 'Who can believe a woman could do this?' (5.2.135). No doubt his line gave voice to the thoughts of many in the audience. However, Evadne's act of vengeance is hardly a proto-feminist act. In the early part of the play, she has been married off to Amintor so that the King can covertly continue his relationship with her, and Amintor is shocked to discover that she will not sleep with him because of her status as the king's mistress. Evadne is shamed into taking her revenge on the king by her brother Melantius, Amintor's closest friend; Melantius forces her to acknowledge her own 'monstrous' nature. Although the sense of guilt Melantius awakens in her is what motivates her, she is essentially engaged in a vindication not of her own honour, but of Amintor's. And the lesson she offers to the audience? 'Let no woman dare/From this hour be disloyal' (5.1.15–16). When she returns to Amintor, '*with bloody hands, carrying a knife*' (5.3.107 s.d.), announcing the king's death, he rejects her as 'a monster of cruelty' (158). Having sacrificed everything for her true husband's honour in vain, and her mind and spirit broken, Evadne's only exit is suicide.

Mother's love, mother's fury

As I noted earlier, the female revenger has remained largely beyond the boundaries of mainstream film, residing in the underground domain that houses the likes of *I Spit on Your Grave*, *Ms. 45: Angel of Vengeance* and *Thriller: A Cruel Film*, the latter an acknowledged influence on Quentin Tarantino's work. By the time Tarantino began work on his own take on the female revenger plot, he had become one of the most familiar celebrities of popular culture in the 1990s, thanks to his two hit movies *Reservoir Dogs* (1992) and *Pulp Fiction* (1994). After the more subdued *Jackie Brown* (1997), however, Tarantino remained inactive as a director for six years before returning with his most ambitious work to date, the two *Kill Bill* movies.[4] The films are noteworthy for their largely successful attempt at filleting obscure, cult and exploitation movies, and refashioning them into well-honed, shiny blockbusters (whatever one might think of the content of his films, Tarantino's visual sense is hard to fault).

Tarantino was very clear that what he was presenting was a revenge movie: 'You've heard of mother's love. This is mother's fury,' he told The Associated Press.[5] The film is prefaced by a title card that reads, 'Revenge is a dish best served cold', a phrase with a long history in a number of Western cultures, but probably first put into print in de LaClos's play *Les Liaisons Dangereuses* (1782). Tarantino, however, in a move that epitomises his approach to popular culture, chooses to credit it as an 'old Klingon proverb', referencing its inclusion in *Star Trek II: The Wrath of Khan* (1982). The first part of the movie is very direct in the execution of its revenge plot: although it does not proceed strictly chronologically, we soon learn that The Bride (Uma Thurman), a member of the Deadly Viper Assassination Squad, has become pregnant by the squad's leader, Bill (David Carradine). She attempts to leave to begin a new life with a new man, but Bill tracks her down, the squad slaughters her wedding party and puts a bullet through her head. The Bride awakens from a coma four years later and goes on a 'rip-roaring rampage of revenge' (as she calls it herself, in a monologue to camera), killing Vernita Green (aka Copperhead, played by Vivica A. Fox), O-Ren-Ishii (aka Cottonmouth, Lucy Liu) and Elle Driver (aka California Mountain Snake, Daryl Hannah). Of the two male members of the team, Budd (aka Sidewinder, Michael Madsen) is killed in a double-cross by Elle, and the second film ends with The Bride confronting Bill, defeating him with a legendary kung fu technique taught to her (but not to Bill) by the martial arts master who instructed both of them. Along the way, The Bride discovers that the child she believed dead is actually alive, and living with her father, Bill. The final resolution of her revenge is complicated by her reunion with her daughter, B.B.

In terms of feminism, the movie's status is problematic. Tarantino declined to call the film feminist, reflecting, 'I would probably use the term girl power.'[6] Uma Thurman was more optimistic about the film's prospects as a document of empowerment, giving the example of high school discourse she had heard, with girls 'referring to defending themselves [and] saying they were gonna do an "Uma" on that person'.[7] Still, in terms of what occurs on screen, the film's gender politics are never this straightforward. There is a casual misogyny among the men – note the discourse of the medical orderly, Buck, and his customer in *Vol. 1*, mirrored almost exactly in the conversation between Budd and his accomplice as they gaze at The Bride's prostrate body in *Vol. 2*. We learn that kung fu master, Tai Pei (Gordon Liu), 'despises women'. Meanwhile, the key female players, particularly in The Bride's confrontations with Verdina Green and Elle Driver, repeatedly refer, tiresomely, to one another as 'bitch'.[8] However, one of the most interesting aspects of *Kill Bill* in terms of gendered revenge is its persistent deferral of conflict between male and female. Although there is an early scene at the hospital, when The Bride takes revenge on the orderly who has routinely prostituted her comatose body, her two key targets in the first part are female: Vernita Green and O-Ren Ishii. Although she slays or maims most of the predominantly male personnel of O-Ren Ishii's gang, the Crazy 88 (it is a moot point whether there are in fact eighty-eight of them), this is a showcase for her swordswomanship, not enactment of vengeance. Even here, the set-piece is her face-off against the killer in a schoolgirl outfit, Go Go Yubari (Chiaki Kuriyama). When she catches up with Budd in *Vol. 2*, he defeats her with casual ease, and he eventually dies at the hands of Elle Driver, not The Bride. Much was made in the film's pre-publicity – in interviews with director and cast – of what Tarantino refers to as the two movies' 'bitch fights'. His remark that the fight between Elle and The Bride as scripted 'was already brutal and they're so beautiful, it hurts all the more actually, it's even more painful', fits very neatly into the familiar trope of the spectacle of the suffering, beautiful woman.[9] Indeed, the first film begins with a devastating image of The Bride's face, smashed and bloody, picked out in highly defined black and white, as she lies on the floor of the chapel, panting, just before Bill shoots her in the head. The Sheriff at the crime scene refers to her as 'a blood-spattered angel'.

Tarantino's enthusiasm for his 'bitch fights' mirrors his thoughts on Uma Thurman's punishing training and acting schedule. This extract from an interview with Thurman is revealing:

> He would laugh to me about the scene where I'm in the car, I'm struggling. He goes, 'I was watching this footage and you were

struggling and I see your tears run down your face and you've got this weird muscle you've developed in your hand, I never saw that. I loved when you're sweating and you look awful, it was so great. And then I realized I made you do it 15 more times.' So we explored every single moment to the nth degree... And for me, just having to make contact with these guys training me and having to actually contact a body with a sword, and with Quentin who's relentless, 'Harder, harder, more, more, more, harder.' Oh geez, I'm not hitting him any harder than that, no.[10]

This quotation is rich in subtext; it brings to mind the film's opening monologue – Bill standing above The Bride as she lies battered and bleeding, and his assurance to her that 'there's nothing sadistic in my actions... this is me at my most masochistic'. It also opens up an interesting angle on the production of the film, akin to the mirroring of fact and fiction in the treatment of Amy/Susan George in *Straw Dogs*, discussed in Chapter 8, although the power relations between Tarantino and Thurman shift and swing much more dynamically than in the case of Peckinpah and George. The parallels between Bill/The Bride and Tarantino/Thurman, are many, however, especially in terms of ownership (Bill's decision to wipe out the wedding party is essentially a tantrum, an act of childish, raging possessiveness). The film's own website notes that Tarantino refers to Thurman as 'my actress',[11] and in interviews he has frequently called her his 'muse' and his 'Marlene Dietrich'. The parallels intensify still further the complex power games at the heart of the movie's production, and particular scenes in the film, most obviously the flashback to the wedding rehearsal in *Vol. 2*, when The Bride attempts to cast Bill in the role of her father, something he accepts as a deceitful role-play, but which he evidently rejects with sour contempt.

The Bride's showdown with Bill is, finally, not an all-conquering triumph, but rather a poignant farewell to her former lover. The so-called five-point palm exploding-heart technique is a tribute to the kung fu movies that Tarantino adores, but it is also something more. All the other members of the squad realise what The Bride's elopement did to Bill in the first place: it broke his heart (Budd uses the precise phrase as he buries her alive near the beginning of *Vol. 2*). Though the exploding heart technique kills its victim five paces after the blow is struck, Bill's five pace journey began over four years earlier, when he took his own 'most masochistic' revenge on The Bride for leaving him. The kung fu blow is also a welcome counter to the obsession with Hatari Hanzo samurai swords, which are used throughout the films so blatantly as signifiers of phallic power that one can almost hear Tarantino laugh as he imagines those academics willing to take popular culture seriously, picking up and running with the subtext.[12]

Central to the conception, if not the execution, of the *Kill Bill* movies, however, is not the wronged woman, but the vengeful mother. When The Bride wakes from her coma, her first thought, after a queasily comic tap on her metal-plated head, is for her unborn child, and the discovery of her empty womb is a trigger for a *tour de force* performance of rage and emotional pain. In terms of the film's sequencing, the point is made some time before this, since it shifts directly from the blood-spattered Bride prologue to her arrival at Vernita Green's house, where the show-down takes place in what is signposted for the audience as a comfortable family home with outdoor toys littering the lawn. Idyllic domesticity is shattered, literally, in the house-wrecking fight between The Bride and her enemy, but the fight is interrupted by the return of Vernita's daughter, Nicki, from school, and the women retire to the kitchen for coffee in a parody of neighbourly convention, before hostilities suddenly resume, Green's shot from a hidden pistol going wide, and The Bride's throwing-knife burying itself deep in Green's chest. Despite the liberal blood-letting that will follow in the two volumes of *Kill Bill* (almost four hours of screen time), perhaps no scene is quite as shocking as the camera pan that reveals Nicki, standing in the kitchen doorway, watching her mother die.

In Shakespeare's *Titus Andronicus*, his most vengeful female character, Tamora, Queen of the Goths, is also motivated by the fury of a mother deprived of her child. Taken prisoner along with her three sons, she is brought into Rome by the victorious general, Titus. When Titus demands the death of her eldest son, Alarbus, as tribute to his own sons who have fallen in battle, she pleads for him to be spared: 'Victorious Titus, rue the tears I shed,/A mother's tears in passion for her son' (1.1.105–6). Her tears and petitions are in vain, however, and Alarbus is taken away, his limbs lopped off, his body cut open, and his entrails and body parts burned. Tamora's revenge, when it comes, is terrible, topped only by Titus's nightmarishly inventive retaliation. The play is a carnival of horrors, mutilation, decapitation and cannibalism, but the blood-letting is as nothing when compared to the anguished scene earlier in the play in which Titus's daughter, cornered in the forest by Tamora and her sons Chiron and Demetrius, pleads for mercy as they kill her husband and then prepare to make his 'dead trunk pillow to [their] lust' (2.3.130).

She turns to Tamora and begs the queen to save her from the horror and shame that awaits her:

> 'Tis present death I beg, and one thing more
> That womanhood denies my tongue to tell.
> O, keep me from their worse-than-killing lust,
> And tumble me into some loathsome pit,
> Where never man's eye may behold my body;
> Do this, and be a charitable murderer. (2.3.173–8)

The text presents Lavinia's plea as an appeal from one woman to another, with Lavinia assuming that Tamora will understand what are framed as uniquely feminised fears and vulnerabilities. Tamora, however, is unmoved, and her sons carry Lavinia away. Having satisfied their lust, these scholars of myth and legend not only cut out her tongue (the fate of Philomela when raped by Tereus) but lop off her hands too (Philomela revealed the identity of her rapist by weaving her story into a tapestry). When Lavinia returns to the stage, her literally unspeakable psychic pain is voiced by a man, her uncle Marcus, in a sixty-line soliloquy. And yet Marcus's eloquence is as nothing when set against Lavinia's earlier pleas; and none of the sadism that follows can match Tamora's stony cruelty in her rejection of them. Lavinia watches as her father takes revenge on the rapists, and she even holds the bowl to catch their blood when he slits their throats. What does she communicate through her face, through her eyes? Satisfaction, horror, or numbed blankness? By now, it hardly matters. She is only another instrument in the hands of the male revenger, and when it is her turn to become another of Titus's object lessons, she dies without any sign of protest or dissent. She does not even live long enough to see her father kill the woman who urged her sons to do with her as they wished, 'The worse to her, the better loved of me' (2.3.167).

In his *Theses on the Philosophy of History*, Walter Benjamin writes:

> The true picture of the past flits by. The past can be seized only as an image which flashes up at the instant when it can be recognized and is never seen again. For every image of the past that is not recognized by the present as one of its own concerns threatens to disappear irretrievably'.[13]

At the climax of Julie Taymor's film version of *Titus* (1999), there is a startling moment of camera trickery. Tamora and Titus are dead. Titus's last remaining son, Lucius, rams a serving spoon into the emperor Satur-ninus's mouth, forcing it straight through his skull. Lucius spits on him as Saturninus's chair tips back and the scene abruptly slows and freezes; after a split second, with the camera wheeling around the table, Lucius, in rapid motion against the frozen tableau, draws his pistol and shoots Saturninus in the head. The camera crash-zooms out, and we find ourselves not on a film set, but in an amphitheatre, with a Croatian audience watching this play of unremitting brutality. It is a picture from a 400-year-old tragedy flashed up for an instant, but frozen for a moment longer, a gesture of faith, perhaps, that this image might be recognised by the present.

This study has been an attempt to read texts across history as documents that illuminate one another in terms of cultural difference and, at the same time, often mirror shameful correlations between the different time periods. Such correlations can provoke pessimism, and invite retreat into unhelpful universalism. Or they may remind us of the abiding need for wider, greater and faster social and political change. While the precise contours and dynamics of each of the ideological concerns outlined in this study remain historically contingent, there are nevertheless striking parallels and points of convergence between the genre of early modern revenge tragedy and the wider cultural phenomenon of violent cinema. They have much to tell us about who we were, who we are, and what we might become.

List of Play and Film Texts

Plays

Antonio's Revenge (John Marston, 1600)
Apius and Virginia (R.B., c.1575)
Arden of Faversham (Anon, 1592)
The Atheist's Tragedy (Cyril Tourneur, 1609–10)
Battle of Alcazar (George Peele, c.1592)
Cambyses (Thomas Preston, c.1560)
The Changeling (Thomas Middleton and William Rowley, 1622)
Doctor Faustus (Christopher Marlowe, 1588)
The Duchess of Malfi (John Webster, 1614)
A Game at Chess (Thomas Middleton, 1624)
Hamlet (William Shakespeare, 1601)
Henry V (William Shakespeare, 1599)
Henry VIII (William Shakespeare, 1613)
The Insatiate Countess (John Marston, c.1608–10)
The Isle of Dogs (Ben Jonson and Thomas Nashe, 1597)
The Jew of Malta (Christopher Marlowe, 1589)
King Lear (William Shakespeare, 1605)
The Maid's Tragedy (Francis Beaumont and John Fletcher, 1611)
The Maiden's Tragedy (Thomas Middleton, 1610)
The Merchant of Venice (William Shakespeare, 1596)
Othello (William Shakespeare, 1603)
The Revenge of Bussy d'Ambois (George Chapman, 1607)
The Revenger's Tragedy (Thomas Middleton, 1606)
Richard III (William Shakespeare, 1593)
Romeo and Juliet (William Shakespeare, 1595)
Sejanus, His Fall (Ben Jonson, 1603)
Sir John van Olden Barnavelt (John Fletcher and Philip Massinger, 1619)
The Spanish Tragedy (Thomas Kyd, 1584)
Tamburlaine, Parts One and *Two* (Christopher Marlowe, 1587)
Titus Andronicus (William Shakespeare, 1592)
The Tragedy of Hoffman (Henry Chettle, 1602)
The Virgin Martyr (Thomas Dekker, 1620)
Volpone (Ben Jonson, 1606)
A Woman Killed with Kindness (Thomas Heywood, 1603)
The White Devil (John Webster, 1612)
The Winter's Tale (William Shakespeare, 1609)
Women Beware Women (Thomas Middleton, 1621)
A Yorkshire Tragedy (Thomas Middleton, 1608)

Films

The Accused (Jonathan Kaplan, 1988)
Alien (Ridley Scott, 1979)
Alien 3 (David Fincher, 1992)
Alien Resurrection (Jean-Pierre Jeunet, 1997)
Aliens (James Cameron, 1986)
An American Werewolf in London (John Landis, 1981)
Attack of the Crab Monsters (Roger Corman, 1957)
Autopsy (Juan Logar, 1973)
Bad Boys II (Michael Bay, 2003)
Baise-Moi (Virginie Despentes and Coralie Trinh Thi, 2000)
The Beast from 20,000 Fathoms (Eugène Lourié, 1953)
Billy Jack (Tom Laughlin, 1971)
Black Widow (Bob Rafelson, 1987)
Blink (Michael Apted, 1994)
Blood Feast (Herschell Gordon Lewis, 1963)
Body of Evidence (Uli Edel, 1993)
Bonnie and Clyde (Arthur Penn, 1967)
Bound (Andy Wachowski, 1996)
Bowling for Columbine (Michael Moore, 2002)
Bram Stoker's Dracula (Francis Ford Coppola, 1992)
The Brood (David Cronenberg, 1979)
Cannibal (Ruggero Deodato, 1976)
Cannibal Ferox (Umberto Lenzi, 1980)
Cannibal Holocaust (Ruggero Deodato, 1979)
Capturing the Friedmans (Andrew Jarecki, 2003)
Carrie (Brian de Palma, 1976)
Charlie's Angels (McG, 2000)
Charlie's Angels: Full Throttle (McG, 2003)
Cherry Falls (Geoffrey Wright, 2000)
Chinatown (Roman Polanski, 1974)
Comanche Station (Budd Boetticher, 1960)
The Company of Wolves (Neil Jordan, 1984)
Daredevil (Mark Steven Johnson, 2003)
Dawn of the Dead (George A. Romero, 1978)
The Day After Tomorrow (Roland Emmerich, 2004)
Dawn of the Dead (Zack Snyder, 2004)
Day of the Dead (George A. Romero, 1985)
Dead Calm (Phillip Noyce, 1989)
The Dead Pool (Buddy Van Horn, 1988)
Dead Ringers (David Cronenberg, 1988)
Death of a Gunfighter (Don Siegel, Alan Smithee, Robert J. Totten, 1969)
Death Wish (Michael Winner, 1974)
Death Wish II (Michael Winner, 1982)
Death Wish 3 (Michael Winner, 1985)
Death Wish 4: The Crackdown (J. Lee Thompson, 1987)
Death Wish V: The Face of Death (Allan A. Goldstein, 1994)
Deliverance (John Boorman, 1972)

Die Hard (John McTiernan, 1988)
Die Hard 2: Die Harder (Renny Harlin, 1990)
Die Hard with a Vengeance (John McTiernan, 1995)
Dirty Harry (Don Siegel, 1971)
Disclosure (Barry Levinson, 1994)
Double Indemnity (Billy Wilder, 1944)
Dressed to Kill (Brian de Palma, 1980)
Easy Rider (Dennis Hopper, 1969)
The Enforcer (James Fargo, 1976)
Enough (Michael Apted, 2002)
Executive Action (David Miller, 1973)
The Exorcist (William Friedkin, 1973)
Extremities (Robert M. Young, 1986)
An Eye for An Eye (John Schlesinger, 1995)
Faces of Death (Conan Lecilaire, 1978)
Fahrenheit 9/11 (Michael Moore, 2004)
Fatal Attraction (Adrian Lyne, 1987)
Femme Fatale (Brian de Palma, 2002)
Final Destination (James Wong, 2000)
Final Destination 2 (David R. Ellis, 2003)
The Fly (Kurt Neumann, 1958)
The Fly (David Cronenberg, 1986)
Event Horizon (Paul W. S. Anderson, 1997)
A Fistful of Dollars (Sergio Leone, 1964)
For a Few Dollars More (Sergio Leone, 1965)
Freddy vs. Jason (RonnyYu, 2003)
Friday the 13th (Sean S. Cunnigham, 1980)
Friday the 13th Part 2 (Steve Miner, 1981)
Friday the 13th Part 3 (Steve Miner, 1982)
Ghost Ship (Steve Beck, 2002)
Gimme Shelter (Albert Maysles, David Maysles, Charlotte Mitchell Zwerin, 1970)
The Godfather (Francis Ford Coppola, 1972)
Godzilla (Terrell O. Morse, 1956)
The Good, the Bad and the Ugly (Sergio Leone, 1966)
Halloween (John Carpenter, 1978)
The Hand That Rocks the Cradle (Curtis Hanson, 1992)
Hang 'Em High (Ted Post, 1968)
Haute Tension (aka *Switchblade Romance*) (Alexandre Aja, 2004)
Hear No Evil (Robert Greenwald, 1993)
Heaven's Gate (Michael Cimino, 1981)
High Noon (Fred Zinnemann, 1952)
High Plains Drifter (Clint Eastwood, 1973)
The Howling (Joe Dante, 1981)
I Spit on Your Grave (Meir Zarchi, 1977)
Interview with the Vampire (Neil Jordan, 1994)
Invasion of the Body Snatchers (1956)
Irréversible (Gaspar Noé, 2002)
It Came from Outer Space (Jack Arnold, 1953)
Jackie Brown (Quentin Tarantino, 1997)

Jason X (James Isaac, 2002)
Jaws (Steven Spielberg, 1975)
Jeepers Creepers (Victor Salva, 2001)
Jeepers Creepers 2 (Victor Salva, 2003)
Joe (John G. Avildsen, 1970)
Joe Kidd (John Sturges, 1972)
Kill Bill Vol. 1 (Quentin Tarantino, 2003)
Kill Bill Vol. 2 (Quentin Tarantino, 2004)
Lady Snowblood (Toshiya Fujita, 1973)
Lara Croft Tomb Raider: The Cradle of Life (Jan de Bont, 2003)
Lara Croft: Tomb Raider (Simon West, 2002)
Last House on the Left (Wes Craven, 1972)
The Last Seduction (John Dahl, 1994)
Lethal Weapon 1–4 (all Richard Donner, 1987, 1989, 1992, 1998)
Lipstick (Lamont Johnson, 1976)
The Long Kiss Goodnight (Renny Harlin, 1996)
The Lost Boys (Joel Schumacher, 1987)
Magnum Force (Ted Post, 1973)
A Man Apart (F. Gary Gray, 2003)
The Man from Laramie (Anthony Mann, 1955)
Man of the West (Anthony Mann, 1958)
Man on Fire (Tony Scott, 2004)
The Matrix (Andy Wachowski, 1999)
Ms. 45: Angel of Vengeance (Abel Ferrara, 1981)
Murder by Numbers (Barbet Schroeder, 2002)
Mute Witness (Anthony Waller, 1994)
My Bloody Valentine (Georges Mihalka, 1981)
My Darling Clementine (John Ford, 1946)
Near Dark (Kathryn Bieglow, 1987)
A Nightmare on Elm Street (Wes Craven, 1984)
A Nightmare on Elm Street 3: Dream Warriors (Chuck Russell, 1987)
Night of the Living Dead (George A. Romero, 1968)
Once Upon a Time in the West (Sergio Leone, 1968)
The Outlaw Josey Wales (Clint Eastwood, 1976)
Pale Rider (Clint Eastwood, 1985)
Panic Room (David Fincher, 2002)
The Parallax View (Alan J. Pakula, 1974)
The Passion of the Christ (Mel Gibson, 2004)
Point Blank (John Boorman, 1967)
Poison Ivy (Andy Ruben, Katt Shea Ruben, 1992)
Psycho (Alfred Hitchcock, 1960)
Pulp Fiction (Quentin Tarantino, 1994)
The Punisher (Jonathan Hensleigh, 2004)
Rabid (David Cronenberg, 1975)
Red Planet Mars (Harry Horner, 1952)
Resident Evil (Paul W. S. Anderson, 2002)
Resident Evil: Apocalypse (Alexander Witt, 2004)
Return of the Living Dead (Dan O'Bannon, 1985)
Robocop (Paul Verhoeven, 1987)

Roger and Me (Michael Moore, 1989)
Scanners (David Cronenberg, 1981)
Scary Movie (Keenen Ivory Wayans, 2000)
Scary Movie 2 (Keenen Ivory Wayans, 2001)
Scary Movie 3 (Jerry Zucker, David Zucker, 2003)
Scream 1–3 (all Wes Craven, 1996, 1997, 2000)
Se7en (David Fincher, 1995)
Sea of Love (Harold Becker, 1989)
Shakespeare in Love (John Madden, 1998)
Shane (George Stevens, 1953)
Shrek 2 (Andrew Adamson et al, 2004)
Sleepaway Camp (Robert Hiltzik, 1980)
Sleeping with the Enemy (Joseph Ruben, 1991)
Sliver (Phillip Noyce, 1993)
Society (Brian Yuzna, 1989)
Spiderman (Sam Raimi, 2002)
A Stranger is Watching (Sean S. Cunningham, 1982)
Straw Dogs (Sam Peckinpah, 1971)
Sudden Impact (Clint Eastwood, 1983)
Supersize Me (Morgan Spurlock, 2003)
Taxi Driver (Martin Scorsese, 1976)
Terminator 2: Judgement Day (James Cameron, 1991)
Terror Train (Roger Spottiswoode, 1980)
Texas Chainsaw Massacre (Tobe Hooper, 1974)
The Searchers (John Ford, 1956)
The Silence of the Lambs (Jonathan Demme, 1991)
The Slumber Party Massacre (Amy Jones and Aaron Lipstadt, 1982)
The Thing (Christian Nyby, 1951)
The Thing (John Carpenter, 1982)
The Wild Bunch (Sam Peckinpah, 1969)
Them! (Gordon M. Douglas, 1954)
Thriller: A Cruel Picture (Bo A. Vibenius, 1973)
Touching the Void (Kevin MacDonald, 2003)
Twisted (Philip Kaufman, 2004)
Valentine (Jamie Blanks, 2001)
Walking Tall (Phil Karlson, 1973)
Walking Tall (Kevin Bray, 2004)
Wes Craven's New Nightmare (Wes Craven, 1994)
What Women Want (Nora Ephron, 2000)
When a Stranger Calls (Fred Walton, 1979)
Wild Things (John McNaughton, 1998)
Winchester '73 (Anthony Mann, 1950)
Woodstock (Michael Wadleigh, 1970)
Wrong Turn (Rob Schmidt, 2003)
X-Men (Bryan Singer, 2000)
X2: X-Men United (Bryan Singer, 2003)
Zombie Flesh Eaters (Lucio Fulci, 1979, aka *Zombie* or *Zombi* 2)

Notes and References

Introduction

1. Walter Benjamin, 'Theses on the Philosophy of History', in Douglas Tallack (ed.), *Critical Theory: A Reader* (Hemel Hempstead: Harvester Wheatsheaf, 1995), p. 281.
2. 'Pakistan: Honour Killings of Girls and Women', Amnesty International, 1 September 1999, http://web.amnesty.org/library/Index/engASA330181999, accessed 18 December 2004.
3. 'Law punishes victims of rape in Pakistan', Amnesty International, July 2004, http://web.amnesty.org/wire/July2004/Pakistan, accessed 18 December 2004.
4. In the more familiar version of the story, Virginius in fact kills his daughter Virginia so that he will not have to hand her over to Appius Claudius. Eugene M. Waith explains that both versions were current in Shakespeare's time; see Eugene M. Waith (ed.), *Titus Andronicus* (Oxford University Press, 1984; World's Classics paperback edition 1994), p. 187.
5. From the Rape, Abuse and Incest National Network website: http://www.rainn.org/statistics.html, accessed 6 January 2005.
6. Jean Howard, 'The New Historicism in Renaissance studies', in Arthur F. Kinney and Don S. Collins (eds), *Renaissance Historicism* (Amherst, Mass.: Massachusetts University Press, 1987), p. 33.
7. For example, John Kerrigan, *Revenge Tragedy: Aeschylus to Armageddon* (Oxford: Clarendon Press, 1997), pp. 1, 25, 321, 328; Katharine Eisaman Maus (ed.), *Four Revenge Tragedies* (Oxford University Press, 1995), p. xi; Jonathan Bate (ed.), *Titus Andronicus*, Arden Shakespeare: Third Series (London: Routledge, 1995), p. 2; Robert N. Watson, 'Tragedy', in A. R. Braunmuller and Michael Hattaway (eds), *The Cambridge Companion to English Renaissance Drama* (Cambridge University Press, 1990), p. 317.
8. Maus (1995), *Four Revenge Tragedies*.
9. Gamini Salgado, *Three Revenge Tragedies* (Harmondsworth: Penguin, 2004; first published 1965).
10. Fredson Bowers, *Elizabethan Revenge Tragedy 1587–1642* (Princeton, NJ: Princeton University Press, 1966; first edn 1940), p. 62.
11. For a very full and accessible philosophical engagement with these debates, see Noel Carroll, *A Philosophy of Mass Art* (Oxford: Clarendon Press, 1998). For further discussion of popular culture in relation to early modern drama, see Michael Bristol, 'Theater and Popular Culture', in John D. Cox and David Scott Kastan (eds), *A New History of Early English Drama* (New York: Columbia University Press, 1997), pp. 231–48.
12. Michael Ryan and Douglas Kellner, *Camera Politica: The Politics and Ideology of Contemporary Hollywood Film* (Bloomington, Ind.: Indiana University Press, 1990), p. 168.
13. Michael Bristol, *Carnival and Theatre* (London: Routledge, 1985), pp. 111–12.

14. Robert Kolker, *A Cinema of Loneliness: Penn, Stone, Kubrick, Scorsese, Spielberg, Altman* (third edn) (Oxford University Press, 2000), p. 11.
15. Ibid., p. 14.
16. Nigel Wheale, *Writing and Society: Literacy, Print and Politics in Britain 1590–1660* (London: Routledge, 1999), p. 10.
17. Franco Moretti, *Signs Taken for Wonders: Essays in the Sociology of Literary Forms* (London: Verso, 1983), p. 68.
18. C. L. Barber, *Creating Elizabethan Tragedy: The Theater of Marlowe and Kyd*, ed. Richard Wheeler (Chicago: University of Chicago Press, 1988), p. 160.
19. See Margot Heinemann, *Puritanism and Theatre: Thomas Middleton and Opposition Drama Under the Early Stuarts* (Cambridge University Press, 1980), p. 36.
20. Wheale, *Writing and Society*, p. 72.
21. Tony Bennett (ed.), *Popular Fictions* (London: Routledge, 1990), p. iv.
22. Tom Shone, *Blockbuster: How Hollywood Learned to Stop Worrying and Love the Summer* (London: Simon & Schuster, 2004), p. 294.
23. UK newspaper, *The Independent*, 28 December 2004, p. 5.
24. Gerald Graff, *Beyond the Culture Wars: How Teaching the Conflicts Can Revitalize American Education* (New York: W. W. Norton & Company, 1992), p. 100.
25. Noel Carroll argues that, by presenting the criminal Zodiac as 'evil incarnate', and offering him 'as a paradigm of the urban criminal, the film [*Dirty Harry*] has favourable implications for authoritarian police practices' (*A Philosophy of Mass Art*, pp. 406–7).
26. Gallup figures taken from http://www.gallup-international.com/ContentFiles/millennium15.asp, accessed 5 January 2005.
27. The Harris Poll no. 16, February 26th 2003; http://www.harrisinteractive.com/harris_poll/index.asp?PID = 359, accessed 5 January 2005.
28. In the USA, those under the age of seventeen require an accompanying parent or guardian to see an R-rated film.
29. Matt Zoller Seitz, 'Ribbons of Revenge', New York Press, 23 April 2004, http://www.alternet.org/movies/18496/, accessed 19 Oct 2004.

Chapter 1

1. Comment to the *New York Post* cited at SouthCoastToday.com – http://www.s-t.com/daily/05-96/05-03-96/2goetz.htm, accessed 17 November 2004. The remark is presumably framed as a reference to Richard Nixon's comment, of which it is a misquote, in a press conference in 1962 following his unsuccessful bid to become governor of California. Bernie Goetz returned to New York City to run for the office of mayor in 2001, chiefly on a vegetarianism ticket; he vowed to return in 2005, despite polling only 1,300 votes in the election.
2. René Girard, *Violence and the Sacred*, translated by Patrick Gregory (London: The Athlone Press, 1995; first published in French 1972, English translation 1977), p. 14.
3. See, for example, scholarship including Tim Judah, *Kosovo: War and Revenge* (New Haven, Conn.: Yale University Press, 2000); Christopher Boehm, *Blood Revenge: The Enactment and Management of Conflict in Montenegro and Other Tribal Societies* (Philadelphia: University of Pennsylvania Press, 1987); Marcus Tanner, *Croatia: A Nation Forged in War* (New Haven, Conn.: Yale University

Press, 2001); Misha Glenny, *The Fall of Yugoslavia* (Harmondsworth: Penguin, 1993); fiction including Ismail Kadare, *Elegy for Kosovo* (New York: Arcade Publishing, 2000); Ismail Kadare, *Broken April* (New York: Vintage, 2003); Slavenka Drakulic, *S.: A Novel about the Balkans* (Harmondsworth: Penguin, 2001); poetry, including Semezdin Mehmedinovic, *Sarajevo Blues* (San Francisco: City Lights Books, 1998); and film, including *Before the Rain* (1994) and *Farewell Sarajevo* (1997).

4. John G. Cawelti, 'Myths of Violence in American Popular Culture', *Critical Inquiry*, vol. 1, no. 3 (March 1975), pp. 521–41, reprinted in Cawelti, *Mystery, Violence and Popular Culture* (Madison, Wisc.: The University of Wisconsin Press, 2004), p. 162.
5. See Richard Slotkin, *Gunfighter Nation: The Myth of the Frontier in Twentieth Century America* (New York: Atheneum, 1992).
6. Terence Hawkes, 'On the Way in which Tragedy "Openeth up the Greatest Wounds and Showeth forth the Ulcers that are Covered with Tissue"', *London Review of Books*, vol. 19, no. 24, 11 December 1997, accessed at http://www.lrb.co.uk/v19/n24/hawk01_.html, 5 November 2004.
7. J. W. Lever, *The Tragedy of State: A Study of Jacobean Drama* (Methuen, 1987; first published 1971), pp. 32–3.
8. Romans 12:19, King James version of the Bible.

Chapter 2

1. John Kerrigan, 'Revenge Tragedy Revisited, 1649–1683' in Kerrigan, *On Shakespeare and Early Modern Literature* (Oxford University Press, 2004), pp. 231–2.
2. Fredson Bowers, *Elizabethan Revenge Tragedy 1587–1642* (Princeton, NJ: Princeton University Press, 1966; first edn 1940), p. 3.
3. René Girard, *Violence and the Sacred*, translated by Patrick Gregory (London: The Athlone Press, 1995; first published in French 1972, English translation 1977), p. 17.
4. Bowers, *Elizabethan Revenge Tragedy*, pp. 4–5.
5. Ibid., pp. 6–7.
6. Ibid., pp. 7–8.
7. Ibid., p. 13. See also Eleanor Prosser, *Hamlet and Revenge* (2nd edn) (Stanford, Calif.: Stanford University Press, 1971; first published 1967), pp. 3–21.
8. Prosser, *Hamlet and Revenge*, p. 10.
9. Kerrigan, 'Revenge Tragedy Revisited', p. 249.
10. Katharine Eisaman Maus (ed.), 'Introduction', *Four Revenge Tragedies* (Oxford University Press, World's Classics, 1995), p. xiv.
11. Bowers, *Elizabethan Revenge Tragedy*, p. 10.
12. See Bowers, *Elizabethan Revenge Tragedy*, pp. 3–61; Lily B. Campbell, 'Theories of Revenge in Elizabethan England', *Modern Philology*, vol. 28 (1931), pp. 281–96; Willard Farnham, *The Medieval Heritage of Elizabethan Tragedy* (Berkeley, Calif.: University of California Press, 1936), pp. 343–51.
13. Jong-Hwan Kim, 'Waiting for Justice: Shakespeare's *Hamlet* and the Elizabethan Ethics of Revenge', *English Language and Literature*, vol. 43 (1997), p. 788.
14. Lawrence Stone, *The Crisis of the Aristocracy, 1558–1641* (abridged edn) (Oxford University Press, 1967; first published 1965), p. 117.

15. V. G. Kiernan, *The Duel in European History* (Oxford University Press, 1988), pp. 82–3.
16. Maus, *Four Revenge Tragedies*, p. xiv.
17. Peter Corbin, '"A Dog's Obeyed in Office": Kingship and Authority in Jacobean Tragedy', in James Hogg (ed.), *Jacobean Drama as Social Criticism* (Lewiston, NY/Salzburg: Edwin Mellen Press, 1995), p. 66.
18. Lawrence Stone, *Crisis of the Aristocracy*, p. 114.
19. Francis Bacon, 'On Revenge', *The Essays, or Counsels Civil and Moral* (ed. Brian Vickers) (Oxford University Press, World's Classics, 1999), p. 10.
20. Prosser, *Hamlet and Revenge*, p. 70.
21. Girard, *Violence and the Sacred*, p. 15.
22. Eileen Allman, *Jacobean Revenge Tragedy and the Politics of Virtue* (Newark: University of Delaware Press, 1999), p. 34.
23. http://www.sensesofcinema.com/contents/03/24/cox_davies.html, accessed 12 October 2004.
24. J. W. Lever, *The Tragedy of State: A Study of Jacobean Drama* (London: Methuen, 1987; first published 1971), p. 20.
25. Ibid., p. 30.
26. Linda Levy Peck, *Court Patronage and Corruption in Early Stuart England* (London: Routledge, 1993; first published 1990), pp. 32–3.
27. John Oglander, *A Royalist's Notebook: The Commonplace Book of Sir John Oglander, Kt. of Nunwell* (ed. Francis Bamford) (New York: B. Blom, 1971), cited by Alvin Kernan, *Shakespeare, The King's Playwright: Theater in the Stuart Court, 1603–1613* (New Haven, Conn.: Yale University Press, 1995), pp. 119–20.
28. Cited in S. R. Gardiner, *History of England from the Accession of James I to the Outbreak of the Civil War, Vol. III* (London: Longman, Green & Co., 1883–4), p. 98.
29. Kernan, *Shakespeare, The King's Playwright*, p. 129.
30. See Lever, *Tragedy of State*, pp. 35–6; also numerous historical accounts, notably Linda Levy Peck, *Court Patronage and Corruption in Early Stuart England* (London: Routledge, 1993).
31. Sir John Harrington, letter describing the Revels at King James's Court, in Russ McDonald (ed.), *The Bedford Companion to Shakespeare: An Introduction with Documents* (2nd edn) (Boston, Mass.: Bedford/St. Martin's Press, 2001), p. 334.
32. Sir Anthony Weldon's description, from *The Court and Character of King James* (1649), is cited by Kernan, *Shakespeare, The King's Playwright*, p. 107. It may not be too fanciful to connect this description of James with Vindice's remark as the poison coated on Gloriana's skull burns away the Duke's face in *The Revenger's Tragedy*: 'My tongue!' gasps the Duke; 'Your tongue?,' Vindice replies; ''twill teach you to kiss closer,/Not like a slobbering Dutchman' (3.5.160–2).
33. Lever, *The Tragedy of State*, p. 87.
34. Cristina Malcolmson, '"As Tame as the Ladies": Politics and Gender in *The Changeling*', *English Literary Renaissance*, vol. 20; no. 2 (Spring 1990), p. 325. See also Margot Heinemann, *Puritanism and Theatre: Thomas Middleton and Opposition Drama under the Early Stuarts* (Cambridge University Press, 1980), pp. 178–9; and J. L. Simmons, 'Diabolical Realism in Middleton and Rowley's *The Changeling*', *Renaissance Drama*, new series 11 (1980), pp. 290–306.

35. Jennifer Woodward, 'Images of a Dead Queen – Historical Record of Mourning Ceremony for Queen Elizabeth I of England', *History Today*, November 1997, at http://www.findarticles.com/p/articles/mi_m1373/is_n11_v47/ai_19987419/pg_3, accessed 20 October 2004.
36. Cited in Levy Peck, *Court Patronage*, pp. 181–2.
37. See, for example, Ernst H. Kantorowicz, *The King's Two Bodies: A Study in Mediaeval Political Theology* (Princeton, NJ: Princeton University Press, 1998; first published 1957); Marie Axton, *The Queen's Two Bodies: Drama and the Elizabethan Succession* (London: Royal Historical Society, 1978); Albert Rolls, *The Theory of the King's Two Bodies in the Age of Shakespeare* (Lewiston, NY: Edwin Mellen Press, 2000).
38. Levy Peck, *Court Patronage*, ch. 8, *passim*.

Chapter 3

1. See, for example, Richard Maxwell Brown, *Strain of Violence: Historical Studies of American Violence and Vigilantism* (Oxford University Press, 1975); Robert P. Ingalls, *Urban Vigilantes in the New South: Tampa, 1882–1936* (Gainesville, Fla.: University Press of Florida, 1993); Christopher Waldrep, *Night Riders: Defending Community in the Black Patch, 1890–1915* (Durham, NC: Duke University Press, 1993); William C. Culberson, *Vigilantism: Political History of Private Power in America* (New York: Greenwood Press, 1990).
2. John G. Cawelti, 'Myths of Violence in American Popular Culture', *Critical Inquiry*, vol. 1, no. 3 (March 1975), pp. 521–41, reprinted in Cawelti, *Mystery, Violence and Popular Culture* (Madison, Wisc.: University of Wisconsin Press, 2004), pp. 164–5.
3. Richard Kazis, 'The Rambo Spirit', *New Internationalist*, vol. 154, December 1985, accessed at http://www.newint.org/issue154/rambo.htm, 17 November 2004.
4. http://www.law.berkeley.edu/institutes/csls/zimringchapter6.doc, accessed 7 October 2004.
5. J. Hoberman, *The Dream Life: Movies, Media, and the Mythology of the Sixties* (New York: The New Press, 2003), p. 321.
6. Ibid., p. 322.
7. The last three mentioned belong to another sub-genre, that of the rape-revenge film. It is interesting to note the ways in which these films invert or endorse the sexual politics that structure plays such as *The Duchess of Malfi* and *The Changeling*. See Carol J. Clover's extensive discussion in her *Men, Women and Chainsaws: Gender in the Modern Horror Film* (London: BFI Publishing, 1992).
8. Seth Cagin and Philip Dray, *Hollywood Films of the Seventies: Sex, Drugs, Rock'n'Roll and Politics* (New York: Harper & Row, 1984), p. 212.
9. Michael Ryan and Douglas Kellner, *Camera Politica: The Politics and Ideology of Contemporary Hollywood Film* (Bloomington, Ind.: Indiana University Press, 1990), p. 313.
10. Cited at http://www.clinteastwood.net/welcome2.html, accessed 17 November 2004.
11. Playboy interview with Clint Eastwood, February 1974, cited in Gary Crowdus (ed.), *The Political Companion to American Film* (London: Fitzroy Dearborn, 1994), p. 126.

12. Cited in Crowdus, *Political Companion*, p. 127.
13. Cited at http://www.the-dirtiest.com/presiden.htm, accessed 10 November 2004.
14. Hoberman, *The Dream Life*, p. 328.
15. Hoberman, *The Dream Life*, p. 373.

Chapter 4

1. Letter to M. Scott 5 January 1972. Reproduced on Criterion Collection DVD edition of *Straw Dogs*, 2003.
2. Katharine Eisaman Maus, 'Introduction', *Four Revenge Tragedies* (Oxford University Press, World's Classics, 1995), p. xi.
3. In the discussion that follows, the non-gender-specific forms are generally not utilised, since examples of female revengers are scarce. Discussion of these largely anomalous figures is reserved for the book's conclusion.
4. Seth Cagin and Philp Dray, *Hollywood Films of the Seventies: Sex, Drugs, Rock'n'Roll and Politics* (New York: Harper & Row, 1984), pp. 215–16.
5. John Locke, 'The Second Treatise of Civil Government', in Peter Laslett (ed.) *Two Treatises of Government* (Cambridge University Press, 1988; first published in this edn 1960), para. 7, p. 271.
6. Ibid., para. 222, pp. 412–13.
7. *Basilikon Doron* was intended by James as a private document, written for the instruction of his son Henry, who, as it turned out, died before his father. Interest in the document led to its publication in 1603, immediately after Queen Elizabeth's death.
8. C. L. Barber, *Creating Elizabethan Tragedy: The Theater of Marlowe and Kyd* (ed. Richard Wheeler) (Chicago: University of Chicago Press, 1988), p. 135.
9. James Shapiro, '"Tragedies naturally performed": Kyd's Representation of Violence', in David Scott Kastan and Peter Stallybrass (eds), *Staging the Renaissance: Reinterpretations of Elizabethan and Jacobean Drama* (London: Routledge, 1991), p. 103.
10. Quotation cited at http://www.melonfarmers.co.uk/in03a.htm, accessed 30 November 2004.
11. J. W. Lever, *The Tragedy of State: A Study of Jacobean Drama* (London: Methuen 1987; first published 1971), p. 68.
12. Dieter Mehl, 'Corruption, retribution and justice in *Measure for Measure* and *The Revenger's Tragedy*', in E. A. J. Honigmann (ed.), *Shakespeare and his Contemporaries: Essays in Comparison* (Manchester: Manchester University Press, 1986), pp. 119, 118.
13. Maus, Introduction, *Four Revenge Tragedies*, p. xi.
14. See Alan Sinfield, *Faultlines: Cultural Materialism and the Politics of Dissident Reading* (Oxford: Clarendon Press, 1992), pp. 38–47.
15. Maus (ed.), Introduction, *Four Revenge Tragedies*, pp. xiv-xv.
16. Review in *Variety* magazine, 1 January 1974, at http://www.variety.com/index.asp?layout=upsell_review&reviewID=VE1117790317&cs=1, accessed 12 January 2005.
17. Cited at http://www.dallasobserver.com/issues/2004–04–15/film/film3.html, accessed 19 November 2004.

18. Yvonne Tasker, *Spectacular Bodies: Gender, Genre and the Action Cinema* (London: Routledge, 1993), p. 32.
19. Tim Miner, DVD commentary, Criterion Collection DVD release of *Robocop*, 1998.

Chapter 5

1. See Charles K. B. Barton, *Getting Even: Revenge as a Form of Justice* (Chicago: Open Court, 1999); Peter A. French, *The Virtues of Vengeance* (University Press of Kansas, 2001).
2. French, *The Virtues of Vengeance*, p. 226.
3. 'Doctor driven out of home by vigilantes', *Guardian*, 30 August 2000; http://www.guardian.co.uk/child/story/0,7369,361031,00.html, accessed 29 November 2004.
4. Eleanor Prosser, *Hamlet and Revenge* (2nd edn) (Stanford, Calif.: Stanford University Press, 1971; first published 1967), p. 40.
5. Fredson Bowers, *Elizabethan Revenge Tragedy 1587–1642* (Princeton, NJ: Princeton University Press, 1966; first edn 1940), p. 184.
6. See Robert C. Jones, *Engagement with Knavery: Point of View in* Richard III, The Jew of Malta, Volpone *and* The Revenger's Tragedy (Durham, NC: Duke University Press, 1986), Introduction, esp. pp. 1–12.
7. Cited in Gary Crowdus (ed.), *The Political Companion to American Film* (London: Fitzroy Dearborn, 1994), p. 126.
8. From the original press materials, cited at http://www.the-dirtiest.com/director.htm, accessed 10 November 2004.
9. From *The Ladies' Home Journal*; cited in Crowdus, *Political Companion*, p. 127.
10. Susan Jeffords, *Hard Bodies: Hollywood Masculinity in the Reagan Era* (Brunswick, NJ: Rutgers University Press, 1994), p. 19.
11. G. Wilson Knight, cited in John Jump (ed.), *Hamlet: A Selection of Critical Essays* (London: Macmillan, 1968; eighth reprint 1983), p. 41, first published in *The Wheel of Fire* (London: Methuen, 1930).
12. A. C. Bradley, cited in Jump (1968), *Hamlet: . . . Essays*, p. 38, first published in *Shakespearean Tragedy* (London: Macmillan, 1904).
13. Michael Ryan and Douglas Kellner, *Camera Politica: The Politics and Ideology of Contemporary Hollywood Film* (Bloomington, Ind.: Indiana University Press, 1990), p. 87.
14. As Callahan and his partner Gonzalez follow a man they believe may be Scorpio, Harry climbs up to observe through a window and is mistaken for a Peeping Tom by residents. Gonzalez rescues him from a beating, and muses aloud on 'another thought . . . about why they call you "Dirty Harry"'. Later, while staking out Scorpio from a rooftop, Harry and his binoculars are diverted by the view of a naked woman at a swingers' party.
15. Robert Kolker, *A Cinema of Loneliness: Penn, Stone, Kubrick, Scorsese, Spielberg, Altman* (3rd edn) (Oxford University Press, 2000), pp. 226–7.
16. Robert Kolker, *A Cinema of Loneliness*, p. 228.
17. Joan Mellen, *Big Bad Wolves: Masculinity in the American Film* (London: Elm Tree Books, 1978), pp. 309–10.

18. John G. Cawelti, 'Myths of Violence in American Popular Culture', *Critical Inquiry*, Vol. 1, no. 3 (March 1975), pp. 521–41; reprinted in Cawelti, *Mystery, Violence and Popular Culture* (Madison, Wisc.: University of Wisconsin Press, 2004), p. 163.
19. Terry Eagleton, *Sweet Violence: The Idea of the Tragic* (Oxford: Basil Blackwell, 2003), p. 151.
20. Friedrich Nietzsche, *Beyond Good and Evil: Prelude to a Philosophy of the Future*, trans. and ed. by R. J. Hollingdale (Harmondsworth: Penguin, 1986; first published 1973), Aphorism 146, p. 84.
21. Ryan and Kellner, *Camera Politica*, p. 46.
22. Johnann Wolfgang von Goethe, *Wilhelm Meister: Apprenticeship and Travels* (London: Foulis, 1947), p. 212.
23. Charles Marowitz, 'Introduction', in *The Marowitz Shakespeare* (London: Marion Boyars, 1990), p. 13.
24. Marowitz, '*Hamlet*', in *The Marowitz Shakespeare*, p. 52.
25. See Bowers, *Elizabethan Revenge Tragedy*, p. 10, and further discussion in my earlier chapter, pp. 30–1.
26. http://www.sensesofcinema.com/contents/03/24/cox_davies.html, accessed 12 October 2004.
27. Leighton Grist, '*Unforgiven*', in Ian Cameron and Douglas Pye (eds), *The Movie Book of the Western* (London: Studio Vista, Cassell, 1996), p. 294.
28. Quoted at http://www.cinemareview.com/production.asp?prodid=2485, accessed 7 October 2004.
29. Ibid.
30. Richard A. Clarke, *Against All Enemies: Inside America's War on Terror* (London: The Free Press, 2004), p. 24.
31. From George W. Bush's address to Congress, 21 September 2001.
32. R. James Woolsey, 'Where's the Posse?', *Wall Street Journal*, 25 February 2002, accessed at http://www.opinionjournal.com/editorial/feature.html?id=105001690, 22 October 2004.
33. Scott Galupo, 'Back with a Vengeance: Vigilantes out for Blood', *Washington Times*, 16 April 2004, accessed at http://www.washingtontimes.com/entertainment/20040415-103107-4467r.htm, 22 October 2004.
34. Charles Taylor, 'Payback Time', 14 May 2004: http://www.salon.com/ent/feature/2004/05/14/fire/print.html, accessed 7 October 2004.
35. http://www.orlandosentinel.com/entertainment/movies/orl-calfire23_mvrv042304apr23,0,6234191.story?coll=orl-calmoviestop, accessed 12 October 2004.
36. The words of General Raymond Odierno, commander of the 4th Infantry Division, which helped to carry out the raid that led to the capture of Saddam, quoted by CNN.com on 14 December 2003: http://www.cnn.com/2003/WORLD/meast/12/14/sprj.irq.main/, accessed 24 November 2004.
37. Robert N. Watson, 'Tragedy', in A. R. Braunmuller and Michael Hattaway (eds), *The Cambridge Companion to English Renaissance Drama* (Cambridge University Press, 1990), p. 318.
38. J. Hoberman, *The Dream Life: Movies, Media, and the Mythology of the Sixties* (New York: The New Press, 2003), p. 323.
39. Joan Mellen, *Big Bad Wolves*, pp. 309–10, 310–11.

Chapter 6

1. Jean E. Howard and Phyllis Rackin, 'Gender and Nation: Anticipations of Modernity in the Second Tetralogy', in Kate Chedgzoy (ed.), *Shakespeare, Feminism and Gender: A New Casebook* (Basingstoke: Palgrave, 2001), pp. 93–4.

2. Marion Wynne-Davies, '"The Swallowing Womb": Consumed and Consuming Women in *Titus Andronicus*', in Valerie Wayne (ed.), *The Matter of Difference: Materialist Feminist Criticism of Shakespeare* (Hemel Hempstead: Harvester Wheatsheaf, 1991), p. 129.

3. See Celia R. Daileader, *Eroticism on the Renaissance Stage* (Cambridge University Press, 1998), appendix I.

4. See Carol Clover, *Men Women and Chainsaws: Gender in the Modern Horror Film* (London: BFI Publishing, 1992).

5. Molly Haskell, *From Reverence to Rape: The Treatment of Women in the Movies* (2nd edn) (Chicago: University of Chicago Press, 1974, 1987).

6. Kathleen MacLuskie, 'Drama and Sexual Politics: The Case of Webster's Duchess', in Dympna Callaghan (ed.), *The Duchess of Malfi: A New Casebook* (Basingstoke and London: Macmillan, 2000), p. 105.

7. Jocelyn Catty, *Writing Rape, Writing Women in Early Modern England: Unbridled Speech* (Basingstoke: Macmillan, 1999), p. 11.

8. D. E. Underdown, 'The Taming of the Scold: The Enforcement of Patriarchal Authority in Early Modern England', in Anthony Fletcher and John Stevenson (eds), *Order and Disorder in Early Modern England* (Cambridge University Press, 1985), quoted by Theresia de Vroom, 'Female Heroism in Heywood's Tragic Farce of Adultery: *A Woman Killed with Kindness*', in Naomi Conn Liebler (ed.), *The Female Tragic Hero in English Renaissance Drama* (Basingstoke: Palgrave, 2002), p. 122.

9. Underdown, 'The Taming of the Scold', p. 120.

10. Steven Mullaney, 'Mourning and Misogyny: *Hamlet* and the Final Progress of Elizabeth I', in Kate Chedgzoy (ed.), *Shakespeare, Feminism and Gender: Contemporary Critical Essays* (Basingstoke: Palgrave, 2001), p. 162.

11. 'H. M.', 'Analytical Essays on the Early English Dramatists', *Blackwood's Edinburgh Magazine* (1818), reprinted in R. V. Holdsworth (ed.), *Webster: The White Devil and The Duchess of Malfi: A Casebook* (London: Macmillan, 1975), pp. 34–5.

12. Gayle Greene, 'Women on Trial in Shakespeare and Webster: "The Mettle of [their] Sex"', *Topics: A Journal of Liberal Arts*, vol. 36 (1982), p. 15.

13. Mary Beth Rose, 'Heroics of Marriage in Renaissance Tragedy', in D. Callaghan (ed.), *The Duchess of Malfi: A New Casebook* (Basingstoke and London: Macmillan, 2000), p. 129.

14. Deborah Burks, '"I'll want my will else": *The Changeling* and Women's Complicity with their Rapists', *English Literary History*, vol. 62 (1995), pp. 759–90.

15. See Gayle Rubin, 'The Traffic in Women: Notes on the "Political Economy" of Sex', in Rayna R. Riter (ed.), *Toward an Anthropology of Women* (New York: Monthly Review Press), 1975, pp. 157–210.

16. Karen Bamford, *Sexual Violence on the Jacobean Stage* (Basingstoke: Palgrave, 2000), p. 8.

17. Joan Smith, *Misogynies* (London: Faber & Faber, 1989), p. 3.
18. Catty, *Writing Rape*, p. 11.
19. Gail Kern Paster, *The Body Embarrassed: Drama and the Disciplines of Shame in Early Modern England* (Ithaca, NY: Cornell University Press, 1993), p. 25.
20. Theodora Jankowski, 'Defining/Confining the Duchess: Negotiating the Female Body in John Webster's *The Duchess of Malfi*', *Studies in Philology*, vol. 87 (1990), p. 228.
21. Jankowski, 'Defining/Confining', p. 229.
22. Naomi Conn Liebler cites Linda Bamber's *Comic Women, Tragic Men* (Stanford, Calif.: Stanford University Press, 1982) as being representative of this approach, and notes Dympna Callaghan's reinscription of the position in *Shakespeare Without Women* (London: Routledge, 2000). Elizabeth D. Harvey's position in *Ventriloquized Voices* (London: Routledge, 1992) is more radical in terms of gender politics, but it works with similar assumptions.
23. Stephen Orgel, *Impersonations: The Performance of Gender in Shakespeare's England* (Cambridge University Press, 1996), p. 8, cited in Liebler (1982) Introduction, *The Female Tragic Hero*, p. 3.
24. Alison Findlay, *A Feminist Perspective on Renaissance Drama* (Oxford: Blackwell, 1999), p. 3.

Chapter 7

1. Molly Haskell, *From Reverence to Rape: The Treatment of Women in the Movies* (2nd edn) (Chicago: University of Chicago Press, 1974, 1987), pp. 39–40.
2. Sara Eaton, 'Defacing the Feminine in Renaissance Tragedy', in Valerie Wayne (ed.), *The Matter of Difference: Materialist Feminist Criticism of Shakespeare* (Hemel Hempstead: Harvester Wheatsheaf, 1991), p. 183.
3. http://www.amnesty.org/svaw/vaw/global.shtml, accessed 20 September 2004.
4. http://www.unfpa.org/swp/2000/pdf/english/chapter3.pdf, accessed 20 November 2004.
5. http://www.amnesty.org/svaw/vaw/causes.shtml, accessed 20 September 2004.
6. Marc O'Day, 'Beauty in Motion: Gender, Spectacle and Action Babe Cinema', in Yvonne Tasker (ed.), *Action and Adventure Cinema* (London: Routledge, 2004), p. 201.
7. Carol M. Dole, 'The Gun and the Badge: Hollywood and the Female Lawman', in Martha McCaughey and Neal King (eds), *Reel Knockouts: Violent Women in the Movies* (Austin, Tx: University of Texas Press, 2001), p. 87.
8. Elizabeth Young, '*The Silence of the Lambs* and the Flaying of Feminist Theory', *Camera Obscura*, vol. 27 (September 1992), pp. 5–35.
9. Yvonne Tasker, *Working Girls: Gender and Sexuality in Popular Cinema* (London: Routledge, 1998), p. 25.
10. *Sleeping with the Enemy* took over US$102m at the US Box Office and was one of the top-grossing films of 1991; *Enough* had a relatively meagre return of around US$39 million, scoring greater success on home video release.
11. Jessica Farb and Felice Cherry, 'Fight or Flight: Wives in Crisis in *Sleeping with the Enemy*', http://www.unc.edu/~jfarb/SWEFINAL.htm, accessed 13 November 2003.

12. Jacinda Read, *The New Avengers: Feminism, Femininity and the Rape–Revenge Cycle* (Manchester: Manchester University Press, 2000), p. 65.
13. Phyllis Frus, 'Documenting Domestic Violence in American Films', in J. David Slocum (ed.), *Violence and American Cinema* (London: Routledge, 2001), p. 237.
14. Lynda Hart, *Fatal Women: Lesbian Sexuality and the Mark of Aggression* (London: Routledge, 1994).
15. Read, *The New Avengers*, p. 69.
16. See interviews with Apted and Lopez at http://www.sonypictures.com/movies/enough/behindthescenes.php, accessed 22 November 2003, and frequent references throughout Apted's commentary on the DVD release.
17. Interview with Irwin Winkler at http://www.sonypictures.com/movies/enough/behindthescenes.php, accessed 22 November 2003.
18. Read, *The New Avengers*, ch. 2, esp. pp. 58–60.
19. It would seem that, by the end of the film, he is rewarded for his patience and restraint: the end credits sequence depicts him on a boat with Slim and Gracie in happy family mode.

Chapter 8

1. Interview with William Murray, *Playboy*, August 1972, cited in David Weddle, *If They Move ... Kill 'Em: The Life and Times of Sam Peckinpah* (London: Faber & Faber, 1996), p. 440.
2. Jean E. Howard and Phyllis Rackin, 'Gender and Nation: Anticipations of Modernity in the Second Tetralogy', in Kate Chedgzoy (ed.), *Shakespeare, Feminism and Gender: A New Casebook* (Basingstoke: Palgrave, 2001), p. 110.
3. Deborah Burks, '"I'll want my will else": *The Changeling* and Women's Complicity with their Rapists', *English Literary History*, vol. 62 (1995), p. 765.
4. Amy Louise Erickson, *Women and Property in Early Modern England* (London: Routledge, 1993), p. 233.
5. Marion Wynn-Davies, '"The Swallowing Womb": Consumed and Consuming Women in *Titus Andronicus*', in Valerie Wayne (ed.), *The Matter of Difference: Materialist Feminist Criticism of Shakespeare* (Hemel Hempstead: Harvester Wheatsheaf, 1991), pp. 130–1.
6. Ibid., p. 131.
7. Anne Laurence, *Women in England 1500–1760: A Social History* (London: Phoenix, 1996; first published 1994), p. 262.
8. Karen Bamford, *Sexual Violence on the Jacobean Stage* (Basingstoke and London: Macmillan, 2000), p. 9.
9. Sara Eaton, 'Beatrice-Joanna and the Rhetoric of Love in *The Changeling*', *Theatre Journal*, vol. 36, no. 3 (1984), p. 372.
10. Lisa Hopkins, *The Female Hero in English Renaissance Tragedy* (Basingstoke: Palgrave, 2002), pp. 13–14.
11. Barker, Roberta, and David Nicol, 'Does Beatrice Joanna Have a Subtext?: *The Changeling* on the London Stage', *Early Modern Literary Studies*, vol. 10, no. 1 (May, 2004) 3.1–43, at http://purl.oclc.org/emls/10–1/barknico.htm, accessed 12 January 2005.
12. Barker and Nicol, 'Does Beatrice', para. 38.

13. Barker and Nicol, 'Does Beatrice', para. 3.
14. *Man Trap*, Channel 4 UK TV documentary, first broadcast July 2003.
15. Carol Clover, *Men Women and Chainsaws: Gender in the Modern Horror Film* (London: BFI Publishing, 1992), p. 115.
16. Molly Haskell, *From Reverence to Rape: The Treatment of Women in the Movies* (2nd edn) (Chicago: University of Chicago Press, 1974, 1987), p. 363.
17. Bernard F. Dukore, *Sam Peckinpah's Feature Films* (Urbana, Ill. and Chicago: University of Illinois Press 1999), p. 33.
18. http://www.geocities.com/paulinekaelreviews/s9.html, accessed 27 August 2003.
19. Clover, *Men, Women and Chainsaws*, p. 139.
20. Linda Ruth Williams, 'Women Can Only Misbehave – Peckinpah, 'Straw Dogs', Feminism and Violence', *Sight and Sound*, vol. 5, no. 2, February 1995, pp. 26–7.
21. http://www.sundayherald.com/print31037, accessed 1 September 2003.
22. Barker and Nicol, 'Does Beatrice', para. 39.
23. Williams, 'Women Can Only Misbehave', p. 27.
24. Pier Paolo Frassinelli, 'Realism, Desire and Reification: Thomas Middleton's *A Chaste Maid in Cheapside*', *Early Modern Literary Studies*, vol. 8, no. 3 (January 2003); 5.1–26, at http://purl.oclc.org/emls/08–3/fraschas.htm>, para. 23, accessed 12 January 2005.
25. In my experience, this moment generally provokes the most heated debate among students. One particular year, a young female student was the first to give voice to this point of view, and immediately several male students (a minority in the class) spoke up in agreement, one of them noting that he had not wanted to say so at first; clearly, the fact that a female had given the idea an airing established an atmosphere in which he and his fellow males could speak their minds. Another female student, a few years older than the majority of the class, very quickly jumped in on the discussion, horrified at what she perceived as blatant sexism.
26. Mohammad Kowsar, 'Middleton and Rowley's *The Changeling*: The Besieged Temple', *Criticism*, vol. 28 (1986), pp. 145–64.
27. Cristina Malcolmson, '"As Tame as the Ladies": Politics and Gender in *The Changeling*', *English Literary Renaissance*, vol. 20, no. 2 (Spring 1990), p. 330.
28. Thanks to Bethyn Casey for email discussion of this aspect of Amy's character.
29. Williams, 'Women Can Only Misbehave', p. 27.
30. Jocelyn Catty, *Writing Rape, Writing Women in Early Modern England: Unbridled Speech* (Basingstoke: Macmillan, 1999), p. 108.
31. Burks, '"I'll want my will else"', p. 163.
32. Catty, *Writing Rape*, p. 3.
33. Ibid., p. 3.
34. N. W. Bawcutt (ed.), *The Changeling* (Manchester: Manchester University Press, Revels Student Edition, 1998), p. 91, note on 4.1.1.
35. Ovid, *Ars Amatoria*, 1.673; the translation given in Ovid, *The Love Poems*, trans. A. D. Melville (Oxford University Press, World's Classics, 1990), reads, '"Brute force!" you'll say: it's force that women want', and continues, 'They love refusing what they long to grant' (p. 195).
36. Karen Bamford, *Sexual Violence on the Jacobean Stage* (Basingstoke: Macmillan, 2000), p. 32.
37. Williams, 'Women', p. 26.

38. Venner hands Scutt his wages after Sumner has fired and paid them off ('Here you go, Norman'), and that evening they are seen standing together watching Amy as she passes by at the church social. When Harry gives the news that Henry is at Trencher's Farm, Scutt passes a slight but unmistakable signal to Venner.

39. Interview with Del Henney, Channel 4 documentary, *Man Trap*, 2003.

40. Weddle, *If They Move . . .* , p. 424.

41. Susan George, interview for the documentary *Man Trap*, Channel 4, 2003.

42. Weddle, *If They Move . . .* , p. 422.

43. Weddle, *If They Move . . .* , p. 423.

44. Weddle, *If They Move . . .* , p. 423.

45. Weddle, *If They Move . . .* , p. 423.

46. Weddle, *If They Move . . .* , p. 423.

47. Sarah Projansky, *Watching Rape: Film and Television in Postfeminist Culture* (New York: New York University Press, 2001), p. 95.

48. Ibid., p. 95.

49. Weddle, *If They Move . . .* , p. 424.

50. Gail Kern Paster, *The Body Embarrassed: Drama and the Disciplines of Shame in Early Modern England* (Ithaca, NY: Cornell University Press, 1993), p. 89.

51. Projansky, *Watching Rape*, p. 36.

Chapter 9

1. David Gunby, David Carnegie and Anthony Hammond (eds), *The Works of John Webster Vol. 1: The White Devil & The Duchess of Malfi* (Cambridge University Press, 1995), pp. 59, 76.

2. John Russell Brown (ed.), *The Duchess of Malfi* (London: Methuen, 1964), p. 92.

3. Roma Gill, '"Quaintly Done": A Reading of *The White Devil*', *Essays and Studies* vol. XIX (1966), reprinted in R. V. Holdsworth (ed.), *Webster: The White Devil and The Duchess of Malfi: A Casebook* (London: Macmillan, 1975), p. 155.

4. Catherine Belsey, *The Subject of Tragedy: Identity and Difference in Renaissance Drama* (London: Routledge 1985), p. 164.

5. Belsey, *Subject*, p. 165.

6. Christina Luckyj, 'Gender, Rhetoric and Performance in John Webster's *The White Devil*', in Viviani Comensoli and Anne Russell (eds), *Enacting Gender on the English Renaissance Stage* (Urbana, Ill. and Chicago: University of Illinois, 1999), p. 218.

7. Gayle Greene, 'Women on Trial in Shakespeare and Webster: "The Mettle of [their] Sex"', *Topics: A Journal of Liberal Arts*, vol. 36 (1982), p. 15.

8. Laura L. Behling, '"S/He Scandals our Proceedings": The Anxiety of Alternative Sexualities in *The White Devil* and *The Duchess of Malfi*', *English Language Notes*, June 1996, p. 30.

9. Kate Aughterson, *Renaissance Woman: A Sourcebook: Constructions of Femininity in England* (London: Routledge, 1995), p. 229.

10. Jonathan Dollimore, *Radical Tragedy: Religion, Ideology and Power in the Drama of Shakespeare and His Contemporaries* (2nd edn) (Hemel Hempstead: Harvester Wheatsheaf, 1989), p. 235.

11. Gunby *et al.*, *Works*, p. 75.
12. A remarkable prototype of the "Mexican stand-off" familiar from such films as *The Good, the Bad and the Ugly* (1966) and *Reservoir Dogs* (1992).
13. Paul Taylor, *Independent*, 20 June 1991; cited in Christina Luckyj (ed.), *The White Devil*, New Mermaids edn (2nd edn) (London: A & C Black, 1996), p. 149, note on 5.6.203–2.
14. Interviewed as part of feature 'Naked Hollywood', *Empire* magazine, no. 36, June 1992, p. 60.
15. E. Ann Kaplan, 'Introduction to the New Edition', in E. Ann Kaplan (ed.), *Women in Film Noir: New Edition* (London: BFI Publishing, 1998), p. 1.
16. Kate Stables, 'The Postmodern Always Rings Twice: Constructing the *Femme Fatale* in 90s Cinema', in Kaplan (ed.), *Women in Film Noir*, p. 164.
17. See, for example, Thomas Austin, '"Desperate to See It": Straight Men Watching *Basic Instinct*', in Melvyn Stokes and Richard Maltby (eds), *Identifying Hollywood's Audiences: Cultural Identity and the Movies* (London: BFI Publishing, 1999); and Thomas Austin, 'Gendered (Dis)pleasures: *Basic Instinct* and Female Spectators', *Journal of Popular British Cinema*, vol. 2 (1999), pp. 4–21.
18. Mary Ann Doane, *Femmes Fatales: Feminism, Film Studies and Psychoanalysis* (London: Routledge, 1992), p. 3.
19. Doane, *Femmes Fatales*, p. 1.
20. Janey Place, 'Women in *Film Noir*' in Kaplan (ed.), *Women in Film Noir*, p. 47.
21. Yvonne Tasker, *Working Girls: Gender and Sexuality in Popular Cinema* (London: Routledge, 1998), p. 120.
22. Tasker, *Working Girls*, p. 120.
23. Stables, 'The Postmodern', p. 165.
24. Doane, *Femmes Fatales*, p. 2.
25. 'H.M.', 'Analytical Essays on the Early English Dramatists', *Blackwood's Edinburgh Magazine* (1818), reprinted in R. V. Holdsworth (ed.), pp. 34–5.
26. Gunby *et al.*, *Works*, p. 71.
27. Christine Gledhill, '*Klute* 1: A Contemporary Film Noir and Feminist Criticism', in Kaplan (ed.), *Women in Film Noir*, p. 31.
28. Alexander Dyce, 'Introduction to *The Works of John Webster*' (1830), reprinted in R. V. Holdsworth (ed.), p. 37.
29. Charles Kingsley, 'Plays and Puritans', *North British Review* (1856), reprinted in R. V. Holdsworth (ed.), p. 39.
30. 'H.M.', Analytical Essays, pp. 34–5.
31. Interview with Paul Verhoeven, http://www.totaldvd.net/features/interviews/200206PaulVerhoeven.php, accessed 1 December 2003.
32. Camille Paglia, commentary track of 10th Anniversary Special Edition DVD, Momentum Pictures, 2002.
33. Paglia, commentary.
34. Paglia, commentary.
35. Rowland Wymer, *Webster and Ford* (Basingstoke and London: Macmillan, 1995), p. 40.
36. Luckyj, 'Gender, Rhetoric and Performance', p. 225.
37. Jane Edwardes, *Time Out*, 1 May 1996, and Benedict Nightingale, *The Times*, 27 April 1996.
38. Martin Orkin, 'As if a Man Should Spit against the Wind', in Naomi Conn Liebler (ed.), *The Female Tragic Hero in English Renaissance Drama* (Basingstoke: Palgrave, 2002), p. 142.

39. Benedict Nightingale, 'Review', *The New Statesman*, 21 November 1969, reprinted in in R. V. Holdsworth (ed.), p. 238.
40. Dyce, 'Introduction', p. 37.
41. Dollimore, *Radical Tragedy*, p. 235.
42. Paul Verhoeven, commentary track of 10th Anniversary Special Edition DVD.
43. Place, 'Women in *Film Noir*', p. 45.
44. Verhoeven, commentary track.
45. Place, 'Women in *Film Noir*', p. 45.
46. Stables, 'The Postmodern', p. 177.
47. Place, 'Women in *Film Noir*,' p. 36.
48. Place, Women in *Film Noir*,' p. 36.
49. Verhoeven, commentary track.

Chapter 10

1. Andrew Tudor, 'Why Horror? The Peculiar Pleasures of a Popular Genre', in Mark Jancovich (ed.), *Horror: The Film Reader* (London: Routledge, 2002), p. 53.
2. Cited at http://www.grandguignol.com/history.htm, accessed 12 January 2005.
3. *Night of the Living Dead* (1968), *Dawn of the Dead* (1978), *Day of the Dead* (1985). A fourth instalment, *Land of the Dead*, was released in 2005.
4. Carol Clover, *Men, Women, and Chainsaws: Gender in the Modern Horror Film* (London: BFI Publishing, 1992), p. 32.
5. John Marston, *The Malcontent and Other Plays* (ed. Keith Sturgess) (Oxford University Press, World's Classics, 1997), p. 113.
6. Cynthia Marshall, *The Shattering of the Self: Violence, Subjectivity, & Early Modern Texts* (Baltimore, Md./London: Johns Hopkins University Press, 2002), p. 5.
7. Quoted in D. J. Hogan, *Dark Romance: Sexuality in the Horror Film* (Jefferson, NC: McFarland, 1986), p. 241.
8. Notably *Spiderman* (2002), *X-Men* and its sequel (2000, 2003), *Hulk* (2003) and *Daredevil* (2003).
9. Paul Wells, *The Horror Genre from Beelzebub to Blair Witch* (London: Wallflower Publishing, 2000), p. 10.
10. Wells, *The Horror Genre*, p. 10.
11. *Final Destination* is also highly self-referential, even naming each of its characters after classic horror film directors and actors: Lewton, Browning, Schreck, Hitchcock, and so on.
12. Andrew Tudor, 'From Paranoia to Postmodernism? The Horror Movie in Late Modern Society', in Steve Neale (ed.), *Genre and Contemporary Hollywood* (London: BFI Publishing, 2002), p. 116.
13. Terry Eagleton, *After Theory* (London: Allen Lane, 2003), pp. 155–6.
14. Eagleton, *After Theory*, p. 164.
15. Robert N. Watson, 'Tragedy', in A. R. Braunmuller and Michael Hattaway (eds) *The Cambridge Companion to English Renaissance Drama* (Cambridge University Press, 1990), p. 319.
16. Fredson Bowers, *Elizabethan Revenge Tragedy 1587–1642* (Princeton, NJ: Princeton University Press, 1966; first edn 1940), pp. 154–5.

17. Ian Jack, 'The Case of John Webster', *Scrutiny*, vol. XVI (1949), p. 43;
    L. G. Salingar, 'Tourneur and the Tragedy of Revenge', in Boris Ford (ed.), *The
    Age of Shakespeare*, The Pelican Guide to English Literature (Harmondsworth:
    Pelican, 1955; revised edn 1982), p. 451.
18. M. C. Bradbrook, *Themes and Conventions of Elizabethan Tragedy* (Cambridge
    University Press, 1966; first published 1935), p. 240.
19. Bradbrook, *Themes*, p. 243.
20. Jonathan Bate (ed.), *Titus Andronicus*, Arden 3rd series (London: Routledge,
    1995), p. 3.
21. James B. Twitchell, *Preposterous Violence: Fables of Aggression in Modern
    Culture* (Oxford University Press, 1989), p. 207.
22. Wells, *The Horror Genre*, p. 93.

Chapter 11

1. Nicholas Culpepper, cited in Jonathan Sawday, *The Body Emblazoned: Dissection and the Human Body in Renaissance Culture* (London: Routledge, 1996;
   first published 1995), p. 233.
2. Sawday, *Body Emblazoned*, p. 88.
3. Philipe Ariès, *The Hour of Our Death* (New York: Alfred A. Knopf, 1981),
   p. 369.
4. Kate Cregan, 'Blood and Circuses', in Elizabeth Klaver (ed.), *Images of the
   Corpse from the Renaissance to Cyberspace* (Madison, Wisc.: University of
   Wisconsin Press, 2004), p. 45.
5. For further discussion of the anatomy lecture as performance, see also
   Michael Neill, *Issues of Death: Mortality and Identity in English Renaissance
   Tragedy* (Oxford University Press, 1997), pp. 114–22; William Heckscher,
   Rembrandt's Anatomy of Dr. Nicolaas Tulp (New York: New York University
   Press, 1957); Sawday, *Body Emblazoned*, pp. 42–8.
6. Kate Cregan, 'Blood and Circuses', p. 42.
7. Francis Barker, *The Tremulous Private Body: Essays on Subjection* (Ann Arbor,
   Mich.: University of Michigan Press, 1995), p. 66.
8. See, in particular, Molly Easo Smith, 'The Theater and the Scaffold: Death as
   Spectacle in *The Spanish Tragedy*', *Studies in English Literature, 1500–1900*,
   vol. 32 (1992), pp. 217–32.
9. This discussion is indebted to Michael Neill's comprehensive analysis of the
   phenomenon in ch. 2 of his *Issues of Death*.
10. René Weis, editing the Oxford World's Classics edition of Webster's plays,
    chooses to omit the word 'artificial' from the First Quarto's stage direction,
    believing that 'motionless actors would almost certainly have played the
    parts of Antonio and the children' (René Weis, *The Duchess of Malfi and
    Other Plays*, (Oxford University Press, 1996, World's Classics), p. 397).
11. J. D. Martinez, 'The Fallacy of Contextual Analysis as a Means of Evaluating
    Dramatized Violence' in John W. Frick (ed.), *Theatre Symposium 7: Theatre
    and Violence* (Tuscaloosa, Ala.: Southeastern Theatre Conference and The
    University of Alabama Press, 1999), p. 77.
12. Jean MacIntyre and Garrett P. J. Epp, '"Cloathes worth all the rest":
    Costumes and Properties', in John D. Cox and David Scott Kastan (eds), *A*

New History of Early English Drama (New York: Columbia University Press, 1997), p. 281.

13. Andrew Gurr, *The Shakespearean Stage 1574–1642* (3rd edn) (Cambridge University Press, 1992), p. 182.

14. Colleen Kelly, 'Figuring the Fight: Recovering Shakespeare's Theatrical Swordplay', *Theatre Symposium*, vol. 7, p. 99.

15. Gurr, *Shakespearean Stage*, p. 183.

16. Alan C. Dessen, *Recovering Shakespeare's Theatrical Vocabulary* (Cambridge University Press, 1995), pp. 249–50n.

17. Cited in MacIntyre and Epp, '"Cloathes worth . . ."', in Cox and Kastan (eds), *A New History*, p. 281.

18. Keith Sturgess, *Jacobean Private Theatre* (London: Routledge & Kegan Paul, 1987), p. 119.

19. Although the play is not mentioned by name, we do know that it was being staged by Marlowe's company, the Lord Admiral's Men, at this time, making *Tamburlaine* a likely candidate.

20. Carol J. Clover, *Men, Women and Chainsaws: Gender in the Modern Horror Film* (London: BFI Publishing, 1992), p. 32.

21. Sawday, p. 5.

22. Paul Wells, *The Horror Genre from Beelzebub to Blair Witch* (London: Wallflower Publishing, 2000), p. 87.

23. 'Skinless Wonders', *Observer*, 21 May 2001, at http://observer.guardian.co.uk/review/story/0,6903,493200,00.html, accessed 12 December 2004.

24. Ibid.

25. Vivian C. Sobchack, 'The Violent Dance: A Personal Memoir of Death in the Movies', in Stephen Prince (ed.), *Screening Violence* (Brunswick, NJ: Rutgers University Press, 2000), p. 119.

26. William Paul, *Laughing Screaming: Modern Hollywood Horror and Comedy* (New York: Columbia University Press, 1994), pp. 293–4.

27. Robert Kolker, *A Cinema of Loneliness: Penn, Stone, Kubrick, Scorsese, Spielberg, Altman* (3rd edn) (Oxford University Press, 2000), p. 50.

28. Pete Boss, 'Vile Bodies and Bad Medicine', *Screen*, vol. 27, no. 1 (January/February 1986), p. 16.

29. Noel Carroll, *The Philosophy of Horror, or Paradoxes of the Heart* (London: Routledge, 1990), p. 195.

30. Wells, *The Horror Genre*, p. 21.

31. Clover, *Men, Women and Chainsaws*, p. 41.

32. Cynthia Marshall, *The Shattering of the Self: Violence, Subjectivity, & Early Modern Texts* (Baltimore, Md./London: Johns Hopkins University Press, 2002), p. 3.

33. For a full survey of this phenomenon, see Nicholas Brooke, *Horrid Laughter in Jacobean Tragedy* (London: Open Books, 1979).

34. There is an analogous scene in Tarantino's *Pulp Fiction* (1994), when Vincent Vega (John Travolta) accidentally shoots informer Marvin in the head as he sits in the back of their car. Again, the scene's comic-horrific impact is based on the gap between the seriousness of the incident, and Vega and Jules Winnfield's (Samuel L. Jackson) ill-matched response of annoyance and irritation.

35. Quentin Tarantino, commentary track for Momentum Pictures 2004 DVD release of *Reservoir Dogs*.

Chapter 12

1. Michael Neill, *Issues of Death: Mortality and Identity in English Renaissance Tragedy* (Oxford University Press, 1997); Robert N. Watson, *The Rest is Silence: Death as Annihilation in the English Renaissance* (Berkeley and Los Angeles, Calif.: University of California Press, 1994; paperback 1999).

2. The DVD documentary also explains how an additional, time-marking scene had to be inserted after surveys of test audiences, since the shock impact was so devastating that the film needed to allow time for the audience to recover before proceeding with the narrative.

3. Maurice Charney, 'The Persuasiveness of Violence in Elizabethan Plays', *Renaissance Drama*, New Series, II, 1969, pp. 63–4.

4. Charney, 'The Persuasiveness of Violence', pp. 64–5.

5. Mark Jancovich (ed.), *Horror: The Film Reader* (London: Routledge, 2002), p. 67.

6. Jancovich, *Horror: The Film Reader*, p. 65.

7. René Girard, *Violence and the Sacred* trans. by Patrick Gregory, London: The Athlone Press, paperback edn, 1995; first published in English 1977; originally published in Paris, 1972), p. 33.

8. Girard, *Violence and the Sacred*, p. 34.

9. See Julia Kristeva, *Powers of Horror: An Essay on Abjection* (New York: Columbia University Press, 1982); Barbara Creed, *The Monstrous-Feminine: Film, Feminism, Psychoanalysis* (London: Routledge, 1993); and Xavier Mendik, 'From the Monstrous Mother to the "Third Sex": Female Abjection in the Films of Dario Argento', in A. Black (ed.), Book Two *Necronomicon: The Journal of Horror and Erotic Cinema* (London: Creation Books, 1998), pp.110–33.

10. Barbara Creed, 'Horror and the Monstrous-Feminine: An Imaginary Abjection', in Jancovich (ed.), *Horror: The Film Reader*, p. 75. First published in *Screen*, vol. 27, no. 1, January–February (1986), pp. 44–54.

11. Creed, 'Horror and the Monstrous-Feminine', p. 74.

12. Tony Williams, *Hearths of Darkness: The Family in the American Horror Film* (Cranbury, N.J.: Associated University Presses, 1996), p. 20.

13. See, for example, Clover, *Men, Women and Chainsaws*, ch. 1; Tania Modleski, 'The Terror of Pleasure: The Contemporary Horror Film and Postmodern Theory', in Ken Gelder (ed.), *The Horror Reader* (London: Routledge, 2000), p. 291; Paul Wells, *The Horror Genre from Beelzebub to Blair Witch* (London: Wallflower Publishing, 2000), pp. 78–80; Peter Hutchings, *The Horror Film* (Harlow: Pearson Education, 2004), ch. 9.

14. See Carol J. Clover, *Men, Women and Chainsaws: Gender in the Modern Horror Film* (London: BFI Publishing 1992), ch. 1.

15. Michael Ryan and Douglas Kellner, *Camera Politica: The Politics and Ideology of Contemporary Hollywood Film* (Bloomington, Ind.: Indiana University Press, 1990), pp. 192–3.

16. Robin Wood, 'Returning the Look: "Eyes of a Stranger"', in Gregory A. Waller (ed.), *American Horrors: Essays on the Modern American Horror Film* (Chicago: University of Illinois Press, 1987), p. 80.

17. Williams, *Hearths of Darkness*, p. 221.

18. See Barry S. Sapolsky and Fred Molitor, 'Current Trends in Contemporary Horror Films', in James B. Weaver III and Ron Tamborini (eds.), *Horror Films:*

Current Research on Audience Preferences and Reactions (Mahwah, NJ: Lawrence Erlbaum Associates, 1996), pp. 103–25.

19. Clover, *Men, Women and Chainsaws*, p. 35.
20. Roger Ebert, 'Why Movies Aren't Safe Anymore', *American Film*, March 1981, p. 56.
21. Wells, *The Horror Genre*, p. 79.
22. Hélène Cixous (trans. Barbara Kerslake), 'Aller à la Mer', *Modern Drama*, vol. 24, no. 4, p. 546.
23. Neill, *Issues of Death*, p. 373.
24. Jonathan Sawday, *The Body Emblazoned: Dissection and the Human Body in Renaissance Culture* (London: Routledge, 1996; first published 1995), p. 87.
25. Sara Eaton, 'Defacing the Feminine in Renaissance Tragedy', in Valerie Wayne (ed.), *The Matter of Difference: Materialist Feminist Criticism of Shakespeare* (Hemel Hempstead: Harvester Wheatsheaf, 1991), p. 193.
26. Michel Foucault, *Discipline and Punish*, trans. Alan Sheridan (first published London, 1977; 1991 reprint, London: Penguin Books), p. 50.

Conclusion

1. Beaumont and Fletcher, *The Maid's Tragedy*, 5.1.45–6. The parallel scene is the opening sequence of *Basic Instinct* (1992).
2. Beaumont and Fletcher, *The Maid's Tragedy*, 5.1.54–6.
3. Beaumont and Fletcher, *The Maid's Tragedy*, 5.1.98–9.
4. The original film was chopped in half at the insistence of his executive producer, with the two parts released six months apart, in 2003 and 2004.
5. CNN.com, Thursday, 9 October 2003, http://www.cnn.com/2003/SHOWBIZ/ Movies/10/09/sprj.caf03.tarantino.revenge.ap/, accessed 7 January 2005.
6. Matthew Turner, *Kill Bill* Interview with Quentin Tarantino and Uma Thurman, http://www.viewlondon.co.uk/home_feat_int_killbill.asp, accessed 7 January 2005.
7. Scott Huver, 'Bridal Chatter', http://www.hollywood.com/features/t1/nav/5/id/ 1749456/p/1, accessed 7 January 2005.
8. Interestingly, this seems not to have triggered a debate among feminists to rival the furious exchanges (notably between Tarantino himself and Spike Lee) over the writer-director's predilection for the term 'nigger' in *Pulp Fiction*.
9. Fred Topel, interview with Quentin Tarantino, 5 October 2003, http:// actionadventure.about.com/cs/weeklystories/a/aa100503_2.htm, accessed 7 January 2005.
10. Fred Topel, 'Strong Thurman', Interview with Uma Thurman 27 September 2003, http://actionadventure.about.com/cs/weeklystories/a/aa092703_2.htm, accessed 7 January 2005.
11. http://killbill.movies.go.com/vol2/castcrew/qt.html, accessed 7 January 2005.
12. I shall resist the temptation to do so here, mentioning only in passing Bill's onanistic caressing of his sword hilt in *Vol. 1* (we do not see his face in the first film), O-Ren Ishii's appropriation of male power via the decapitation of the one Yakuza boss who resists her leadership on the basis of her gender and her race, and the sexually-charged conversation between Elle and Budd as he negotiates the sale of the Hanzo sword he confiscates from The Bride.

Incidentally, one reporter reflecting on stories of Uma Thurman's split with Ethan Hawke invoked a similar sub-text, remarking, 'When you see her in *Kill Bill*, you'll wonder if she just used her Samurai skills to kick Ethan's ass' (Fred Topel, 'Strong Thurman', Interview with Uma Thurman 27 September 2003, http://actionadventure.about.com/cs/weeklystories/a/aa092703_2.htm, accessed 7 January 2005.

13. Walter Benjamin, 'Theses on the Philosophy of History', in Douglas Tallack (ed.), *Critical Theory: A Reader* (Hemel Hempstead: Harvester Wheatsheaf, 1995), p. 279.

Bibliography

Primary sources: play texts

Quotations in the text are from Oxford World's Classics editions of the plays, except where noted.

Ford, John, *'Tis Pity She's a Whore* (ed. Simon Barker) (London: Routledge, 1997).

Kyd, Thomas, *The Spanish Tragedy* (ed. J. R. Mulryne) (London: A. & C. Black, 1970; 6th impression 1987).

Marlowe, Christopher, *Doctor Faustus and Other Plays* (ed. David Bevington and Eric Rasmussen) (Oxford University Press, World's Classics, 1995).

Marowitz, Charles, *The Marowitz Shakespeare* (London: Marion Boyars, 1990).

Marston, John, *The Malcontent and Other Plays* (ed. Keith Sturgess) (Oxford University Press, World's Classics, 1997).

Maus, Katharine Eisaman (ed.), *Four Revenge Tragedies* (Oxford University Press, 1995).

Middleton, Thomas, *The Changeling* (ed. N. W. Bawcutt) (Manchester: Manchester University Press, Revels Student Edition, 1998).

Middleton, Thomas, *Women Beware Women and Other Plays* (ed. Richard Dutton) (Oxford: Oxford University Press, World's Classics, 1999).

Salgado, Gamini, *Three Revenge Tragedies* (Harmondsworth: Penguin, 2004; first published 1965).

Shakespeare, William, *Hamlet* (ed. G. R. Hibbard) (Oxford University Press, World's Classics, 1994; first published 1987).

Shakespeare, William, *Macbeth* (ed. Nicholas Brooke) (Oxford University Press, World's Classics, 1994; first published 1990).

Shakespeare, William, *Titus Andronicus* (ed. Jonathan Bate), Arden Shakespeare: 3rd Series (London: Routledge, 1995).

Shakespeare, William, *Titus Andronicus* (ed. Eugene M. Waith) (Oxford University Press, 1984, World's Classics paperback edition, 1994).

Webster, John, *The Duchess of Malfi* (ed. John Russell Brown) (London: Methuen, 1964).

Webster, John, *The Works of John Webster, Vol. One: The White Devil & The Duchess of Malfi* (ed. D. Gunby, David Carnegie and Anthony Hammond) (Cambridge University Press, 1995).

Webster, John, *The White Devil* (ed. Christina Luckyj) (New Mermaids Edition, London: A & C Black; 2nd edn, 1996a).

Webster, John, *The Duchess of Malfi and Other Plays* (ed. René Weis) (Oxford University Press, World's Classics, 1996b).

Wiggins, Martin (ed.), *Four Jacobean Sex Tragedies* (Oxford University Press, World's Classics, 1998).

Primary sources: other

Bacon, Francis, *The Essays, or Counsels Civil and Moral* (ed. Brian Vickers) (Oxford University Press, World's Classics, 1999).
Drakulic, Slavenka, *S.: A Novel about the Balkans* (Harmondsworth: Penguin, 2001).
Kadare, Ismail, *Elegy for Kosovo* (New York: Arcade, 2000).
Kadare, Ismail, *Broken April* (New York: Vintage, 2003).
Locke, John, *The Second Treatise of Civil Government*, in *Two Treatises of Government* (ed. Peter Laslett) (Cambridge University Press, 1988; first published in this edition 1960).
Mehmedinovic, Semezdin, *Sarajevo Blues* (San Francisco: City Lights Books, 1998).
Nietzsche, Friedrich, *Beyond Good and Evil: Prelude to a Philosophy of the Future* (trans. and ed. R. J. Hollingdale) (Harmondsworth: Penguin, 1986; first published 1973).
Ovid, *The Love Poems* (trans. A. D. Melville) (Oxford University Press, World's Classics, 1990).

Secondary sources

Allman, Eileen, *Jacobean Revenge Tragedy and the Politics of Virtue* (Newark, Del.: University of Delaware Press, 1999).
Ariès, Philipe, *The Hour of Our Death* (New York: Alfred A. Knopf, 1981).
Aughterson, Kate, *Renaissance Woman: A Sourcebook: Constructions of Femininity in England* (London: Routledge, 1995).
Austin, Thomas, 'Gendered (Dis)pleasures: *Basic Instinct* and Female Spectators', *Journal of Popular British Cinema*, vol. 2 (1999a), pp. 4–21.
Austin, Thomas, '"Desperate to See It": Straight Men Watching *Basic Instinct*', in Melvyn Stokes and Richard Maltby (eds), *Identifying Hollywood's Audiences: Cultural Identity and the Movies* (London: BFI Publishing, 1999b), pp. 147–61.
Axton, Marie, *The Queen's Two Bodies: Drama and the Elizabethan Succession* (London: Royal Historical Society, 1978).
Bamford, Karen, *Sexual Violence on the Jacobean Stage* (Basingstoke and London: Macmillan, 2000).
Bamber, Linda, *Comic Women, Tragic Men* (Stanford, Calif.: Stanford University Press, 1982).
Barber, C. L., *Creating Elizabethan Tragedy: The Theater of Marlowe and Kyd* (ed. Richard Wheeler) (Chicago: University of Chicago Press, 1988).
Barker, Francis, *The Tremulous Private Body: Essays on Subjection* (Ann Arbor, Mich.: University of Michigan Press, 1995).
Barker, Roberta and David Nicol, 'Does Beatrice Joanna Have a Subtext?: *The Changeling* on the London Stage', *Early Modern Literary Studies*, vol. 10, no. 1 (May, 2004) 3.1–43.
Barton, Charles K. B., *Getting Even: Revenge as a Form of Justice* (Chicago: Open Court, 1999).
Behling, Laura L., '"S/He Scandals our Proceedings": The Anxiety of Alternative Sexualities in *The White Devil* and *The Duchess of Malfi*', *English Language Notes*, June 1996, pp. 24–43.

Belsey, Catherine, *The Subject of Tragedy: Identity and Difference in Renaissance Drama* (London: Routledge 1985).

Benjamin, Walter, *Theses on the Philosophy of History*, in Douglas Tallack (ed.), *Critical Theory: A Reader* (Hemel Hempstead: Harvester Wheatsheaf, 1995), pp. 278–86.

Bennett, Tony (ed.), *Popular Fictions* (London: Routledge, 1990).

Boehm, Christopher, *Blood Revenge: The Enactment and Management of Conflict in Montenegro and Other Tribal Societies* (Philadelphia: University of Pennsylvania Press, 1987).

Boss, Pete, 'Vile Bodies and Bad Medicine', *Screen*, vol. 27, no. 1 (January/February 1986), pp. 14–24.

Bowers, Fredson, *Elizabethan Revenge Tragedy 1587–1642* (Princeton, NJ: Princeton University Press, 1966; first edition, 1940).

Bradbrook, M. C., *Themes and Conventions of Elizabethan Tragedy* (Cambridge University Press, 1966; first published 1935).

Bristol, Michael, *Carnival and Theatre* (London: Routledge, 1985).

Bristol, Michael, 'Theater and Popular Culture', in John D. Cox and David Scott Kastan (eds), *A New History of Early English Drama* (New York: Columbia University Press, 1997), pp. 231–48.

Brooke, Nicholas, *Horrid Laughter in Jacobean Tragedy* (London: Open Books, 1979).

Brown, Richard Maxwell, *Strain of Violence: Historical Studies of American Violence and Vigilantism* (Oxford University Press, 1975).

Burks, Deborah, '"I'll want my will else": *The Changeling* and Women's Complicity with their Rapists', *English Literary History*, vol. 62 (1995), pp. 759–90.

Cagin, Seth and Philp Dray, *Hollywood Films of the Seventies: Sex, Drugs, Rock'n'Roll and Politics* (New York: Harper & Row, 1984).

Callaghan, Dympna, *Shakespeare Without Women* (London: Routledge, 2000).

Campbell, Lily B., 'Theories of Revenge in Elizabethan England', *Modern Philology*, vol. 28 (1931), pp. 281–96.

Carroll, Noel, *The Philosophy of Horror, or Paradoxes of the Heart* (London: Routledge, 1990).

Carroll, Noel, *A Philosophy of Mass Art* (Oxford: Clarendon Press, 1998).

Catty, Jocelyn, *Writing Rape, Writing Women in Early Modern England: Unbridled Speech* (London: Macmillan, 1999).

Cawelti, John, *Mystery, Violence and Popular Culture* (Madison, Wisc.: University of Wisconsin Press, 2004).

Charney, Maurice, 'The Persuasiveness of Violence in Elizabethan Plays', *Renaissance Drama*, New Series, vol. II, 1969, pp. 59–70.

Cixous, Hélène, 'Aller à la Mer' (trans. Barbara Kerslake), *Modern Drama*, vol. 24, no. 4 (December 1984), pp. 546–8.

Clarke, Richard A., *Against All Enemies: Inside America's War on Terror* (London: The Free Press, 2004).

Clover, Carol J., *Men, Women and Chainsaws: Gender in the Modern Horror Film* (London: BFI Publishing, 1992).

Corbin, Peter, '"A Dog's Obeyed in Office": Kingship and Authority in Jacobean Tragedy', in James Hogg (ed.), *Jacobean Drama as Social Criticism* (Lewiston, NY/Salzburg: Edwin Mellen Press, 1995), pp. 59–72.

Creed, Barbara, 'Horror and the Monstrous-Feminine: An Imaginary Abjection', in Mark Jancovich (ed.), *Horror: The Film Reader* (London: Routledge, 2002). First published in *Screen*, vol. 27, no. 1, January–February (1986), pp. 44–54.

Creed, Barbara, *The Monstrous-Feminine: Film, Feminism, Psychoanalysis* (London: Routledge, 1993).

Cregan, Kate, 'Blood and Circuses', in Elizabeth Klaver (ed.), *Images of the Corpse from the Renaissance to Cyberspace* (Madison, Wisc.: University of Wisconsin Press, 2004), pp. 39–62.

Crowdus, Gary (ed.), *The Political Companion to American Film* (London: Fitzroy Dearborn, 1994).

Culberson, William C., *Vigilantism: Political History of Private Power in America* (New York: Greenwood Press, 1990).

Daileader, Celia R., *Eroticism on the Renaissance Stage* (Cambridge University Press, 1998).

Dessen, Alan C., *Recovering Shakespeare's Theatrical Vocabulary* (Cambridge University Press, 1995).

Doane, Mary Ann, *Femmes Fatales: Feminism, Film Studies and Psychoanalysis* (London: Routledge, 1992).

Dole, Carole M., 'The Gun and the Badge: Hollywood and the Female Lawman', in Martha McCaughey and Neal King (eds), *Reel Knockouts: Violent Women in the Movies* (Austin, Tx: University of Texas Press, 2001).

Dollimore, Jonathan, *Radical Tragedy* (2nd edn) (Hemel Hempstead: Harvester Wheatsheaf, 1989).

Dukore, Bernard F., *Sam Peckinpah's Feature Films* (Urbana, Ill. and Chicago: University of Illinois Press, 1999).

Dyce, Alexander, 'Introduction to *The Works of John Webster*' (1830), reprinted in R. V. Holdsworth (ed.), *Webster*: The White Devil *and* The Duchess of Malfi: *A Casebook* (Basingstoke : Macmillan , 1975), pp. 37–8.

Eagleton, Terry, *After Theory* (London: Allen Lane, 2003a).

Eagleton, Terry, *Sweet Violence: The Idea of the Tragic* (Oxford: Basil Blackwell, 2003b).

Eaton, Sara, 'Beatrice-Joanna and the Rhetoric of Love in *The Changeling*', *Theatre Journal*, vol. 36, no. 3 (1984), pp. 371–82.

Eaton, Sara, 'Defacing the Feminine in Renaissance Tragedy', in Valerie Wayne (ed.), *The Matter of Difference: Materialist Feminist Criticism of Shakespeare* (Hemel Hempstead: Harvester Wheatsheaf, 1991), pp. 181–98.

Ebert, Roger, 'Why Movies Aren't Safe Anymore', *American Film*, March 1981, pp. 54–56.

Erickson, Amy Louise, *Women and Property in Early Modern England* (London: Routledge, 1993).

Farb, Jessica and Felice Cherry, 'Fight or Flight: Wives in Crisis in *Sleeping with the Enemy*'; http://www.unc.edu/~jfarb/SWEFINAL.htm, accessed 13 November 2003.

Farnham, Willard, *The Medieval Heritage of Elizabethan Tragedy* (Berkeley, Calif.: University of California Press, 1936).

Findlay, Alison, *A Feminist Perspective on Renaissance Drama* (Oxford: Basil Blackwell, 1999).

Foucault, Michel, *Discipline and Punish* (trans. Alan Sheridan) (first published London, 1977; Penguin reprint 1991).

Frassinelli, Pier Paolo, 'Realism, Desire and Reification: Thomas Middleton's *A Chaste Maid in Cheapside*', *Early Modern Literary Studies*, vol. 8, no. 3 (January, 2003), pp. 5.1–26.

French, Peter A., *The Virtues of Vengeance* (University Press of Kansas, 2001).

Frus, Phyllis, 'Documenting Domestic Violence in American Films', in J. David Slocum (ed.), *Violence and American Cinema* (London: Routledge, 2001), pp. 226–44.

Gardiner, S. R., *History of England from the Accession of James I to the Outbreak of the Civil War*, Vol. III (London: Longman, Green & Co., 1883–4).

Gill, Roma, '"Quaintly Done": A Reading of *The White Devil*', in *Essays and Studies* XIX (1966), reprinted in R. V. Holdsworth (ed.), *Webster: The White Devil and The Duchess of Malfi: A Casebook* (London: Macmillan, 1975), pp. 145–63.

Girard, René, *Violence and the Sacred* (trans. Patrick Gregory) (London: The Athlone Press, 1995; first published in French, 1972; English translation, 1977).

Gledhill, Christine, '*Klute* 1: A Contemporary Film Noir and Feminist Criticism', in Kaplan(ed.), *Women in Film Noir: New Edition* (London: BFI Publishing, 1998), pp. 20–34.

Glenny, Misha, *The Fall of Yugoslavia* (Harmondsworth: Penguin, 1993).

von Goethe, Johnann Wolfgang, *Wilhelm Meister: Apprenticeship and Travels* (London: Foulis, 1947).

Graff, Gerald, *Beyond the Culture Wars: How Teaching the Conflicts Can Revitalize American Education* (New York: W. W. Norton, 1992).

Greene, Gayle, 'Women on Trial in Shakespeare and Webster: "The Mettle of [their] Sex"', *Topics: A Journal of Liberal Arts*, vol. 36 (1982).

Grist, Leighton, '*Unforgiven*', in Ian Cameron and Douglas Pye (eds), *The Movie Book of the Western* (London: Studio Vista, Cassell, 1996).

Gurr, Andrew, *The Shakespearean Stage 1574–1642* (3rd edn) (Cambridge University Press, 1992).

'H.M.', 'Analytical Essays on the Early English Dramatists', *Blackwood's Edinburgh Magazine* (1818), reprinted in R. V. Holdsworth (ed.), *Webster: The White Devil and The Duchess of Malfi: A Casebook* (London: Macmillan, 1975), pp. 34–5.

Hart, Lynda, *Fatal Women: Lesbian Sexuality and the Mark of Aggression* (London: Routledge, 1994).

Harvey, Elizabeth D., *Ventriloquized Voices* (London: Routledge, 1992).

Haskell, Molly, *From Reverence to Rape: The Treatment of Women in the Movies* (2nd edn) (Chicago: University of Chicago Press, 1974, 1987).

Hawkes, Terence, 'On the Way in which Tragedy "Openeth up the Greatest Wounds and Showeth forth the Ulcers that are Covered with Tissue"', *London Review of Books*, vol. 19, no. 24, 11 December 1997, accessed at http://www.lrb.co.uk/v19/n24/hawk01_.html, 5 November 2004.

Heckscher, William, *Rembrandt's Anatomy of Dr. Nicolaas Tulp* (New York: New York University Press, 1957).

Heinemann, Margot, *Puritanism and Theatre: Thomas Middleton and Opposition Drama Under the Early Stuarts* (Cambridge University Press, 1980).

Hoberman, J., *The Dream Life: Movies, Media, and the Mythology of the Sixties* (New York: The New Press, 2003).

Hogan, D. J., *Dark Romance: Sexuality in the Horror Film* (Jefferson, NC: McFarland, 1986).

Holdsworth, R. V. (ed.), *Webster: The White Devil and The Duchess of Malfi: A Casebook* (London: Macmillan, 1975).

Hopkins, Lisa, *The Female Hero in English Renaissance Tragedy* (Basingstoke: Palgrave, 2002).

Horkheimer, Max and Theodor W. Adorno, *Dialectic of Enlightenment* (Stanford, Calif: Stanford University Press, 2002).

Howard, Jean E., 'The New Historicism in Renaissance Studies', in Arthur F. Kinney and Don S. Collins (eds), *Renaissance Historicism* (Amherst, Mass.: Massachusetts University Press 1987), pp. 3–33.

Howard, Jean E. and Phyllis Rackin, 'Gender and Nation: Anticipations of Modernity in the Second Tetralogy', in Kate Chedgzoy (ed.), *Shakespeare, Feminism and Gender: A New Casebook* (Basingstoke: Palgrave, 2001), pp. 93–114.

Peter Hutchings, *The Horror Film* (Harlow: Pearson Education, 2004).

Ingalls, Robert P., *Urban Vigilantes in the New South: Tampa, 1882–1936* (Gainesville, Fla.: University Press of Florida, 1993).

Jack, Ian, 'The Case of John Webster', *Scrutiny*, vol. XVI (1949), pp. 38–43.

Jancovich, Mark (ed.), *Horror: The Film Reader* (London: Routledge, 2002).

Jankowski, Theodora, 'Defining/Confining the Duchess: Negotiating the Female Body in John Webster's *The Duchess of Malfi*', *Studies in Philology*, vol. 87 (1990), pp. 221–45.

Jeffords, Susan, *Hard Bodies: Hollywood Masculinity in the Reagan Era* (Brunswick, NJ: Rutgers University Press, 1994).

Jones, Robert C., *Engagement with Knavery: Point of View in* Richard III, The Jew of Malta, Volpone *and* The Revenger's Tragedy (Durham, NC: Duke University Press, 1986).

Judah, Tim, *Kosovo: War and Revenge* (New Haven, Conn.: Yale University Press, 2000).

Jump, John (ed.), *Hamlet: A Selection of Critical Essays* (London: Macmillan, 1968, 8th reprint 1983).

Kantorowicz, Ernst H., *The King's Two Bodies: A Study in Mediaeval Political Theology* (Princeton, NJ: Princeton University Press, 1998; first published 1957).

Kaplan, E. Ann (ed.), *Women in Film Noir: New Edition* (London: BFI Publishing, 1998).

Kelly, Colleen, 'Figuring the Fight: Recovering Shakespeare's Theatrical Swordplay', in John W. Frick (ed.), *Theatre Symposium 7: Theatre and Violence* (Tuscaloosa, Ala.: Southeastern Theatre Conference/The University of Alabama Press, 1999), pp. 96–108.

Kernan, Alvin, *Shakespeare, The King's Playwright: Theater in the Stuart Court, 1603–1613* (New Haven, Conn.: Yale University Press, 1995).

Kerrigan, John, *Revenge Tragedy: Aeschylus to Armageddon* (Oxford: Clarendon Press, 1997).

Kerrigan, John, 'Revenge Tragedy Revisited, 1649–1683', in *On Shakespeare and Early Modern Literature* (Oxford University Press, 2004), pp. 230–54.

Kiernan, V. G., *The Duel in European History* (Oxford University Press, 1988).

Kim, Jong-Hwan, 'Waiting for Justice: Shakespeare's *Hamlet* and the Elizabethan Ethics of Revenge', *English Language and Literature*, vol. 43 (1997), pp. 781–97.

Kingsley, Charles, 'Plays and Puritans', *North British Review* (1856), reprinted in R. V. Holdsworth (ed.), *Webster: The White Devil and The Duchess of Malfi: A Casebook* (London: Macmillan, 1975).

Kolker, Robert, *A Cinema of Loneliness: Penn, Stone, Kubrick, Scorsese, Spielberg, Altman* (3rd edn) (Oxford University Press, 2000).

Kowsar, Mohammad, 'Middleton and Rowley's *The Changeling*: The Besieged Temple', *Criticism*, vol. 28 (1986), pp. 145–64.

Kristeva, Julia, *Powers of Horror: An Essay on Abjection* (New York: Columbia University Press, 1982).

Laurence, Anne, *Women in England 1500–1760: A Social History* (London: Phoenix, 1996; first published 1994).

Lever, J. W., *The Tragedy of State: A Study of Jacobean Drama* (London: Methuen 1987; first published 1971).

Levy Peck, Linda, *Court Patronage and Corruption in Early Stuart England* (London: Routledge, 1993; first published 1990).

Liebler, Naomi Conn, 'Introduction', in *The Female Tragic Hero in English Renaissance Drama* (Basingstoke: Palgrave, 2002).

Luckyj, Christina, 'Gender, Rhetoric and Performance in John Webster's *The White Devil*', in Viviani Comensoli and Anne Russell (eds), *Enacting Gender on the English Renaissance Stage* (Urbana, Ill. and Chicago: University of Illinois, 1999), pp. 218–232.

McDonald, Russ (ed.), *The Bedford Companion to Shakespeare: An Introduction with Documents* (2nd edn) (Boston, Mass.: Bedford/St. Martin's Press, 2001).

MacIntyre, Jean and Garrett P. J. Epp, '"Cloathes worth all the rest": Costumes and Properties', in John D. Cox and David Scott Kastan (eds), *A New History of Early English Drama* (New York: Columbia University Press, 1997), pp. 269–86.

MacLuskie, Kathleen, 'Drama and Sexual Politics: The Case of Webster's Duchess', in Dympna Callaghan (ed.), *The Duchess of Malfi: A New Casebook* (Basingstoke and London: Macmillan, 2000), pp. 104–21.

Malcolmson, Cristina, '"As Tame as the Ladies": Politics and Gender in *The Changeling*', *English Literary Renaissance*, vol. 20; no. 2 (Spring 1990), pp. 320–39.

Marshall, Cynthia, *The Shattering of the Self: Violence, Subjectivity, & Early Modern Texts* (Baltimore, Md./London: Johns Hopkins University Press, 2002).

Martinez, J. D., 'The Fallacy of Contextual Analysis as a Means of Evaluating Dramatized Violence', in John W. Frick (ed.), *Theatre Symposium 7: Theatre and Violence* (Tuscaloosa, Ala.: Southeastern Theatre Conference/The University of Alabama Press, 1999), pp. 76–85.

Mehl, Dieter, 'Corruption, retribution and justice in *Measure for Measure* and *The Revenger's Tragedy*', in E. A. J. Honigmann (ed.), *Shakespeare and his Contemporaries: Essays in Comparison* (Manchester: Manchester University Press, 1986).

Mellen, Joan, *Big Bad Wolves: Masculinity in the American Film* (London: Elm Tree Books, 1978).

Mendik, Xavier, 'From the Monstrous Mother to the "Third Sex": Female Abjection in the Films of Dario Argento', in A. Black (ed.), *Necronomicon: The Journal of Horror and Erotic Cinema, Book Two* (London: Creation Books, 1998), pp. 110–33.

Modleski, Tania, 'The Terror of Pleasure: the Contemporary Horror Film and Postmodern Theory', in Ken Gelder (ed.), *The Horror Reader* (London: Routledge, 2000), pp. 285–93.

Moretti, Franco, *Signs Taken for Wonders: Essays in the Sociology of Literary Forms* (London: Verso, 1983).

Mullaney, Steven, 'Mourning and Misogyny: *Hamlet* and the Final Progress of Elizabeth I', in Kate Chedgzoy (ed.), *Shakespeare, Feminism and Gender: Contemporary Critical Essays* (Basingstoke: Palgrave, 2001), pp. 161–83.

'Naked Hollywood', *Empire* magazine, no. 36 (June 1992), pp. 54–60.

Neill, Michael, *Issues of Death: Mortality and Identity in English Renaissance Tragedy* (Oxford University Press, 1997).

O'Day, Marc, 'Beauty in Motion: Gender, Spectacle and Action Babe Cinema', in Yvonne Tasker (ed.), *Action and Adventure Cinema* (London: Routledge, 2004), pp. 201–18.

Orgel, Stephen, *Impersonations: The Performance of Gender in Shakespeare's England* (Cambridge University Press, 1996).

Orkin, Martin, 'As if a Man Should Spit against the Wind', in Naomi Conn Liebler (ed.), *The Female Tragic Hero in English Renaissance Drama* (Basingstoke: Palgrave, 2002), pp. 141–59.

Paster, Gail Kern, *The Body Embarrassed: Drama and the Disciplines of Shame in Early Modern England* (Ithaca, NY: Cornell University Press, 1993).

Paul, William, *Laughing Screaming: Modern Hollywood Horror and Comedy* (New York: Columbia University Press, 1994).

Peck, Linda Levy, *Court Patronage and Corruption in Early Stuart England* (London: Routledge, 1993).

Place, Janey, 'Women in *Film Noir*', in E. Ann Kaplan (ed.), *Women in Film Noir* (London: British Film Institute, 1978), pp. 47–68.

Projansky, Sarah, *Watching Rape: Film and Television in Postfeminist Culture* (New York: New York University Press, 2001).

Prosser, Eleanor, *Hamlet and Revenge* (2nd edn) (Stanford, Calif.: Stanford University Press, 1971; first published 1967).

Read, Jacinda, *The New Avengers: Feminism, Femininity and the Rape–Revenge Cycle* (Manchester: Manchester University Press, 2000).

Rolls, Albert, *The Theory of the King's Two Bodies in the Age of Shakespeare* (Lewiston, NY: Edwin Mellen Press, 2000).

Rose, Mary Beth, 'Heroics of Marriage in Renaissance Tragedy', in D. Callaghan (ed.), *The Duchess of Malfi: A New Casebook* (Basingstoke and London: Macmillan, 2000), pp. 122–43.

Rubin, Gayle, 'The Traffic in Women: Notes on the "Political Economy" of Sex', in Rayna R. Riter (ed.), *Toward an Anthropology of Women* (New York: Monthly Review Press, 1975), pp. 157–210.

Ryan, Michael and Douglas Kellner, *Camera Politica: The Politics and Ideology of Contemporary Hollywood Film* (Bloomington, Ind.: Indiana University Press, 1990).

Salingar, L. G., 'Tourneur and the Tragedy of Revenge', in Boris Ford (ed.), *The Age of Shakespeare*, The Pelican Guide to English Literature (Harmondsworth: Pelican, 1955; revd edn 1982), pp. 436–56.

Sapolsky, Barry S. and Fred Molitor, 'Current Trends in Contemporary Horror Films', in James B. Weaver III and Ron Tamborini (eds), *Horror Films: Current Research on Audience Preferences and Reactions* (Mahwah, NJ: Lawrence Erlbaum Associates, 1996), pp. 103–25.

Sawday, Jonathan, *The Body Emblazoned: Dissection and the Human Body in Renaissance Culture* (London: Routledge, 1996; first published 1995).

Shapiro, James, '"Tragedies naturally performed": Kyd's Representation of Violence', in David Scott Kastan and Peter Stallybrass (eds), *Staging the Renaissance: Reinterpretations of Elizabethan and Jacobean Drama* (London: Routledge, 1991).

Shone, Tom, *Blockbuster: How Hollywood Learned to Stop Worrying and Love the Summer* (London: Simon & Schuster, 2004).

Simkin, Stevie (ed.), *Revenge Tragedy: Contemporary Critical Essays* (Basingstoke: Palgrave, 2001).

Simmons, J. L., 'Diabolical Realism in Middleton and Rowley's *The Changeling*', *Renaissance Drama*, new series 11 (1980), pp. 290–306.

Sinfield, Alan, *Faultlines: Cultural Materialism and the Politics of Dissident Reading* (Oxford: Clarendon Press, 1992).

Slotkin, Richard, *Gunfighter Nation: The Myth of the Frontier in Twentieth Century America* (New York: Atheneum, 1992).

Smith, Joan, *Misogynies* (London: Faber & Faber, 1989).

Smith, Molly Easo, 'The Theater and the Scaffold: Death as Spectacle in *The Spanish Tragedy*', *Studies in English Literature, 1500–1900*, vol. 32 (1992), pp. 217–32.

Sobchack, Vivian C., 'The Violent Dance: A Personal Memoir of Death in the Movies', in Stephen Prince (ed.), *Screening Violence* (Brunswick, NJ: Rutgers University Press, 2000), pp. 110–24.

Stables, Kate, 'The Postmodern Always Rings Twice: Constructing the *Femme Fatale* in 90s Cinema', in E. Ann Kaplan (ed.), *Women in Film Noir: New Edition* (London: BFI Publishing, 1998), pp. 164–82.

Stone, Lawrence, *The Crisis of the Aristocracy, 1558–1641* (Abridged edn, Oxford University Press, 1967; first published 1965).

Sturgess, Keith, *Jacobean Private Theatre* (London: Routledge & Kegan Paul, 1987).

Tallack, Douglas (ed.), *Critical Theory: A Reader* (Hemel Hempstead: Harvester Wheatsheaf, 1995).

Tanner, Marcus, *Croatia: A Nation Forged in War* (New Haven, Conn.: Yale University Press, 2001).

Tasker, Yvonne, *Spectacular Bodies: Gender, Genre and the Action Cinema* (London: Routledge, 1993).

Tasker, Yvonne, *Working Girls: Gender and Sexuality in Popular Cinema* (London: Routledge, 1998).

Tudor, Andrew, 'From Paranoia to Postmodernism? The Horror Movie in Late Modern Society', in Steve Neale (ed.), *Genre and Contemporary Hollywood* (London: BFI Publishing, 2002a), pp. 105–16.

Tudor, Andrew, 'Why Horror? The Peculiar Pleasures of a Popular Genre', in Mark Jancovich (ed.), *Horror: The Film Reader* (London: Routledge, 2002b), pp. 47–55.

Twitchell, James B., *Preposterous Violence: Fables of Aggression in Modern Culture* (Oxford University Press, 1989).

de Vroom, Theresia, 'Female Heroism in Heywood's Tragic Farce of Adultery: *A Woman Killed with Kindness*', in Naomi Conn Liebler (ed.), *The Female Tragic Hero in English Renaissance Drama* (Basingstoke: Palgrave, 2002), pp. 119–40.

Waldrep, Christopher, *Night Riders: Defending Community in the Black Patch, 1890–1915* (Durham, NC: Duke University Press, 1993).

Watson, Robert N., 'Tragedy', in A. R. Braunmuller and Michael Hattaway (eds), *The Cambridge Companion to English Renaissance Drama* (Cambridge University Press, 1990).

Watson, Robert N., *The Rest is Silence: Death as Annihilation in the English Renaissance* (Berkeley/Los Angeles: University of California Press, 1994; paperback 1999).

Weddle, David, *If They Move ... Kill 'Em: The Life and Times of Sam Peckinpah* (London: Faber & Faber, 1996).

Wells, Paul, *The Horror Genre from Beelzebub to Blair Witch* (London: Wallflower Publishing, 2000).

Wheale, Nigel, *Writing and Society: Literacy, Print and Politics in Britain 1590–1660* (London: Routledge, 1999).

Williams, Linda Ruth, 'Women Can Only Misbehave – Peckinpah, 'Straw Dogs', Feminism and Violence', *Sight and Sound*, vol. 5, no. 2 (February 1995), pp. 26–7.

Williams, Tony, *Hearths of Darkness: The Family in the American Horror Film* (Madison, NJ.: Associated University Presses, 1996).

Wood, Robin, 'Returning the Look: "Eyes of a Stranger"', in Gregory A. Waller (ed.), *American Horrors: Essays on the Modern American Horror Film* (Chicago: University of Illinois Press, 1987), pp. 79–85.

Woodward, Jennifer, 'Images of a Dead Queen – Historical Record of Mourning Ceremony for Queen Elizabeth I of England', *History Today*, November 1997, at http://www.findarticles.com/p/articles/mi_m1373/is_n11_v47/ai_19987419/pg_3, accessed 20 Oct 2004.

Wymer, Rowland, *Webster and Ford* (Basingstoke and London: Macmillan, 1995), p. 40.

Wynne-Davies, Marion, '"The Swallowing Womb": Consumed and Consuming Women in *Titus Andronicus*', in Valerie Wayne (ed.), *The Matter of Difference: Materialist Feminist Criticism of Shakespeare* (Hemel Hempstead: Harvester Wheatsheaf, 1991), pp. 129–51.

Young, Elizabeth, '*The Silence of the Lambs* and the Flaying of Feminist Theory', *Camera Obscura*, vol. 27 (September 1992), pp. 5–35.

Internet resources

http://actionadventure.about.com/
http://www.allmovie.com
http://www.alternet.org/
http://web.amnesty.org/
http://www.cinemareview.com/
http://www.clinteastwood.net/
http://www.cnn.com/
http://www.dallasobserver.com/
http://www.the-dirtiest.com/
http://www.gallup-international.com/
http://www.geocities.com/paulinekaelreviews
http://www.grandguignol.com/
http://www.harrisinteractive.com/
http://www.hollywood.com/
http://www.imdb.com/
http://killbill.movies.go.com/
http://www.law.berkeley.edu/
http://www.melonfarmers.co.uk/
http://www.newint.org/
http://www.opinionjournal.com/
http://www.orlandosentinel.com/
http://www.rainn.org/
http://www.rottentomatoes.com/
http://www.salon.com/
http://www.sensesofcinema.com/
http://www.sonypictures.com/
http://www.s-t.com/
http://www.totaldvd.net/
http://www.unfpa.org/
http://www.viewlondon.co.uk/
http://www.variety.com/
http://www.washingtontimes.com/

Index